ISLAM

Islam: The Key Concepts is a clear and concise guide to the religion and culture of Islam. Kecia Ali and Oliver Leaman explore this highly topical subject focusing on key issues including:

- the Qur'an
- faith
- theology
- gender
- fundamentalism
- philosophy
- jihad
- Islam in America
- Islam in Europe
- Islamic law

This is the ideal study resource and includes a concise introduction, an alphabetical list of relevant terms (fully cross-referenced), a short bibliographical guide together with the bibliography itself and an index.

Kecia Ali is the author of *Sexual Ethics and Islam: Feminist Reflections on Qur'an, Hadith, and Jurisprudence* (2006). She is currently Assistant Professor of Religion at Boston University. She previously held research and teaching fellowships at Brandeis University and Harvard Divinity School.

Oliver Leaman teaches at the University of Kentucky and writes mainly on Islamic thought. His most recent relevant publication is his edited volume, *The Qur'an: An Encyclopedia* (Routledge, 2005).

Also available from Routledge

Islam: the Basics
Colin Turner
978–0–415–34106–6

The Qur'an: the Basics
Massimo Campanini
978–0–415–41163–9

Fifty Key Figures in Islam
Roy Jackson
978–0–415–35468–4

Fifty Eastern Thinkers
Diané Collinson, Robert Wilkinson and Kathryn Plant
978–0–415–20284–8

Religion: the Basics
Malory Nye
978–0–415–26379–5

Judaism: the Basics
Jacob Neusner
978–0–415–40176–0

Fifty Key Jewish Thinkers, 2nd edition
Dan Cohn-Sherbok
978–0–415–77141–2

Roman Catholicism: the Basics
Michael Walsh
978–0–415–26381–8

Fifty Key Christian Thinkers
Peter McEnhill and George Newlands
978–0–415–17050–5

The Bible in Western Culture
Dee Dyas and Esther Hughes
978–0–415–32618–6

ISLAM

The Key Concepts

Kecia Ali and Oliver Leaman

Routledge
Taylor & Francis Group

LONDON AND NEW YORK

First published 2008
by Routledge
2 Park Square, Milton Park, Oxon OX14 4RN

Simultaneously published in the USA and Canada
by Routledge
270 Madison Ave, New York, NY10016

Routledge is an imprint of the Taylor & Francis Group, an informa business

© 2008 Kecia Ali and Oliver Leaman

Typeset in Bembo by The Running Head Limited, Cambridge,
www.therunninghead.com
Printed and bound in Great Britain by TJ International Ltd,
Padstow, Cornwall

British Library Cataloguing in Publication Data
A catalogue record for this book is available from the British Library

Library of Congress Cataloging in Publication Data
Ali, Kecia
Islam: the key concepts / Kecia Ali & Oliver Leaman.
p. cm.
Includes bibliographical references and index.
1. Islam—21st century. 2. Islam—Essence, genius, nature.
3. Koran—Criticism, interpretation, etc.
I. Leaman, Oliver, 1950–. II. Title.
BP161.3.A376 2007
297.03—dc22
2007015404

ISBN10: 0-415-39638-7 (hbk)
ISBN10: 0-415-39639-5 (pbk)
ISBN10: 0-203-93423-7 (ebk)

ISBN13: 978-0-415-39638-7 (hbk)
ISBN13: 978-0-415-39639-4 (pbk)
ISBN13: 978-0-203-93423-4 (ebk)

CONTENTS

FOREWORD

We wrote this book because many of our students are puzzled by what they find in the Qur'an and while studying Islam, and require a concise guide to the key concepts of the Book and the religion. Armed with this guide, it is to be hoped that they will be able to appreciate the form and matter of the Qur'an and Islam more adequately. In particular, we hope that it will help them to gain an appreciation of the interconnections that exist between the main ideas found in the Qur'an and within the heritage of Muslim thought. This book is meant to be a starting point only, and it is our hope that readers will proceed to more detailed and complex works on those topics that captivate their interest.

On the concepts: the selection of which ideas to discuss is always subjective. We have limited ourselves to 123 concepts, including all of those topics that we considered essential and others that we thought very important. To a certain extent, this book's areas of focus reflect our own specializations: philosophy, law, Qur'an, and gender. There may be some terms we have included that others think are marginal; likewise, we are bound to have left out some terms that others would consider vital. The index of topics will guide readers to discussions of terms that appear in other entries but did not merit entries of their own in a work of this brevity.

We have each written part of this book and also collaborated on many sections. We have read each other's work and everything has been edited by both of us. Any errors should be laid at our door. We should like to thank Lesley Riddle and Gemma Dunn at Routledge for their help and encouragement along the way, together with Carole Drummond from The Running Head, and Dr John Gaunt, for what has been, we hope in the view of our readers, a fruitful cooperative enterprise.

Kecia Ali
Oliver Leaman
February 2007

INTRODUCTION

The purpose of this book is to help those coming to the Qur'an or the study of Islam for perhaps the first time, or who do not have an extensive knowledge of the religion or the Book, to find an explanation of some of the most important concepts. We are aware throughout of how complicated many of the key concepts are. What we have done here is merely to skim the surface of the richness that lies within these central terms, and their role in the Book specifically and Islam more broadly. There is plenty of further reading indicated and readers should have no difficulty in following up references in other and more extensive texts. *The Qur'an: An Encyclopedia*, with which we have both been involved, has detailed bibliographical information and will be useful in this regard as will the other reference texts listed below.

Theological concepts are frequently controversial and difficult to understand without grasping the precise context in which they figure. A difficulty in presenting brief and distinct information on each such term is that it fails to help readers see how they relate to each other, and what point in general is being made when they are used. We have used cross-referencing wherever possible, as described below. Yet some inevitable repetition of information occurs in the various entries. We are aware that we are producing no more than a thin slice of what counts as commentary on the Qur'an and Islam, and are unable here to represent in any way the depth of the original. For those particularly interested in scripture, reading our book without reading the Qur'an is likely to be unprofitable; reading them together is what we have in mind. For those with more historical or sociological concerns, our intent is to provide an overview that allows the reader to orient herself or himself in a vast terrain.

HOW TO USE THIS BOOK

Rather than reading this book from start to finish, we expect that most readers will turn to those entries that are of particular interest to them, finding topics in the list of entries or the subject index that appears at the end of the volume. Each entry, in turn, will lead elsewhere through cross-references within the entry or at its conclusion.

Terms that appear in **bold** are either main entries or refer to main entries that appear elsewhere. Linked terms that do not actually appear in an entry are indicated at the end of each entry with the prefix "See also: . . ." Ubiquitous terms like God, Islam, and Qur'an have not been cross-referenced.

We have used important Arabic terms, always explained, and have avoided macrons and diacritics. We have not italicized those Arabic terms that occur frequently, e.g., hadith and surah. Where terms have standard forms in English, such as fatwa and ulama, we have used those.

Names are sometimes given in their English form (e.g., Abraham) and sometimes in their Arabic form (Ibrahim) to replicate the variety of forms of expression that readers will meet.

Quotations and references to the Qur'an appear with chapter (surah) and the verse (ayah): surah:ayah. Where translated passages from the Qur'an appear, the translation is usually our own. However, on occasion we have drawn from other translators including A.J. Arberry.

Dates are usually given thus: *hijri* date/Gregorian date, i.e. AH/CE. The *hijri* date is the date in accordance with the Islamic calendar, starting with the migration of the Prophet Muhammad and his supporters to Medina in 622 CE. Where only one date is given, it is the common era date.

GENERAL REFERENCES

The following works have a great deal of information on the topics of this book. We have not given specific references to them in the suggestions for further reading that follow entries, as we would have had to cite them for every entry.

For the Qur'an specifically, readers will find the following sources useful:

The Qur'an: An Encyclopedia, ed. O. Leaman, London: Routledge, 2006. A one-volume work designed to deal with key figures, ideas, terms, and concepts related to the Qur'an and its history and interpretation.

Encyclopedia of the Qur'an, ed. J. McAuliffe, Leiden: Brill, 2001–6. Although written by specialists and intended to be of use to those with academic interest in the study of Islam, the entries are geared to be useful to students and others with more general interests as well. Unlike in the *Encylopedia of Islam*, terms for entries are given in English; an extensive volume with cross-referencing to Arabic terms is available.

Concordance of the Qur'an, H. Kassis, Berkeley: University of California Press, 1982. This unique reference work allows readers to search in English for Qur'anic terms by using transliterated Arabic triliteral roots. The inclusion of partial quotations from relevant verses makes it easy to see at a glance which entries are relevant for one's interest.

Dictionary of Qur'anic Terms and Concepts, M. Mir, New York: Garland, 1987. An inclusive reference for terms specifically related to the Qur'an and its interpretive tradition.

In addition to the *Journal of Qur'anic Studies* published by Edinburgh University Press, most of the main Islamic studies journals have material on the Qur'an.

More general works:

Biographical Encyclopedia of Islamic Philosophers, ed. O. Leaman, London: Continuum, 2006.

Encyclopedia of Islam, Leiden: Brill, 1st edn, 1913–16; 2nd edn 1960–.

A note on translations of the Qur'an

The Qur'an has been translated into English many times and there are distinct merits to each of the available translations. The translations by M. Asad, A.J. Arberry, and M.M. Pickthall are well respected. A Saudi-government subsidized version based on the translation by Abdullah Yusuf Ali circulates widely; the original Ali translation is very popular with Muslim readers. Newer renderings by Ahmed Ali, M. Abdul Haleem, and T. Cleary have their partisans, as do other more established translations, such as that by N. Dawood. The bibliography contains full publication information for these and other translations.

Several online sites also make English translations of the Qur'an available, sometimes with multiple versions side-by-side. Some sites have keyword search options or topical indices, which are helpful to those looking for information on particular topics.

On suggested further reading

The suggestions for further reading that accompany most entries correspond to entries in the bibliography. We have emphasized works that are written in English and likely to be widely available although we have included more specialized sources when we deemed it appropriate. We have included in the bibliography those Arabic texts that we drew on specifically as sources ourselves, but have generally refrained from providing citations to secondary literature in other languages.

LIST OF KEY CONCEPTS

ISLAM

The Key Concepts

ABROGATION

Abrogation (*naskh*) is the process through which specific **revelations** are replaced by others. Abrogation can apply to entire revelations—for instance, the Qur'an both corrects and perfects earlier scriptures— or to particular sections of one revelation, where one verse or set of verses replaces another. Though increasingly controversial in modern Muslim thought, due in part to a defensive stance on the origins of the Qur'anic text, abrogation in this latter sense was widely accepted by premodern **Sunni** exegetes, and became an important herme- neutical tool for jurists as they formulated rulings. **Shi'i** scholars in general have been less inclined to accept it, using other interpretive techniques to reconcile divergent passages; the traditionally trained Shi'i scholar Abu al-Qasim al-Khu'i (d. 1992) rejected abrogation altogether. Even among those who agreed as to the existence of abro- gation, disagreements persisted as to which were the abrogated verses (*mansukh*) and which were abrogating (*nasikh*).

The notion that some scriptures replace or modify others is most clearly articulated in Q. 2:106, which declares, "for whatever verse We abrogate or cast into oblivion, We bring a better." This verse has bearing on the broader controversy about the validity of the religions of the **People of the Book** once Muhammad's prophecy exists. The phenomenon of one scripture replacing another in part is not unique to the Qur'an but rather is part of an ongoing prophetic pattern. For instance, Jesus (2:50) both attested to the truthfulness of the Torah and proclaimed new rules, making lawful part of what had previ- ously been forbidden.

The abrogation of some verses by others within the Qur'an has gar- nered the most attention from Muslim scholars, who defined three types. In the first, *naskh al-tilawa wa'l hukm*, both recitation and the associated rule, if any, are removed from the Qur'an. In the second, *naskh al-hukm dun al-tilawa*, the verse remains and continues to be recited but its provisions are superseded by a later revelation. Alcohol is a famous example of progressive revelation; three passages (2:219, 4:43, 5:90–91) discuss intoxication in increasingly restrictive ways and the latter are usually said to abrogate the former. In the third and most controversial type, *naskh al-tilawa dun al-hukm*, a verse is no longer recited but its corresponding rule persists.

Discerning when abrogation exists is vital for legal scholars who must attempt to reconcile potentially contradictory commands. Jurists debated abrogation extensively, disagreeing over whether the Qur'an and **sunnah**, the primary textual sources of the law, could abrogate one another. Al-Shafi'i (d. 204/820) famously held that only Qur'an could abrogate Qur'an and only a new prophetic precedent could cancel an earlier one, but others allowed cross-genre abrogation.

Finally, abrogation appears as a protective measure against corruption of the Qur'anic text. In the "satanic verses" incident—not to be confused with Salman Rushdie's controversial 1988 novel of the same name—Muhammad had recited verses praising three pre-Islamic goddesses in a demonically inspired attempt to conciliate the hostile Meccan tribes. However, God abrogated what **Satan** had caused the Prophet to recite (22:52–54). While some classical Muslim scholars deny that the incident ever occurred, seeing it as a blemish upon Muhammad's reputation, others including Ibn Taymiyyah (d. 728/1328) have viewed it as further evidence for the divinely guarded inviolability of the Qur'anic text.

See also: **fatwa**, *fiqh*, *sunnah*

Further reading: Ahmed 1998; Brown 1998; Burton 1990; Khadduri 1984; al-Khu'i 1998

ADHAN see **prayer**

AESTHETICS

The Qur'an makes it very clear that it does not see itself as poetry, although it does consider itself beautiful in both form and substance. As it was transmitted to the Arabs, a community with a high regard for language, it is appropriate that the language of the Book be impressive to its original audience. It is important for the Book that Muhammad is not a poet (36:69) since otherwise he might have been accused of writing the Book. The beauty of the Book is often taken to be evidence of its veracity, an unusual theological argument, and is an important part of the proof that the Qur'an is unique in nature and has to be God-given.

Islamic aesthetics tends to be Neoplatonic. This approach replaced the earlier theories of thinkers like al-Kindi (d. c. 252/866), for whom beauty was derived from perfection: since God is the most perfect being in the universe, he is also the most beautiful. He is constantly aware of his beauty while we are only occasionally able to come close to experiencing beauty, since it is an essential feature of the deity but its perception is merely an accidental human attribute. This version of Pythagoreanism was replaced by the argument that we operate on the level of imagination, so our ideas of beauty are limited to what we can experience and abstract from those experiences. On the other hand, we can use our material ideas and experiences to construct more abstract and perfect concepts of beauty, and so come closer to the range of completely pure beauty which exists far from and above the material world.

The aesthetics of poetry and the ways in which poetry works logically came in for much discussion. Many of the Islamic philosophers such as al-Farabi, Ibn Sina (Avicenna) and Ibn Rushd (Averroes) were convinced that poetry follows a syllogistic pattern of proof, albeit with far weaker premises than most such reasoning processes and with the conclusion that the audience should be moved to action or have an emotion. Imagination is again crucial here, blending the human ability to be both spiritual and material. Our material ideas reflect our experiences, yet they can be made more abstract. In the process of abstraction, those experiences are extended in novel and exciting ways. Were we to be entirely rational we would not need imagination, and could be spoken to entirely in terms of logic. Since we are emotional creatures we must be addressed at least partially through our emotions. This is where poetry and other art forms come in. They appeal to us both intellectually and emotionally, and persuade us that we should adopt a certain attitude or share a particular feeling.

See also: **beauty**, **philosophy**

Further reading: Kermani 1999; Leaman 2004

AFTERLIFE

The term *akhir* is mentioned in the Qur'an often referring to the Last Day (*al-yawm al-akhir*) or the **day of judgment**. On that day God will replace the world of generation and corruption with the permanent, everlasting world. The dead will be raised and judged. The afterlife (*al-akhirah*) begins with the day of judgment, where God divides those who go to **paradise** (*jannah*) from those who are destined for **hell** (*jahanam*). Belief in the afterlife is essential in Islam, and the Qur'an describes the next life in vivid terms. This world is merely a site for testing and those who have the right beliefs and actions pass the test for an eternal future of happiness.

The next life is mentioned 116 times in the Qur'an, appearing in almost every chapter. Some **surah**s (22, 44, 45, 56, 59, 75, 79, 81, 82, 84, and 88) have a great deal of information on the afterlife. Discussions of the afterlife emphasize the closeness of the event, warning people to be prepared for the imminent day. Verses graphically depict disasters that will occur in the natural world at the hour of judgment and the despair of people in general who have not behaved well and so cannot expect divine succor. Surah 78, by contrast, highlights God's kindness and power. God has made the earth a cradle for human beings; the mountains are supports to protect the balance of the earth; and God has created humans in the form of males and females. He has made the night a time for resting and the day a time for living. Towards the end of the chapter a comparison between the transgressors and the righteous is made. The former will be horribly punished while the latter will receive a great reward. God's activity in **creation** and in guiding human life on earth is thus linked closely to eventual judgment and the afterlife.

Further reading: Cragg 1998; Nursi 1990; al-Razi 1990; Smith and Haddad 1981

AHADITH see **hadith**

AL-AKHIRAH see **afterlife**

ALLAH

God stands at the core of the *shahadah* or profession of faith which constitutes the first of Islam's **five pillars**: "There is no deity but God and Muhammad is His messenger." The statement is repeated by Muslims in their five daily **prayer**s, in the call for prayer, and in their daily lives. Belief in one God differentiates Islam from many of the pre-Islamic religions in Arabia, though the Arabic word for God, "Allah," is apparently pre-Islamic, and was used in combination with the names of other deities until the influence of Islam brought this to an end. The word "Allah" is said to occur only in the singular, although there is a plural of a related term *al-ilah*, i.e. *alihah*. Grammar aside, God in the Qur'an is definitely one and the unity (*tawhid*) of the deity cannot be sufficiently stressed in Islam. Q. 112:1 reflects this in its command "Say: He, God, is One."

As one might expect, the word "Allah" is ubiquitous in the Book. The Qur'an has many references to God and to his close relationship with the world; God is said to be closer to the human being than is the jugular vein (50:16). Everything in the universe is regarded as a sign (*ayah*) of his presence and human beings need to use their intelligence to interpret these signs in the right sort of way. Intelligent reflection on God's signs confirms the existence of God and of the divine and directed nature of the world's design.

Although close to the human being in some respects, God is also incomparable and cannot be completely known. Our **knowledge** of God is limited, but we can reflect on his attributes through meditating on his beautiful names which appear alongside or sometimes as substitutes for the name Allah. God describes himself as the creator and teacher of human beings who through the Qur'an and earlier messages instructs humanity in how to live. He has created us to **worship** him and he notes our conduct and punishes or rewards us accordingly. Many Muslims have a name including that of the deity, such as 'Abdallah (servant of God).

See also: *al-asma' al-husna'*, **creation**, *ikhlas*

ALMSGIVING see **charity**

AMBIGUOUS see *muhkam* and *mutashabih*

ANGELS

Angels are very active in the Qur'an, and are described in a variety of ways. They may have two, three, or four pairs of wings (35:1); they do not need to eat (25:7, 25:20); and they are said to be very beautiful. Sometimes they fight on the side of the righteous (3:124). They note our actions (50:18) and take the souls of the dead and guard over **hell** (32:11, 43:77). These angelic guards are understood to be nineteen in number (74:30). On the **day of judgment** God's throne will be carried by the angels (69:17). The Ark of the Covenant, holding the *sakinah* (inspired peace), will also be borne by the angels (2:248). There is a High Council of angels (37:8, 38:69), who repel eavesdropping demons with bolts of fire. Some angels are described by name, such as the "two angels at Babylon," Harut and Marut, who teach people white magic (2:102). There are also Gabriel and Michael (2:98). The former is associated with the bringing down of **revelation** (26:193 calls him "the faithful spirit"), and in the **hadith** accounts he accompanies Muhammad on his heavenly ascension or *mi'raj*. The Qur'an calls 'Izra'il the angel of death and names Israfil as the angel whose trumpet blast will mark the day of judgment (69:13).

It is an interesting question why an angel was not sent down to accompany the Prophet Muhammad in his task. In 6:8–9 we are told that such an angel would have made it too easy for the audience to accept the message. The only miracle in the Qur'an is taken to be the miracle of the Qur'an itself, its unique and perfect style and composition.

Belief in angels, mentioned alongside that in God, the Last Judgment, the Book and the messengers is incumbent upon Muslims (2:177). God is the enemy of those who oppose his angels (2:98).

The angels are intermediaries between the divine and the lower world. They announce the news of Yahya (John the Baptist) to Zakariyya and Jesus to Mary. Angels may also serve as messengers (sing. *rasul*). However, most messengers mentioned in the Qur'an are human. Passages describe the coming down of the angels and the spirit (*ruh*) during the Night of Power (*laylat al-qadr*), and the descent of the angels, together with the spirit of God's command, to help humanity (16:2, 97:4).

In the story of Adam's creation, which is mentioned in seven distinct places in the Qur'an, angels figure prominently. In 2:30–34 God announces, "I will create a vicegerent on earth," to which the angels reply, "Will You place there someone who will make mischief and shed blood? While we celebrate Your praises?" The narrative continues with God teaching Adam "the names of all things," and then challenging the angels to recite these names. Their inability to comply betrays their simple nature: "We have no knowledge beyond that which You have taught Us." Adam then tells the angels their own names, and they are commanded to prostrate themselves to him, but one of them called Iblis (**Satan**) refuses, saying, "I am better than he is. You created me from fire and him from clay" (7:12). Iblis is cast out of heaven, and will contend with humanity until the Last Day. He is an angel (7:11), but made from fire, like the *jinn* (55:15). In the hadith literature, angels are said to be made from light.

The Muslim philosopher Ibn Sina (Avicenna, d. 428/1037) identified the various spheres of the world as angels, and this sort of language became popular with various thinkers. Al-Suhrawardi (549–587/1154–1191) developed a cosmology of light in which angels play a significant role. Ibn 'Arabi (560–638/1164–1240) distinguished between the angels of the incorporeal world, and contrasted them with those of the physical. The four archangels Gabriel, Michael, 'Izra'il, and Israfil are used to represent the four divine attributes of life, knowledge, will, and power.

See also: *'aqidah*

Further reading: Murata 1991

APOSTASY

Apostasy (*riddah*) is the act of leaving the **faith** of Islam. According to premodern Islamic **jurisprudence**, apostasy is punishable by death in nearly all cases, assuming the apostate is an adult of sound mind who leaves Islam by choice and who does not repent of his or her decision. Both Muslims by birth and by **conversion** can apostatize, though there is usually less opportunity for repentance in the former case. Most evidence for the criminalization of apostasy comes from **hadith**, such as the frequently quoted "Whoever changes his **religion**, kill him," which is found in the two compilations of Bukhari and Muslim.

Classical jurists debated the relationship between apostasy, blasphemy, and **heresy**. In his *Shifa'a*, Qadi 'Iyad (d. 544/1149) weighed various opinions as to whether insulting or cursing Muhammad constituted apostasy. The punishment was more implacable if it did not: while the apostate was usually granted time to repent and return to Islam (jurists debated how long a period for reflection might be granted), a Muslim guilty of blaspheming the Prophet was to be executed without delay. Formal implementation of the death penalty for apostasy and related crimes was historically uncommon though by no means unheard-of. Well-known cases were usually related to conflicts over political and theological authority, as in the execution of the mystic al-Hallaj (d. 309/922), whose utterance "I am the Reality [*al-Haqq*, also **Truth**]" appropriated one of God's divine names.

While in practice accusations of apostasy have usually concerned heretical or blasphemous views, apostasy was most basically conversion to another faith or a declaration of lack of belief in major Muslim articles of faith such as the oneness of God (*tawhid*) or the **prophethood** of Muhammad. In the twentieth century, **Wahhabi** thinkers have widened the scope of offenses deemed to constitute apostasy, in keeping with their narrow views of proper Muslim belief and conduct. Persecution of Muslims who hold unpopular or disapproved views continues in the modern era, as the 1990s case against Egyptian Qur'an scholar Nasr Hamid Abu Zayd (b. 1943) attests. Reacting to Abu Zayd's attempt to interpret the Qur'an as a literary text (while still viewing it as divine in origin), Islamists sued to have his wife **divorce**d from him on the grounds that, as a Muslim woman, she could not be married to an apostate. When a court decided against him, Abu Zayd and his wife emigrated to the Netherlands.

This case constitutes an interesting reversal of an earlier phenomenon combining **marriage** and apostasy. Taking advantage of the

Hanafi **madhhab**'s view that apostasy immediately dissolves a marriage and that female apostates are to be imprisoned indefinitely rather than executed, Indian Muslim women who could not otherwise obtain desired divorces might apostatize, converting to Christianity and thereby dissolving their marriages. A perceived crisis of conversions prompted legal reform—the Dissolution of Muslim Marriages Act of 1939—which increased women's avenues for divorce without leaving the faith.

Apostasy has direct bearing on the issue of freedom of religion. Muslim-majority countries frequently ban proselytizing and the majority of contemporary Muslim scholars uphold the premodern view that apostasy merits death. Others, though, including influential modernists such as Sayyid Ahmad Khan in India, Muhammad 'Abduh and Rashid Rida in Egypt, and Hasan Turabi in the Sudan, have argued for religious freedom, claiming that death for apostasy was a penalty applicable in a particular context of a community where religious allegiances defined political loyalties as well; the punishment for apostasy, in this view, was not for switching one's personal convictions but because it was akin to treason. For them, the Qur'an shows that apostates will be punished in the **afterlife** (e.g., 2:218, 3:86–87), but after dying naturally. The death penalty for apostasy is, in this view, for active violent opposition to the Muslim community (4:89–90). Freedom of religion, including the freedom to leave Islam, is entirely in keeping with the core principle that "there is no compulsion in religion" (2:256).

See also: *al-asma' al-husna'*, *'aqidah*, **faith**

Further reading: Masud et al. 1996; Peters and De Vries 1976–77; Saeed and Saeed 2004

'AQIDAH

'Aqidah (pl. *'aqa'id*) is the Muslim creed. The earliest and simplest creed is the **shahadah** which declares: "I witness that there is no god but God and that Muhammad is the messenger of God."

The *shahadah* is generally considered to be a declaration of faith. It is customarily recited on **conversion** and is part of the daily prayer ritual. It emphasizes as articles of **faith** two basic principles: the unity of God and the prophethood of Muhammad. Later creeds may be substantially more complex, and their particulars will depend on the precise doctrinal line that a particular Muslim follows. Some include topics such as **angels**, revealed scriptures, the **afterlife**, and destiny with the *shahadah* principles. The different schools of thought in Islam often used their definition of creed to present a summary of their basic beliefs, and there are sharp distinctions between various **Sunni** and **Shi'i** views. The latter insist on acceptance of the special significance of the Prophet's family (*ahl al-bayt*) as part of the creed.

See also: **prophethood**, *qadr*, **revelation**, *tawhid*

Further reading: Goldziher 1967; Watt 1994; Wensinck 1965

ASH'ARIYA, ASH'ARITES see **theology**

AL-ASMA' AL-HUSNA'

The phrase *al-asma' al-husna'*—"the most beautiful names"—appears four times in the Qur'an (7:180, 17:110, 20:8, 59:24), always in reference to God: "Oh Muhammad! Call upon God or call upon the Merciful [*al-Rahman*]; whichever you call upon, to Him belong the most beautiful names" (17:110). The Qur'an portrays about fifteen names of God together in the following verses:

> He is Allah, than whom there is no other God, the Knower of the invisible and the visible. He is the Beneficent, the Merciful. He is Allah, than whom there is no other God, the Sovereign Lord, the Holy One, Peace, the Keeper of Faith, the Guardian, the Majestic, the Compeller, and the Superb. Glorified be Allah from all that they ascribe as partner [with Him]. He is Allah, the Creator, the Shaper out of naught, the Fashioner. To Him belong the most beautiful names. All that is in the heavens and the earth glorifies Him, and He is the Mighty, the Wise.
>
> (59:22–24)

Muslim theologians usually speak of ninety-nine names of God. This number comes not from the Qur'an but from a tradition narrated by Abu Hurayra in which the Prophet says: "There are ninety-nine names of God. Whosoever memorizes and accepts these names"—which he goes on to list—"will enter **paradise**." Another version of this **hadith** contains a slightly different set of names. Not counting duplicates, the two versions contain a total of 124 names, and there are some names, such as *al-nasir* (the Helper), *al-mawlah* (the Friend), and *al-ghalib* (the Defeater) cited in the Qur'an but not found in either list. Muslim theologians agree that these traditions are not meant to limit the number of God's names, but to give an idea of his many names. The **Sufi** Abu Bakr al-Wasiti (d. 320/928) expresses this sentiment when he declares, "His names are innumerable."

Scholars sometimes divide God's names into the names of **beauty** (*jamal*) and the names of majesty (*jalal*). The *jalal* names are considered masculine while the *jamal* names are viewed as feminine. Notably, the Merciful (*al-rahman*), perhaps God's most important name, is feminine, though of course God is beyond masculinity and femininity, just as God defies limitation to any of the otherwise contradictory attributes described by the most beautiful names.

Muslim naming practices often draw on the divine names. Individuals may be named according to a quality—*Karim(a)*, "generous," in imitation of God, *al-karim*, the Generous. Pious practices denote the status of the named person as a worshiper, prefacing a divine name with the prefix *'abd* (male slave or servant) or, less commonly, *amat* (female slave or servant). Thus, a male Muslim may be named 'Abdallah (slave or worshiper of God), 'Abd al-Rahman, or 'Abd al-Karim.

Naming is significant in other ways. At the **creation** of the first human being from clay, God teaches Adam "all the names" (2:31). Adam's knowledge of the names is significant as a demonstration of humanity's fitness to serve as God's trustee or representative on earth.

See also: **caliphate**, **worship**

Further reading: al-Ghazali 1995a; Murata 1992

'AWRAH

The term *'awrah* refers to genitals, but may be glossed as "shameful nakedness." Both men and women have parts that are *'awrah* and must be covered. However, in some Muslim texts and social contexts, the female body is uniquely associated with **sex** and shame. A prophetic tradition of somewhat dubious authenticity declares that "Woman is an *'awrah*," or even "Woman is entirely an *'awrah*," and a number of classical jurists were guided by this view. Some thinkers have held that women's voices are *'awrah* when heard by unrelated men.

Although the Qur'an does not express these sentiments, it does differentiate between men and women with regard to modest clothing in the most important reference to *'awrah* (24:31). In this use, however, *'awrah* is not defined; it merely refers to the permissibility of women's "adornments" being viewed by "children who have not yet attained knowledge of women's *'awrah*." (In addition to one verse using the term in an unrelated sense, the term *'awrah* also appears in 24:58 in defining "three times of nakedness" when children are to knock before entering private chambers.)

Later jurists explored the issue of *'awrah* as it related to covering bodies, particularly women's. Multiple variables determine which body parts must be covered, some related to the characteristics of the female in question and others related to specific situations. As to the first, variables include whether a woman was free or enslaved—**slavery** was an integral part of premodern Muslim societies—and her age or physical maturity; it was at puberty, generally, that full covering became obligatory. With free women, the degree of covering required depended on who she was covering herself from and what activity she was engaged in.

Different standards of acceptable exposure were in place for persons at various degrees of closeness. The greatest degree of covering is required when a woman is in the presence of non-*mahram* men other than her husband. (A *mahram* is a relative within the "forbidden degrees," that is, someone too closely related to marry such as a father, father-in-law, uncle, brother, or son.) With *mahram* relatives, a certain degree of relaxation in dress is permissible but with men who are potential **marriage** partners, even a married woman (who might find herself marriageable after widowhood or **divorce**) must cover her body, including her hair. There was general agreement that the hair of a free, post-pubescent female must be covered in front of all non-*mahram* men. (Some premodern jurists made an exception for a woman's male slave-servant, who might be allowed to see her hair, presuming that because of his enslavement he could never be a suitor.)

Whether a woman was obligated to cover her face was more controversial. Most agreed that women's covering of the face was not mandated by the Qur'an or by the Prophet, but many classical jurists held that such covering was nonetheless strongly recommended or even required for women. Al-Razi (543–606/1149–1209) held that by covering her face a woman made clear that she was not sexually available. Notably, a man is permitted and even encouraged to look at the face of a woman he is considering marrying, even if he normally would not be allowed to.

For free women, the breasts were obviously *'awrah*, and the relevant debate was over what constituted the *juyub* (sing. *jayb*) that Q. 24:31 mandates covering. Reflecting the different expectations for women of different statuses, slave women were subject to looser controls on their appearance and mobility. Khaled Abou El Fadl points out that jurists disagreed as to whether enslaved women's breasts constituted *'awrah* and had to be covered in public. Ankles were usually agreed to constitute *'awrah* for free women, but there was debate as to whether the tops of a free woman's feet were *'awrah* or whether they might be seen.

Where women are concerned, the distinction between relatives and non-relatives does not apply. Women can generally see parts of other women except what is between the navel and the knees. However, sometimes a distinction is made between Muslim women and other women in determining what it is acceptable to see.

A husband, and he alone, may see all parts of his wife's body (and vice versa). It is at the very least disapproved for either spouse to look directly at the other's genitals, but this is a matter of modest conduct rather than legal offense.

The rules governing male *'awrah* are much simpler and do not generally vary according to status or setting: a mature male must cover between his navel and his knees. The knees themselves are part of *'awrah* for the Hanafis, and so must be covered, while other **madhhab**s allow the knees to appear. Despite this limited definition of *'awrah*, Muslim men in traditional contexts usually wear concealing clothes frequently including some type of head covering. Men's dress has not become the symbol of Islamic identity that women's has, however, and this combination of social pressure and greater legal attention to women's bodies as potential sources of sexual temptation and resultant social chaos means that *'awrah* continues to be defined as a women's issue.

See also: *fitnah*, *haram*, *hijab*, **morality**

Further reading: Abou El Fadl 2001b; Alvi, Hoodfar, and McDonough 2003

AYAH/AYAT

The term *ayah* (pl. *ayat*), which appears hundreds of times in the Qur'an, has two basic meanings: a "sign" from God and a "verse" of the Qur'an. Q. 2:99 encompasses both meanings when it declares, "We have sent down to you *ayat*." The two definitions of *ayah* are interconnected; **revelation** is itself a sign from God, which points through *ayat*/verses to other *ayat*/signs already existing in nature. These two forms of God's signs strengthen and reinforce one another through the human intellect; *ayat* are said to be for those who think or reflect (2:164, 6:198, 45:13).

"God makes clear His signs to humankind," the Qur'an states (2:187). Some of God's signs are clear in the physical universe. Natural signs appear throughout the Qur'an as evidence of God's majesty and power, as well as mercy. "In the heavens and the earth there are signs for the believers" (45:3). "We have appointed the night and the day as two signs" (17:12).

Other signs involve **prophethood**: "a Messenger to recite Our *ayat* to you (2:151)." Moses is frequently mentioned as a bringer of *ayat*: "We sent Moses with Our signs" (11:96 and 14:5; cf. 7:103, 10:75, 17:101, 23:45). At least one prophet not only recites *ayat*, but is himself a sign: "We made Mary's son, and his mother, to be a sign" (23:50).

Despite the clarity of God's signs, human beings may disregard the evidence of God's presence and command (e.g., 2:61, 27:82, 31:7, 46:26, 54:42, 64:10). Disbelieving in the clear signs that already exist, individuals may challenge prophets to produce signs (26:154). However, some people are stubborn; Q. 2:145 points out that "if you bring to [them] every sign, they will not follow." Denial of God's signs—both natural and revelatory—is a rejection of God: "none denies Our signs but the unbelievers" (29:47; cf., 29:49). Commenting on the relationship between God's signs and *kufr*—which encompasses both unbelief and ingratitude—those who reject God's signs are both ungrateful for these favors and in a state of fundamental denial of God's existence or power.

Ayah is also the technical term for a Qur'anic verse; Q. 11:1 speaks of "a Book whose verses are set clear." The Qur'an is divided into 114 chapters, or **surah**s, of varying lengths, and each surah is divided into a varying number of verses, from a low of three in surah 103 to a high of 286 in surah 2. The *ayat* themselves are also of varying lengths—some are short and rhyming, or contain brief, powerful oath-like statements (e.g., surah 100), while others are long and detailed, such as the discussion of inheritance in 4:11–12.

Further reading: Algar 1998; Robinson 1996

BALAGHAH see **rhetoric**

BARAKAH

Barakah means blessing; something blessed is to be honored and respected. "And We have placed mountains on top of it and We have placed blessings [*barakah*] there" (41:10), where the reference is to the earth, and the ways in which God has created it in such a way as to make life easy for his creatures. "And then We made to inherit those who were weak and oppressed in the eastern and western parts of the earth, in which We had placed blessing [*barakah*]" (7:137), where the Jews are given land and allowed to overcome the apparent might of Pharaoh. Yet these blessings are dependent on the behavior of the recipients: "We would have opened blessings [*barakaht*] for them from the heavens and the earth had they only behaved well, but they did not so they suffered the ultimate fate of disobedience and evil" (7:96).

The word *tabaraka* occurs in the Qur'an only with reference to God or his name. This suggests that all *barakah* belongs to God, that it all originates from him and that he gives *barakah* to various things in his **creation**. For example, rain is blessed since an increase in agriculture and life in general is obtained by it and there is also considerable growth on account of it. "And We sent down blessed rain from the sky and produced from it gardens and grain that are reaped" (50:9). There is not absolute *barakah* and things do not on their own or in and of themselves produce *barakah*. The rain might come down, but if it is not followed up by some sunshine and if the soil is not appropriate, and if there is too much rain, then the crops will not flourish. By contrast, some things always exhibit *barakah*: "Glorified and exalted is he who took his slave [Muhammad] for a journey by night from *masjid al-haram* to *masjid al-aqsah*, the neighborhood of which We have blessed" (17:1). We also read: "Verily the first House [of **worship**] appointed for humankind was that at Bakka [Mecca], full of blessing and guidance for the world [human beings and *jinn*]" (3:96).

See also: *ziyarah*

Further reading: Qutb 1981

BASMALAH

The term *basmalah* is an acronymic abbreviation taken from the first two words of the formula *bi-smi llahi l-rahmani l-rahim*: In the name of God, the Merciful (and) the Compassionate. This invocation precedes each surah in the Qur'an except surah 9 (and it also appears at 27:30). It has become the most widely used Islamic expression of piety. The *basmalah* is a ubiquitous feature of Islamic calligraphy and ornament. It is also used as a magical tool and symbol. Starting an act in the name of God appeals powerfully to God's protection, grace, and mercy. To invoke God's name in the right sort of way suggests that the result could be divine intervention.

The two divine attributes, *rahman* and *rahim*, which appear in the *basmalah* are derived from the same root, associated with *rahmah* or mercy. Qur'anic commentators often note that though the terms are related, these divine names or attributes carry subtle differences of meaning: while *rahman* is an exclusively divine epithet, *rahim* can be attributed to God and his creatures.

Why the *basmalah* is missing in surah 9 is unclear, and is itself the source of much commentary. Some have argued that the subject matter of surah 9, which describes God's wrath and the punishment of idolators, made an allusion to God's mercy inappropriate, yet there are other surahs which combine reports of punishment and **mercy**. Since the *basmalah* is the traditional introduction to each separate surah, other commentators regard surah 8 and surah 9 as originally constituting one surah precisely since the *basmalah* between them is missing.

See also: *al-asma' al-husna'*, **surah**, *tafsir*

Further reading: Algar 1998; Wild 1996

BEAUTY

The word "beauty" (*jamal*) occurs only once in the Qur'an (16:5–6). The context of this admonition to mankind is the divine **creation** of nature and the word "beauty" refers to cattle and their uses. The word *jamil*, usually translated as "beautiful," means in the Qur'an "praiseworthy." *Jamal* is used, however, for those of God's names that refer to certain attributes, in tandem with the term *jalal*: beauty and majesty together constitute a more complete rendering of the divine qualities.

Beauty and goodness are linked in the Qur'an. "God has sent down the fairest discourse as a book, consistent and repetitive, whereat shiver the skins of those who fear their Lord; then their skins and their hearts soften to the remembrance of God" (39:23). The meaning of the words "the fairest discourse" (*ahsan al-hadith*) could include the aesthetic, but also includes the good and morally uplifting. The same is true for the expression "the fairest of stories" (*ahsan al-qasas*; 12:3), with which the Qur'an introduces the long narrative about Joseph and his brothers. The effect of the recitation of the "fairest discourse" is described as sublime. It is in general primarily associated with the

Qur'anic verses describing the catastrophes preceding the **day of judgment** and depicting **hell**. The inimitability of the Qur'an, as far as it was connected to **aesthetics**, lay thus more in its overwhelming and frightening power than in its sweetness.

On a different level, a calligraphic rendering of the Qur'anic text can be a source of great aesthetic gratification. As sculpture and painting in a religious context were frowned upon by many Muslims through the ages, much of the religious–artistic creative energy of Muslim culture went into the highly developed art of calligraphy, above all the calligraphy of the Qur'an. As a mural inscription in a mosque or as a precious page of a manuscript, Qur'anic calligraphy was and is the artistic form of the revealed word of God.

See also: *al-asma' al-husna'*, **morality**

Further reading: Kermani 1999; Leaman 2004

CALIPHATE

The caliph (*khalifah*) is a successor to the Prophet Muhammad in governing the Muslim community. The first four successors to Muhammad—known among **Sunni**s as the "rightly guided caliphs"—were Abu Bakr (ruled 632–634), 'Umar ibn al-Khattab (r. 634–644), 'Uthman ibn 'Affan (r. 644–656), and 'Ali ibn Abi Talib (r. 656–661). Attesting to the importance of family and personal ties in that era, the first two were the Prophet's fathers-in-law and the second two, his sons-in-law. 'Ali, who was also Muhammad's younger cousin, was married to Fatima, the only one of Muhammad's daughters to bear surviving offspring, Hasan and Husayn.

The major split between groups that eventually became the Sunnis and **Shi'ah** happened over the belief of some early Muslims that 'Ali was the rightful ruler of the first community and that the first three caliphs had been usurpers. This disagreement began as infighting and ended in open conflict, causing the first *fitnah*, a period of social disruption and unrest. The caliphate became a Sunni institution, lasting in various forms until the demise of the Ottoman Empire, when it was formally abolished in 1924 by the Turkish government. The Shi'ah referred to their early leaders, who retained a more specifically religious authority, as **imam**s; in place of a caliphate, they had an imamate, with a somewhat different scope of religious and political authority

In addition to its general meaning of succession—related terms appear numerous times in the Qur'an with regard to some communities, prophets, or angels following each other chronologically—the term *khalifah* appears in discussions of human vicegerency on earth. Q. 2:30 famously declares, "I am setting in the earth a viceroy," and 6:65 states, "it is He who appointed you viceroys in the earth" (cf. 10:14, 33:39).

See also: **democracy**

Further reading: Madelung 1997

CALL TO PRAYER see **prayer**

CHARITY

Charity is an obligation for every Muslim, its importance clear in the fact that obligatory almsgiving (*zakat*) is the third of Islam's **five pillars**, after the testimony of faith (*shahadah*) and **prayer**. Indeed, the Qur'an often mentions those who "keep the prayer and pay the *zakat*" together; this common phrase, which appears over two dozen times in the Qur'an (e.g., 2:43, 4:77, 9:11, 21:73, 58:13, 73:20, 98:5), shows the close linkage between one's **obligation**s to God and one's duty to fellow believers. One ought to have the intention of pleasing God when giving alms (30:39); non-payment of alms is linked to lack of belief in the **afterlife** (41:7).

The term *zakat* connotes purification. Calculated at 2.5 percent of accrued wealth (with different percentages for agricultural produce and livestock), and exempting basic items of personal use such as a residence, the *zakat* "purifies" the wealth that remains. In addition to providing for the needy the *zakat* prevents the hoarding of wealth, something repeatedly condemned in the Qur'an (e.g., 9:34) and the **sunnah**. It is incumbent on every Muslim who possesses the requisite amount of wealth. The obligation of *zakat* is individual: a husband does not pay on his wife's wealth, nor a wife on her husband's, as there is no marital property regime.

In medieval times, *zakat* was often collected and distributed by the state through a variety of intermediaries. The list of those who can receive *zakat* includes both the poor and new Muslims (some of these categories are the same as those who may be supported from booty; see 8:41). Any Muslims too poor to pay *zakat* themselves and who have financial obligations are entitled to receive it. In fact, a wife can give charity to her husband if she is wealthy and he is poor.

A Muslim's charitable impulses need not be constrained by the formal obligation of alms. *Sadaqah* is voluntary charity. Tales are told of famous incidents where early Muslims gave away half or all of their possessions. The Prophet's widow Aishah reportedly gave so freely of the large sums she received as pension distributions that when she requested meat for a meal soon after receiving one such payment, her servant informed her that she had no money left with which to purchase it.

Generosity is valued, and the Qur'an condemns those who turn away the needy. It also warns, however, against doing anything for show or following up charitable giving with reminders of one's generosity. **Sufi** thinkers have elaborated on this, noting that one should give charity "without being asked." Anything given after someone has been driven by need to request it is, according to the Sufi scholar al-Sulami (d. 412/1021), "merely reparation for the embarrassment suffered by the asker."

In medieval Muslim societies, charity was often channeled through pious endowments known as *awqaf* (sing. *waqf*). The income from these endowments could be used to provide for family members or the poor, or to support institutions such as hospitals, **mosque**s, places of **education**, or Sufi lodges.

Charity need not necessarily be material; the Prophet reportedly said that a smile can be charity, as can a loving gesture between spouses.

Further reading: Izutsu 1966; Lev 2005; al-Sulami 1983

CLERGY see **ulama**

COMMANDING THE GOOD

Muslims are repeatedly ordered in the Qur'an to "command right and forbid wrong [*amr bi'l-ma'ruf wa nahy 'an al-munkar*]" (e.g., 3:104, 3:110, 3:114, 9:112; see also 9:71 and 9:67, where the order is reversed). The phrase "commanding right" may also be rendered "commanding what is good" or "what is proper": *al-ma'ruf* literally means "what is known" and refers to behavior that is appropriate and honorable according to custom. Q. 2:228, before its famous declaration that men "have a degree over" women, uses the term in this sense in its discussion of marital rights: "women have rights [from men] like the rights men have [from them] according to what is *ma'ruf*."

20

The other element in this equation, "wrong," means something that is disapproved of. It relates to, but is not precisely the same as, *zulm*—oppression. The duty of forbidding wrong can reasonably be summed up in a **hadith** found in *Sahih Muslim*: "Whosoever sees a wrong, let him change it with his hand. If he is not able, then [let him condemn it] with his tongue. If he is not able, then [let him hate it] with his heart, and that is the weakest **faith**." ·

As this hadith shows, there are different ways in which one forbids wrong. The precise scope of the interrelated duties of commanding right and forbidding wrong occupied Muslim thinkers extensively. How ought Muslims from diverse walks of life respond in concrete social interactions with other human beings who are engaged in wrongdoing? Both male and female believers are to command right and forbid wrong (9:71) according to the Qur'an, but medieval scholars tended to view women's duty as more restricted than that of men. More recently, some thinkers have used this verse as evidence for the divinely approved nature of women's social roles.

Q. 3:104 identifies the people who will be successful as those who "invite to good, command what is right, and forbid what is wrong." Q. 3:110 joins "commanding what is right and forbidding what is wrong" with believing in God as a characteristic of "the best of communities." In 3:114, belief in the Last Day and the doing of good deeds are mentioned along with commanding what is good and forbidding wrongdoing as characteristics of "the righteous."

See also: **knowledge, morality, *ummah***

Further reading: Cook 2000b

CONVERSION

Religious conversion is the process of renouncing one's original religious standing or affiliation for the sake of another religious ideal. Conversion appears in different ways in the Qur'an. *Wahy* (**revelation**) is the key factor underlying guidance. The Qur'an argues that guidance is bestowed only by God, and so he is the only source of guidance. "Whomever God leads is indeed led aright, while whomever God sends astray is indeed a loser" (7:178). "Then God sends whom He will astray, and guides aright whom He will. He is the Mighty, the Wise" (14:4; see also 2:120, 10:35, 17:97, 18:17). However, God does not force people to accept guidance; rather, he expects individuals to use their free will and decide what they are going to believe and how they will act. "Lo! We have shown him the way, whether he be grateful or disbelieving" (76:3; also 28:56, 47:17). There is guidance right from the beginning, and we are taken to know how things are just by paying attention to what happens around us and through listening to those who bring messages from God (91:8). Our innate character makes us aware, in varying degrees, of the truth. So conversion is not the acceptance of a new **religion**, but a return to the original religion: the Qur'an suggests that everyone is born a Muslim, or rather that the natural state or *fitrah* of the human being is a state of submission (*islam*) to God. Someone who converts to Islam in a sense remembers her original religion and returns to it. Some English-speaking Muslims prefer the term "reversion" to conversion; others, particularly some African Americans, use the term "transition" to describe the process of coming to identify religiously as Muslims.

God has given us both revelation and also rationality, and with these two factors it should be difficult to understand how we can go awry. "He has shown you [Muhammad] the scripture with truth, confirming what was [revealed] before it just as He revealed the Torah and the Gospel" (3:3), and it is made clear that the Qur'an provides the most direct guidance. "This Qur'an guides in the straightest way, and gives an indication to the believers who do good works that they will receive a great reward" (17:9).

See also: **apostasy**, *fitrah*, **straight path**

Further reading: Köse 1996; Levtzion 1979

CREATION

God is the creator of the universe and humanity, an attribute reflected in the divine name *al-Khaliq*, the Creator. The Qur'an repeatedly mentions God's creative activity. Indeed, the first portion of the Qur'an revealed states: "Read in the Name of your Lord who created, created the human being [*al-insan*] from a clot" (96:1–2).

The creation of humanity is described in numerous verses of the Qur'an. Human beings are variously said to be created from a clot, a drop of fluid, or from dust or clay. Q. 22:5 describes several stages of creation and gestation. God not only originates but also shapes or fashions (*khalaqa fa sawwa*) (7:11) as part of his creative activity. Humanity is distinguished in its creation from other beings; Q. 55:14–15 states that God "created the human being from sounding clay," while the *jinn* are created from a flame or "smokeless fire." **Angels** are created from light.

One important account of creation is found at the beginning of surah 4 ("Women"). Q. 4:1 commands people: "Revere your lord who created you from a single soul (*nafs wahidah*) and created from it its mate and from them both brought forth many men and women." This account does not give a gender for the first created being or its mate (literally, "her" mate since the word *nafs*, the soul or self out of which the first being is created, is grammatically feminine). Feminist commentators have argued on the basis of this and other verses that there is no Qur'anic basis for considering man to have been created first or viewing woman as a secondary being. However, based in part on **hadith** reports that echo the biblical story of the creation of the first woman from Adam's rib, most Muslims believe that Adam is God's first creation. He was followed by his wife who is traditionally called Hawwa, though the Qur'anic text does not name her, referring instead to Adam's "wife" (2:35, 7:19, 20:117).

Q. 4:1 highlights the complementarity of humankind in creation, and the importance of procreation for the continued development of human life on earth, in direct contrast to God's status as creator. God's creative activity is unlike human reproduction; God has no mate, partners, or children (2:116) and was not "born" (112). While Jesus's birth is unusual (Jesus has no father, but is rather a "spirit breathed into Mary" or a "word from God"), it is no more so than the creation of the first human beings; Jesus remains a created servant of God, not a partner or child. Q. 3:59 explicitly likens Jesus to Adam in his relationship to God: "He created him from dust then said to him 'Be,' and he was."

The creation of humanity (for the purpose of stewardship or trusteeship) happens within a universe also created by God. All of creation attests to God's power and authority. Q. 55:6 points to this phenomenon in detail when it describes the stars and trees prostrating before God. All of creation is *muslim*, in the sense of submitting to God, though the sound foundation (*fitrah*) of human beings does not prevent them from deviating.

The purpose of humanity's creation, in fact, is to serve God: "I have not created *jinn* and humankind except to **worship**/serve Me" (51:56); the sentiment appears also in the form of a command: "Worship/serve your Lord who created you" (2:21; see also 41:37).

See also: **caliphate**, **feminism**

Further reading: Wadud 1999

DAR

Dar is a noun meaning a large house, especially one with a courtyard; the term could also refer to a sizeable building comprising several sets of apartments. *Dar al-Islam*, "the abode of Islam," is the territory governed by Muslims with a Muslim leader and adhering to religious law. For medieval Muslim jurists, this was a central concept in structuring the way they conceived of the world. The contrary of *dar al-Islam* is the "abode of war," *dar al–harb*. *Dar al-harb* refers to the country or countries of the unbelievers or the polytheists between whom and the Muslims there are conflicts.

The *shari'ah* or Islamic law has established different sets of laws and codes that apply to Muslims and non-Muslims in either state. Christians and Jews were **People of the Book** regardless of which realm they dwelt in, but those within dar al-Islam had the additional status of *dhimmi* or protected subordinate minority.

Further reading: Lewis 1988

DAR AL-HARB see *dar*

DAR AL-ISLAM see *dar*

DAY OF JUDGMENT

After the death of the world, God will resurrect everyone. In its depiction of the gathering for the day of judgment, the **hadith** literature speaks of an extremely high temperature and people asking for intercession by the prophets. Due to their ablution before the five daily **prayer**s, the Prophet will recognize the members of his community. On this day, divine **justice** will be carried out finally. The Qur'an explains that on this day people will be divided into two groups. Those who receive their books—the accounting of their deeds—through their right hands are the people of **paradise**. They will find what God has prepared for them to reward them for their behavior. The second group will receive their books through their left hands. Their destination is **hell**. The Prophet gives hope to some in this group, indicating that anyone who has **faith**, even as small as a seed of mustard, will not stay there forever. Eventually they will get through the period of punishment and go to heaven. The highest pleasure in heaven is to see God (*ru'yatullah*), although more material descriptions of what life there is like are also given.

In various accounts, Muhammad mentions a number of events that prefigure the final hour: the appearance of the anti-Christ (*al-Dajjal*); the emergence of a beast; the sun rising in the west; the descent of Jesus; the emergence of Gog and Magog; the disappearance of three lands in the east, the west, and the Arabian peninsula; and a fire arising in the south to bring people to the place of the final gathering.

See also: **afterlife**, *ummah*

Further reading: Nursi 1990

DEMOCRACY

In the Qur'an, the righteous are described as managing their affairs through "mutual consultation" or s*hurah* (42:38). The importance of consultation is often taken to prefigure the institution of democracy. The concepts of caliph and **caliphate** are relevant to the development of Islamic ideas about democracy. Caliph was the title of the monarchs who ruled the medieval Muslim world, Muhammad's successors, but the first caliphs were selected by a process of consultation among some of the Prophet's Companions. In the Qur'an, the Arabic words for caliph (*khalifah*) and caliphate (*khilafah*) have a different meaning than "ruler." These terms refer to stewardship, trusteeship, or vicegerency. In this way, Adam, as the first human, is identified as God's caliph or steward on earth (2:30). Muhammad is instructed to remind humans that God made them the caliphs (stewards or trustees) of the earth (6:165). In this way the term caliphate refers to the broad responsibilities of humans to be the stewards of God's creation. Some commentators argue that it follows that Muslims have to be involved in the running of their state and cannot give up this duty to others, since the duty is imposed on them by God.

Many significant concepts of classical Islamic political thought point to the key concerns of democracy. There is a covenant among rulers and ruled (*'ahd*), consensus of the representatives of community (*ijma'*), legitimization of public power through free will (*ikhtiyar*), **justice** (*'adl, 'adalah*), general welfare (*maslahah*), and equality (*musawat*). These concepts can be found in the commentaries and theoretical works inspired by the Qur'an.

See also: *ummah*

Further reading: Campanini 2003; Esposito and Voll 1996; Muqtedar Khan 2006; Mernissi 1992; Mousalli 2001; Sachedina 2001

DEVIL/SATAN

The devil appears in the Qur'an as either Iblis or *al-shaytan* ("the satan"). The Qur'an describes the devil's revolt against God in four sorts of dialogue between God and Iblis (7:12–19, 15:31–40, 17:61–65, 38:71–85). One of the views that emerges is that the devil will be very successful in trying to get human beings to go awry.

Some Qur'anic passages seem to suggest that Iblis before his fall was an **angel**, others that he was a **jinn** or, in 18:50, both. His importance is in resisting God and interfering with divine guidance. He first of all succeeds with Adam and Eve (7:19–22), where he tempts them and lies to them. He is keen on whispering to human beings and persuading them to do the wrong thing.

On the **day of judgment** humanity will be divided into Satan's group (*hizb al-shaytan* 58:19), which will go to **hell**, and God's party (*hizb allah* 58:22), which will enter **paradise**.

The devil is omnipresent and has to be constantly resisted. Special care must be taken in certain activities: "When you recite the Qur'an, seek refuge in God from the accursed Satan" (16:98). Although the devil is powerful, his power will come to an end. After the day of judgment the devil and his hosts will be thrown into hell (26:94–95) just like human sinners.

"Whispering," *waswas*, is used four times in the Qur'an as a verb and once as a noun, functioning as an attribute of Satan. In Qur'an 7:20 and 20:120, Satan whispers to Adam and his wife in the Garden of Eden; in 50:16, also in the context of creation, it is said that God knows that the "self," the human soul, whispers to itself. In 114:4–5, the final surah of the Qur'an, Satan is portrayed as the evil whisperer who insinuates himself into the hearts of people.

See also: *nafs*

Further reading: Awn 1983

DHIKR see **Sufism**

DHIMMI

Dhimmi, a term related to the Arabic word meaning **obligation**, refers to an individual from the **People of the Book** living under the protection of the Muslim state in **Dar** al-Islam. Dhimmi status involves a community's agreement to pay the *jizya*, a type of poll tax, to the Muslim ruler (9:29) and to accept a subordinate status.

Historically, *dhimmi* communities were allowed to manage their own affairs, maintaining their own governing bodies. Under the Ottomans, this was known as the millet system. In some cases, *dhimmi*s sought to have disputes adjudicated in Muslim courts, at times taking advantage of rights not available under their own religious laws. For example, some Christian men availed themselves of Muslim law to practice polygamy or divorce. When commercial or criminal disputes pitted Muslims against non-Muslims, however, *dhimmi*s could be at a real disadvantage in Muslim courts and were sometimes prohibited from testifying.

The extent to which *dhimmi*s were accorded inferior status—or even interacted regularly with Muslims at all—varied a great deal. Medieval Andalusia has a mostly deserved reputation as a place where a productive co-existence emerged, though its egalitarianism and harmony has sometimes been exaggerated. Even there, in times of political uncertainty or strife, *dhimmi*s might find their communities under pressure as well, with symbolic humiliation becoming part of communal life.

In the modern Muslim world, nations have had to decide whether to distinguish between citizens on the basis of religious affiliation. Most do so only with regard to so-called personal-status laws but formally allow equal economic and political rights for non-Muslims.

Further reading: Lewis 1988

DIN see **religion**

DIVORCE

Divorce is explicitly permitted, and closely regulated, by the Qur'an, mostly in surahs 2, 4, and 65. These verses accept, modify, or sometimes prohibit pre-Islamic Arab customs in many areas related to the family, but pay particular attention to **marriage** and divorce. Although divorce has been widely practiced through Muslim history, it has been often discouraged by those quoting Muhammad's declaration, found in the **hadith** compilation of Abu Dawud: "Of all things permitted, divorce is the most repugnant to God."

Although divorce may have been discouraged—one verse (4:35) recommends the appointment of arbiters from the spouses' families to try to resolve disputes—it was nonetheless allowed. The Qur'an's dictates and Muhammad's rulings were solidified by the schools of jurisprudence into three main types: male-initiated repudiation; female-initiated divorce for compensation; and judicial divorce, also usually female-initiated.

The primary form of divorce, *talaq*, is a unilateral repudiation by the husband. In pre-Islamic Arabia, *talaq* featured in those marriages where wives joined their husbands' tribes and where any offspring were part of that tribe. The main Islamic reform was to limit the number of times a husband could pronounce such a form of divorce to three (or, though this was disputed, one "absolute" pronouncement). If a husband made his divorce pronouncement final, the wife had to marry (and be divorced or widowed by) an intermediate husband before she could remarry her original husband.

Since *talaq* was based on an oath—something carrying tremendous weight in Arab society of the time—this form of divorce could also be delegated to the wife herself or made to hinge on some action by the wife or the husband or a third party. Such oaths might be used to restrict wives' behavior ("If you ever do such-and-such, you are divorced") but have also been used to restrict husbands' privileges ("If I ever strike you" or "If I ever take another wife you are divorced"). Oaths might also be used to induce another to perform an act he or she is unwilling to do: "If you don't sew my cloth into a new suit by tomorrow, my wife is divorced" might not actually be meant as divorce, but has been taken to actually incur that consequence by most jurists. This form of divorce, where the point of the statement is not the divorce but the intended persuasion or coercion of a third party, was rejected by some early authorities and has been declared null by a number of modern legislatures.

In the second form of divorce, *khul'*, the wife returns the dower she received at marriage or pays some other mutually agreed compensation in return for divorce. The vast majority of jurists have considered the husband's consent required for *khul'*, limiting its usefulness as a means for wives to get out of marriages. However, twentieth-century reforms in both Pakistan and Egypt have substituted judicial consent for the husband's agreement. The story of Habiba bint Sahl, who approached the Prophet to obtain a divorce from Zayd bin Thabit, offering to return the orchard he had given her as dower, may be invoked to support *khul'* without the husband's consent; some accounts show the Prophet accepting the divorce without consulting Zayd.

Judicial dissolution has been practiced since the early years of Islam. Falling under various headings including *faskh* (annulment) or *tatliq* (divorce pronounced by a judge on the husband's behalf), grounds on which a wife could obtain divorce from an unwilling husband varied dramatically across the classical doctrines of the legal schools. Modern legal reforms have again adapted and adopted grounds from the more liberal schools to make judicial divorce easier for women to obtain.

Even in the premodern period, however, female-initiated divorce was commonplace. It is difficult to judge what percentage of divorces were sought by women, because these cases are overrepresented in court archives. *Talaq* pronouncements by men were extrajudicial. Before modern laws requiring government registration of marriage and divorces, divorce would have only come to the court's attention if there were issues such as unpaid support to resolve. In both *khul'* and judicial divorce, women's possession of independent resources facilitated their getting out of marriages they did not want.

In addition to limiting the number of times a man could divorce and then take back his wife, the Qur'an also instituted a three-menstrual-cycle waiting period before a woman could remarry. The purpose of this *'iddah*, which existed in a slightly different form for widows, was to ascertain the paternity of any children resulting from the union. There was, therefore, no waiting period for women divorced before their marriages were consummated. In such a case, husbands only owed their wives half the agreed dower.

Today, divorced women may be stigmatized or viewed as less desirable spouses in some areas—this is often the case in North American Muslim communities—but this is not universal. Remarriage has historically been the norm for divorced or widowed Muslim women. A medieval woman's marital prospects (and dower amount) might be enhanced if she was a virgin, but her family pedigree and economic status were generally of greater import. With the exception of Aishah, married when she was quite young, all of Muhammad's wives were either divorcees or widows.

See also: **madhhab**

Further reading: Ali 2006; An-Na'im 2002a; Esposito with DeLong-Bas 2001; Rapoport 2005; Sonbol 1996b; Tucker 1998

EDUCATION

A famous **hadith** calls on Muslims to seek knowledge, even if it be found in China. The Qur'an can readily be seen as calling on Muslims to use their reason, intellect, and whatever is the current state of human **knowledge** to try to understand and explore the meanings of God's revelations (25:73). There can be no general incompatibility between

Islam and science since for many centuries the center of scientific investigation internationally was precisely the Islamic world. Some schools or madrasahs that provide a predominantly religious education do not involve themselves much in secular education, but the Qur'an itself provides no support for such a policy. On the contrary, all the evidence suggests that the Qur'an takes a practical attitude to issues like education in general, although of course religious education is regarded as highly significant.

Religious education involves study of the Qur'an, the hadith, the **sunnah** of the Prophet and his *sirah* or biography. Underlying this education is some type of study of the Arabic language which is a foreign tongue for 80 percent of the world's Muslims. Most often, children are taught to recite Arabic, learning rules of pronunciation without any attention to Arabic meaning.

The Qur'an is often learnt by rote, and the status of the teacher may be elevated since he is passing on religious truths, not subjects that may be acquired or rejected casually by the student. It is often argued that the pedagogy is based on the view that knowledge is acquired rather than discovered, and that the student's mind is passive and receptive rather than active and creative, and the general attitude is that all knowledge is seen as unchangeable and books need to be internalized and not questioned.

To the extent this picture is accurate, it reveals a contrast between Islamic and modern education. The former has an otherworldly orientation, promotes Islam, uses curricula largely unchanged since medieval times, and treats knowledge as something to be revealed because of a divine command. The questioning of what is taught is then unwelcome, teaching styles may be authoritarian, education is mainly undifferentiated, and memorization is important. By contrast, modern education has an orientation towards this world, and claims to be directed towards the development of the individual pupil. Curricula change as the subject matter changes, and knowledge is acquired through empirical or deductive methods and treated as a problem-solving tool. Teachers ideally invite student participation and questioning, and the aim is not just to repeat material. Finally, different subjects are clearly distinct from each other, by contrast with the fairly unified notion of religious education.

Hoodbhoy has argued that the two styles of education are in conflict with each other since they differ not only in subject matter but also in style. Students who enter the modern education system from madrasahs are unlikely to do well, as they are accustomed to an entirely different process of education, operating under entirely different sets of rules and expectations.

On the other hand, this view of the clash between the two peda-
gogies, like the clash between civilizations, is regarded by others as
overdone. After all, how much of the so-called modern curriculum
is really taught in accordance with what we are told are the principles of modern education? There is a good deal of rote learning there
also, and students often do not feel that they are encouraged to question or challenge their teachers. Even at the level of tertiary education
many students in the modern system are passive and concentrate on
taking notes and repeating what they hear in the lecture hall. In addition, how much of the religious curriculum is really as traditional as
the stereotype suggests? There is always going to be some mechani-
cal learning when a new language is at issue, and students may also be
encouraged to learn to recite the Qur'an on the way to understanding
it, but these do not in themselves orient the student away from independent thought. There is no evidence that children brought up
within the confines of traditional religious education are any less inno-
vative or active than children brought up within the modern system.

When it was revealed the Qur'an challenged many of the prevailing views of the time and in particular what had up to that point been
authority. The Qur'an argues that individuals should not do what their
fathers had done just because that was the accepted practice, but advocates thinking, reasoning, and arguing until the truth is revealed. It is
difficult to argue, then, that Qur'anic education is in itself opposed to
modern principles of teaching and learning. This is not to ignore that
in many places Qur'anic education follows a traditional model that
does stand in the way of modern education, but then modern education often does not accord in practice with the theory of how it
should operate.

Further reading: Hoodbhoy 1991

EID

There are two Eids or holidays in the Muslim calendar: Eid al-Fitr,
which marks the end of the **fasting** month of Ramadan, and Eid
al-Adha, which follows the **pilgrimage** and commemorates Abraham's willingness to sacrifice his son. Both Eids are the occasion for
congregational **prayer** services which the entire community of Muslims is encouraged to attend.

Sawm (fasting) is the fourth of Islam's **five pillars**: "Fasting is prescribed for you" (2:183). Muslims observe the month of Ramadan,
which is ninth in the lunar calendar, by abstaining from satisfying

bodily appetites from dawn to sunset. Ramadan—the month in which the Qur'an was revealed to Prophet Muhammad as "guidance for humanity" (2:185)—is a time for Qur'anic recitation, self-purification, and charitable acts. Eid al-Fitr falls on the first day of Shawwal, the tenth month in the Islamic calendar, and its celebration marks the collective release from the restrictions of the previous month's fasting. Muslims are encouraged to eat a morning meal before attending the Eid prayer.

Eid al-Adha or Feast of Sacrifice, sometimes also called the "Greater Eid" (Eid al-Kabir), concludes the rituals of pilgrimage (hajj) to Mecca. It celebrates Abraham's resolve to sacrifice his son, usually held to be Ishmael, as a sign of his submission to God. "O my son! I have seen a dream in that I am offering you in sacrifice to God" (37:102). Abraham was about to sacrifice his son when he was stopped by a **revelation** from God. "And We ransomed him with a great sacrifice, [a ram]" (37:105). Muslims often sacrifice an animal and donate most of the meat to the poor, or make a monetary contribution to represent this ceremony. Eid al-Adha occurs on the tenth day of the Islamic month of Dhu'l Hijja. Like Eid al-Fitr, Eid al-Adha also begins with a short prayer followed by a *khutbah* or concluding sermon.

Other customs associated with Eid celebrations vary by country. In many places it is usual to wear new and elaborate clothing to the prayers, and gifts of clothing may be given. Children may receive money or sweets from their parents or other adults. The remainder of Eid day, after the prayer service, is often taken up with visiting friends and family.

ETHICS see **morality**

FAITH

Iman is faith, and the interesting question is: faith in what? Most **Sunni** creeds consider faith to include belief in God, **angels**, his Books, his Messengers, the **day of judgment**, and destiny. The **Shi'i** would add accepting the special status of the Family of the House— that is, Muhammad's descendants through 'Ali and Fatima.

The Book is quite clear on the difference between saying one believes and actually believing: "The desert Arabs said, 'We believe.' Say, 'You have not believed,' but rather say, 'We have submitted,' for faith has not yet entered your hearts" (49:14). This brings out nicely the close links between *islam* (submission) and *iman* (faith). Submission is indeed a critical component of faith, even for those touched by **prophethood**: "Then, when they both had submitted, and he [Abraham] laid [his son] down on his forehead" (37:103).

In some ways faith is easy to acquire since there are so many signs around us in nature and in the Qur'an itself that make a thoughtful person reflect on their origins and design. Those who do not appreciate these signs make more than an intellectual mistake:

> I shall turn away from My signs those who are unjustly proud upon the earth, and if they see the way of rectitude, they do not take it as a way, and if they see the way of error, they take it as a way; that is because they rejected Our signs and did not take sufficient notice of them.
>
> (7:146)

Faith is not just a reflection of our thinking but also of our actions and character. Muslim theologians debated extensively the relationship between faith, actions, and sins. Are deeds required to establish faith? Not according to the Murji'ites, who argued that **sin** committed by one who has faith is no obstacle to remaining a Muslim.

The Mu'tazilites said that a believer who commits a major sin can no longer be considered either a believer but neither is she a disbeliever. They termed such a person a *fasiq* (transgressor), who is between the two stations of belief and unbelief, and represents someone who will remain eternally in **hell**. The Kharijites suggested that a Muslim who deliberately commits a sin becomes a disbeliever, and will remain forever in hell. But the position of most Sunnis is that a Muslim who has committed a sin is still a Muslim, not a disbeliever, although his faith is imperfect. He will not remain forever in hell and we cannot infer from his actions that he is not a believer. After all, "Whoever does an atom's weight of good shall see it" (99:7).

An important school initiated by Abu Hanifa (d. 150/767) and provided with a solid intellectual foundation by al-Maturidi (d. 303/944) argued that even the worst sinner cannot be treated as an unbeliever; the decision as to whether she is really a believer should be left to God (9:106). The later Hanafi school, basing itself largely on the work of al-Maturidi, argued that *iman* or belief does not genuinely increase or decrease, unlike **taqwah** or piety which does fluctuate.

The Ash'arites take the opposite view on *iman*, and they also argue that we are strictly limited in what we can work out by ourselves using reason alone. For the Maturidis, by contrast, we can even without religious instruction or **revelation** know that some things are just wrong. This has interesting implications for the fate of those who do not receive the message of Islam and then die. The Maturidis argue that how one ought to live is broadly so obvious that those who did not live appropriately will be sent to hell, despite their lack of revelation. The Ash'arites would assign them elsewhere, since they cannot be blamed for their actions. The Maturidi approach was strongly opposed by the Hanbalites, who cited **hadith** statements against the Murji'i hesitancy to define belief. In particular, the Qur'anic idea of "judgment is God's alone" (6:57, 12:40, 67) suggests that religious texts alone provide the answer to all such controversies.

At the end of most accounts of *iman* which are sympathetic to the Murji'i perspective comes a political chapter, and this tends to argue for a quietist approach to an evil ruler. The Hanbali position is more revolutionary, often arguing that the believer does not owe allegiance to a sinful ruler if the latter can be classified as *kafir* (unbeliever); on the contrary, the Muslim may well have a duty of disobedience. The Hanafi, and so largely Murji'i, atmosphere of the Ottoman Empire was much better able to live with diversity than other Muslim regimes which insisted on the ruler being a certain sort of believer. If God is to decide on who is a believer or otherwise, and if he is going to wait until the individual dies before examining his heart, who are we to pronounce on the issue? Hanbalis, like the Kharijites, do point out that we can usually derive character from behavior. If the only thing of importance is the intention of the agent, then it would not matter whether those who pray are actually praying in the right direction or whether they are praying behind a just **imam**. One could abandon all ritual and good works if the only thing of significance was intention (as some ridiculed the Murji'i doctrine, it would not matter if one bowed down in front of a shoe, provided that one had the right intention!), and there are many sayings of the Prophet and his Companions which emphasize the importance of correct action in any definition of being a Muslim. In this debate it is not obvious which protagonist is the more "rational" and which the more "traditional." They each take themselves to be both reasonable and grounded in revelation.

See also: *ayah*, *'aqidah*, *kufr*, **theology**

Further reading: Izutsu 1964

FASTING

Fasting, *sawm*, is one of the **five pillars** of Islam. The obligatory fast occurs during the lunar month of Ramadan, when Muslims believe the first **revelation** of the Qur'an occurred. Fasting requires abstention from food, drink, and **sex** between dawn and dusk. The new moon's crescent announces the end of Ramadan and the celebration of **Eid** al-Fitr, the holiday of fastbreaking.

During Ramadan, Muslims wake to eat a pre-dawn meal. In many societies, it is customary to break the fast at sunset with an odd number of dates and a glass of water or milk, as Muhammad and his Companions are said to have done. *Iftar*, or fast-breaking, meals are often social occasions, when family, neighbors, and friends gather to celebrate the release from the day's restrictions. Fasting is thus both an individual **obligation** and a collective occasion; even Muslims who do not regularly pray or pay obligatory alms may keep the annual fast. When Tunisia's president Habib Bourguiba appeared on television in Ramadan during the 1960s drinking orange juice during daytime, he scandalized not only the nation but the entire region.

According to Islamic jurisprudence, all competent adult Muslims are expected to fast except for those who are ill or traveling. Pregnant or lactating women may fast or not, depending on their health, while menstruants are prohibited from fasting due to ritual impurity. All who miss days are required to make them up, except for the frail elderly and those who have permanent health conditions that make fasting impossible; if they can afford to do so, they should pay **charity** in lieu of fasting. Deliberate breaking of the fast without an excuse requires significant atonement; breaking the fast with sex is a more serious offense than ingestion of food or drink. Children are usually gradually introduced to fasting over a period of years as they approach puberty.

In addition to the mandated fast of Ramadan, and optional fasts on days such as the Day of 'Arafat, some Muslims undertake regular voluntary fasts as one element of their **worship**. A pattern of fasting one day on, one day off is sometimes said to be particularly meritorious, as it prevents the individual from simply becoming accustomed to that pattern of eating. Other pious figures, though, are reported to have fasted continuously for years.

Fasting is meant to be a spiritual exercise as well as an act of physical discipline. Hunger and thirst remind Muslims to be grateful for God's bounty and to be aware of those who are in need. Ideally, fasting should not only involve abstention from food and drink but also anger and careless speech.

Further reading: Izutsu 1966

FATWA

For Westerners, the term fatwa is irrevocably linked with the death sentence pronounced on purportedly blasphemous novelist Salman Rushdie by Ayatollah Khomeini, then the spiritual leader of Iran's Islamic revolutionary regime, a few months before his death in 1989. Yet a fatwa is nothing more or less than an opinion on a legal matter, the response to a question put to a mufti, or respondent.

Although the term fatwa itself does not appear in the Qur'an, related verbs appear several times. On one occasion, the Prophet Joseph is commanded to explain or advise about Pharaoh's dreams (12:43, 12:46); on another, the Queen of Sheba seeks guidance from her advisers (27:32). The most important uses, however, occur in contexts where believers are seeking guidance from Muhammad (*istafta'*) (4:127, 4:176, 12:41, 18:22). On two of these occasions, God "pronounces" or "advises" on matters relating to human social conduct: with regard to marital matters (4:127) and with regard to inheritance (4:176; also 37:11, 37:149).

After the Prophet's death, opinions on matters of religious and personal import were sought from his Companions. Later, the process of seeking and receiving guidance became formalized as scholars were trained in law. Scholars have debated the qualifications necessary for a jurist to engage in *ijtihad* or independent legal reasoning. However, given the range of issues most frequently presented to muftis, those who are qualified merely to give accepted answers according to their **madhhab** can handle many questions. In practice, most fatwas are sought on relatively minor and mundane issues—is my ablution valid if I'm wearing nail polish?—and answers are usually terse, often a simple "yes" or "no."

In cases where novel or complicated issues are at stake, especially where the audience is comprised of other scholars, muftis may respond with lengthy scholarly arguments akin to a lawyer's brief or a judge's decision. These fatwas will cite Qur'anic passages, **hadith**, and precedents from other jurists as well as material pertaining to social custom or circumstance. Despite the notion that the "gates of *ijtihad*" were closed in the eleventh or twelfth century, leading to centuries of stagnation in law, in reality legal change and development continued, with fatwa literature instrumental to this process.

Fatwas from prominent scholars have also been critical in the drafting and reform of national legal codes throughout the Muslim world. But fatwa-giving today ranges from institutions such as the **Dar** al-Ifta' in Egypt to the official Saudi fatwa council whose authoritarianism has been forcefully critiqued by Egyptian-American legal scholar Khaled

Abou El Fadl. Books of fatwas from this organization are widely translated and circulated. Forums for the seeking and granting of fatwas
have proliferated dramatically, and include syndicated newspaper col-
umns, radio call-in shows, and online "ask-the-mufti" websites.

While there has historically been an important minority of female
jurists – unlike the dominant classical view that women could not
serve as judges, there were no restrictions on female fatwa-giving,
as fatwas are not binding—in the modern world few women are
recognized as muftis. This has begun to change at the turn of the
twenty-first century, however. In addition to a group of Indian scholars, who are of the limited-mufti type subordinate to a male scholar,
a group of fifty Moroccan women religious leaders (*murshidat*) are in
theory as qualified to provide the same type of religious guidance
as their male counterparts. (The key difference is that they are not
called **imam**s and they do not lead men in **prayer**.) In 2006, the New
York-based American Society for Muslim Advancement (ASMA)
announced its intention to put together an all-female fatwa council.

See also: *fiqh*, *shari'ah*

Further reading: Abou El Fadl 2001a; Bunt 2003; Esack 2005a; Masud, Messick,
and Powers 1996; Skovgaard-Petersen 1997

FEMINISM

Few issues are so contentious among Muslims as those related to women
and **gender**, and the notion of feminism sparks fierce debate. Whether
one ought even speak of feminism in Muslim contexts remains controversial. For some, feminism has no place in Islam but rather is a
Western invention that has led to drastic and unwelcome social
changes. Others hold that feminism and Islam are compatible and
that seen in the proper light Islam is truly feminist. Even setting aside
squabbles over terminology, among advocates for women's rights
there are sharp divisions over both ultimate aims and the strategies to
be used to attain them.

The main division among gender activists is between secularists
who oppose the use of religion in the public sphere, whatever their
private convictions, and those who work within a religious framework, either out of sincere belief that Islam should be part of the public
order or because they believe the use of religious language is the only
viable approach to achieving desired aims. In scholarly discussions
of Muslim women's gender-related activism, some have proposed a

distinction between Muslim feminism—usually secular—and Islamic feminism, where women use religious ideas to reshape norms about acceptable ways to organize the family and society.

Many of those who identify as feminists are scholars or intellectuals, and scholarship has been one important area where feminists have attempted to encourage social change. Muslim feminists have devoted much attention to interpretation of the Qur'an, often to the exclusion of other important texts, including **hadith** and jurisprudence. A number have worked to expose the patriarchal presuppositions of centuries of male exegetes, arguing that the Qur'an "itself" is not oppressive toward women. Seeking to develop an alternative to this male-focused interpretive literature, scholars including Riffat Hassan, Amina Wadud (whose *Qur'an and Woman* is a foundational text in the genre), and Asma Barlas have undertaken their own thematic exegeses of particular verses, focusing on those that discuss **creation**, **marriage**, and the family.

The other major realm of activism has been legal. Women's rights activists often focus on discriminatory legislation governing the family. Organizations such as Sisters in Islam in Malaysia and the international network Women Living Under Muslim Laws have pursued reforms and objected to particular instances of discrimination or unfair treatment. Other reformist thinkers and groups contest dress codes and restrictions on employment or civic activities such as voting that fall primarily on women. Many female activists, however, are primarily concerned with combating other types of social injustice such as poverty or lack of **education**, often for boys as well as girls.

Further reading: Badran 1996; Barlas 2002; Shaikh 2003b; Wadud 1999, 2006; Yamani with Allen 1996

FIQH

Fiqh, derived from the root meaning "to understand," is the term used for jurisprudence. The closest Qur'anic usage (9:122) refers to those who "become learned in religion [*yatafaqqahu*]." Jurisprudence is often said to be the most important of the Islamic sciences and it is part of a cluster of related concepts that structure Muslim legal norms and practices.

Jurisprudence, which solidified into a discipline during the first Muslim centuries, is not precisely equivalent to law in the modern sense. Rather, like Jewish halakhah it governs both social and ritual obligations, and concerns itself with questions of moral and ethical correctness, not only legally binding rights and duties subject to adjudication.

Fiqh is the human attempt to interpret and implement the **shari'ah**, God's revealed law. Unlike *shari'ah*, which is understood to be universal, complete, and perfect, *fiqh* is a human discipline that involves disagreement and development over time. Historically, these differences have resulted in the creation of legal schools (sing. **madhhab**).

Sunni and **Shi'i** models of jurisprudence are similar in many respects. The most striking difference, apart from the specific **hadith** compilations deemed authoritative, are in their approaches to the issue of authority and precedent. Although the view that the "gates of *ijtihad*"—independent legal thought—were closed by medieval Sunni jurists has been effectively debunked by recent scholarship, following precedent (**taqlid**) continued to be important. Among Shi'is, however, the rule is that one must always follow a living *mujtahid*, known as a *marja'-i taqlid* or model for emulation.

In their work, jurists must mediate between the provisions of source texts and the customs and requirements of diverse social circumstances. In developing substantive doctrines—which were argued over and debated across and even within *madhhab* lines—the jurists relied on the theoretical framework known as *usul al-fiqh*, "the roots of jurisprudence." In its developed form, Sunni legal methodology relies on Qur'an and **sunnah**, the two textual roots of the law; *qiyas* or analogy; and consensus, *ijma'*. Some schools rely on supplementary legal principles, such as *'urf* (custom), or *maslahah* (public interest). Modern attempts at legal reform often rely on these subsidiary principles to work around specific doctrines rather than radically reinterpret their bases.

See also: **fatwa**

Further reading: Hallaq 1997; Kamali 1991; Moors 1999; Rippin, Calder, and Mojaddedi, 2003

FITNAH

Fitnah is a state of confusion, dissent, or chaos within the Muslim community. The term is used to describe some of the major conflicts that have occurred in the Islamic world, beginning with the dispute over the **caliphate** in 656–661 CE. This *fitnah*, which culminated in outright civil war, followed the assassination in 656 of the third caliph, 'Uthman. Other early *fitnah*s are the 683–685 CE conflict among the Umayyads for control of the caliphate, the various conflicts in al-Andalus, and the struggle for dominance by the Mu'tazilite theological school. To be considered a *fitnah* it is not enough for there to be a conflict; it is necessary for the conflict to be internal and touch on fundamental disagreements. In the case of the first *fitnah*, the community was divided over matters of retribution and succession to an extent that the survival of the **ummah** seemed threatened. A state of *fitnah* is threatening to proper communal discipline: at 8:39 we are told "and fight them until there is no more *fitnah* and everyone accepts the **religion** of God."

Fitnah is also used in a more restricted sense to refer to the social tumult that can result from improperly restrained sexuality, particularly that of women.

See also: *'awrah*, **suffering**

Further reading: Ayoub 1987; Madigan 2001; Mawdudi 1982

FITRAH

Fitrah is the immutable natural predisposition for good, innate in every human being from birth, or even earlier, from the pre-existent state in which the human soul enters into a covenant with God (7:172). The term *fitrah* designates the human being's essential nature, moral constitution, and original disposition. *Fitrah*, as the primordial nature of the individual, aims at perfection.

Islam is held to be *din al-fitrah*, meaning that human beings are inclined by their inner nature to submit to the will of God; it is inherent in human nature to aspire to the good, to the best sort of end. *Fitrah* is the harmony between the creator and the created, representing a possible balance between how we ought to be and how we are. *Fitrah* is in tune with the nature of **creation** itself, and the role of humanity within creation (30:30).

Sin may come about through ignorance. **Knowledge** can be either acquired (*kasbi*) or innate (*fitri*). Every soul has an innate knowledge of good and evil. Our innate understanding of good and evil is sometimes not strong enough to ensure correct behavior. The passions can confuse or obscure the *fitrah*. We have free will and so can go astray. We are equipped (*bi'l-fitrah*) to understand how things can go wrong. Once we become unaware of what is really happening around us we can fall into sin.

See also: *nafs*, *qadr*, **religion**

Further reading: Mohamed 1996

FIVE PILLARS

According to a well-known **hadith**, Muhammad reportedly declared that Islam is based on five things: bearing witness (*shahadah*) that there is no God but God and that Muhammad is the Messenger of God; praying the five daily **prayers**; paying the obligatory alms (*zakat*), a type of **charity**; making **pilgrimage** to Mecca; and **fasting** from dawn to sunset during the month of Ramadan. These five pillars have become standard for **Sunni** Muslims, but can appear in different order (though the *shahadah* always comes first). A variant of this list found in a text by Abu al-Hasan al-'Amiri (d. 381/992) leaves off the *shahadah*—presumably taking it as a given, as **Shi'i** scholars do in their slightly different list of esentials of **faith**—and includes **jihad** along with prayer, fasting, *zakat*, and pilgrimage in his list of pillars.

FORBIDDEN see **lawful and forbidden**

FUNDAMENTALISM

Fundamentalism is a sweeping term used to describe a range of religious responses to modernity. Some scholars have suggested that the term should be reserved for particular strands of Christianity, while others find it useful for comparative purposes to group movements that display several related traits. In the case of Islam, it has been used to characterize everything from pietistic revivalism to violent extremism.

Another term frequently used to describe Muslim fundamentalism is Islamism, which implies support for an Islamic state. The term Islamist should not be confused with Islamicist, used for a scholar who specializes in the study of Islam.

Some Muslim fundamentalist groups have explicitly political aims, and seek to use the electoral process to gain an "Islamic" government. Other groups stress the creation of religious social norms and focus on reforming individual conduct. They may focus on sex segregation, "moral" conduct by public figures, and cultural production. A minority of groups, including al-Qaeda and Hizbollah, consider the use of violence justified in the pursuit of Islamic rule.

It is assumed by some that most Muslims are fundamentalists or conservatives. Occasionally, authors will write of "orthodox Jews, fundamentalist Christians, and Muslims," as if being Muslim were synonymous with being a fundamentalist.

GENDER

The notion that humanity is divided into male and female and that **sex** or gender is a defining characteristic of human experience is firmly embedded into the Muslim worldview. The extent to which this gender difference, however, implies or requires social hierarchy between men and women is deeply disputed.

The Qur'an speaks of the **creation** of humanity first in a way that is not defined by gender: "He created you from a single self [*nafs*] and of it [literally, her] created its [her] mate" (4:1; the Qur'an refers repeatedly to the creation of mates and spouses "from among your selves/souls," as in 30:21). The text then goes on to distinguish later humans by gender: "and from the two of them many men and women."

Several verses mention men and women together as equal in religious status and reward (e.g., 33:35). Male and female believers are each others' friends or protectors (9:71). Those who do good deeds will be rewarded whether "male or female" (4:124).

The Qur'an also distinguishes between men and women in a number of ways. It refers to male and female obligations in **marriage** and **divorce** differently, allotting husbands obligations as well as privileges beyond those of wives (2:228, 4:34). Within broader kin structures, it is assumed that male relations will, at least usually, be involved in the marriages of females; most Qur'anic discussions of marriage have men "marrying" in the grammatical active voice and women "being married" in the passive voice (e.g., 2:221).

Outside of the family, a few other matters are distinguished by gender. Inheritance usually, though not always, grants a larger share to a male heir than a female, often by a 2:1 ratio (4:11). In witnessing certain commercial transactions, the Qur'an commands that the parties take two men as witnesses "or one man and two women, so that if one of them errs, the other can remind her" (2:282). Although male or female testimony is equated with regard to a husband and wife testifying against each other in certain matters (24:6–9), the two-to-one rule is carried through by jurists in other, non-commercial contexts—where women are allowed to witness at all. Jurists almost uniformly reject women serving as witnesses in cases of *hadd* crimes even though, for instance, the Qur'an does not mention the gender of required witnesses for illicit sex (24:4). Only the Hanafi *madhhab* allows two women to serve as witnesses in marriage, replacing one of the men; the other **Sunni** schools require two male witnesses (while the majority **Shi'i** *madhhab* does not demand witnesses at all).

The Qur'an speaks of difference very clearly in one non-legal circumstance. In the story of Mary's birth, it declares, "And the male is not like the female" (3:36). With regard to fulfilling social roles, however, the Qur'an mostly does not make distinctions.

Michael Sells has pointed out the exquisite interplay of gendered terms in the short hymnic surahs that come at the end of the text but comprise the chronologically earliest portions of the Qur'an. Yet as to the gender of the divine, the Qur'an uses exclusively male pronouns for God, when it speaks of God in the third person ("He," *huwa*); Arabic does not have a neuter. Goddess worship, part of pre-Islamic Arab religion, was a concern for the first Muslims, who were vigilant in their rejection of anything that could compromise their strict view of God's uniqueness and unicity (*tawhid*). It is perhaps not surprising that both the Qur'an and early thinkers strenuously reject any attempt to attribute daughters to God. However, mystical thinkers through the centuries have recognized a feminine element to the divine.

See also: **feminism,** *wali*

Further reading: Barazangi 2004; Murata 1992; Shah 2006; Tucker 1994; Wadud 1999

GRATITUDE see *shukr*

HADD

Hadd means a boundary or limit. It appears in the Qur'an only in the plural as *hudud*, and refers to God's boundaries for proper human conduct. Failure to obey these limits is transgression.

Legally, the term is associated with crimes that are offenses against God, usually with specific punishments set forth in the Qur'an such as amputation of the hand for theft. The more serious crime of highway robbery or brigandage merits amputation of an opposing hand and foot. Unsubstantiated allegation of illicit sexual activity—slander—is punished by eighty lashes (24:4). The Qur'an specifies one hundred lashes for illicit **sex** itself (24:2), when properly proven; stoning, based in the *sunnah*, is the accepted punishment for married individuals. Other crimes such as **apostasy** and alcohol consumption do not have clear Qur'anic punishments. Drinking alcohol or becoming intoxicated is theoretically punished with eighty lashes. This penalty has been sometimes justified by an analogy to slander: people say foolish things when drunk.

What makes something a *hadd* crime as opposed to one that merits discretionary chastisement (*ta'zir*) from the ruler or compensatory damages to another individual? Muslim thinkers divide human **obligation**s into two main categories: those owed to God and those owed to other human beings. *Hadd* punishments are generally for crimes that violate God's rights—though of course not all violations of God's rights result in fixed earthly punishments—and additionally threaten the social order.

Hadd crimes may very well involve injury to another person, but not always. Consensual sex between parties not married to one another, *zina'*, is an offense to God. As it also potentially destabilizes family structures it is punishable by *hadd*. Rape, by contrast, may or may not be treated as a *hadd* crime, by analogy to illicit sex. Some legal schools punish rapists with lashes or stoning (victims are not punished), while others insist on compensation for victims instead. A few jurists argue for both: the victim is due compensation for the injury she suffered but the rapist has also offended God's law and must be punished appropriately.

While the *hadd* punishments are severe, convictions have historically been rare. While jurists certainly upheld the penalties in theory, in practice any opportunity to avert a punishment might be taken. In the case of theft, for instance, stealing from the treasury, or out of hunger, or below a certain amount, would not result in punishment. (The caliph 'Umar is said to have suspended all *hadd* punishments for theft during a famine.) In the case of illicit sex, the majority of jurists insisted on eyewitness testimony or confession rather than relying on circumstantial evidence for conviction.

Although many today find the physically harsh penalties such as lashings or amputation shocking, they were in line with punishments employed in other ancient and premodern societies and set forth in texts such as the Bible. Most modern Muslim societies do not impose these punishments, but rather rely on imprisonment to deal with crimes ranging from theft to illicit sex, when the latter is prosecuted at all. However, implementation of *hadd* punishments is a demand of many **fundamentalist** groups and a component of self-identified Islamic regimes in Iran, Pakistan, and portions of Nigeria. For Islamist activists, these punishments symbolize Islamic identity, much like personal-status laws for **marriage** and child custody.

Others, however, including many lay Muslims, view *hadd* punishments as inappropriate to the modern world. Rejecting them outright, however, causes difficulties with those who call for literal application of Qur'anic rules in all times and places. Swiss Muslim thinker Tariq Ramadan, generally regarded as a moderate figure, caused an uproar in 2005 when he called for a moratorium on *hadd* punishments for illicit sex. Secularists criticized him for not going far enough by supporting the outright abolition of *hadd* punishments, while religious conservatives viewed his call for a moratorium as a capitulation to Western ideology.

Further reading: Haeri 1995; Quraishi 2000; Rizvi 1982; Sanneh 2005; Shah 2006; Sidahmed 2001

HADITH

Hadith are accounts that report the words and deeds of the Prophet and his Companions. They are the primary resource for Muslim knowledge of Muhammad's **sunnah**, or exemplary practice.

Each hadith report contains two parts: a chain of transmitters (*isnad*) and a substantive portion (*matn*). The list of reporters may be longer than the information itself. Classical Muslim hadith scholarship tended to assess a hadith primarily on the basis of the reliability of its named transmitters. A science known as "knowledge of men," *'ilm al-rijal*, marshaled biographical data for this purpose. (Despite the reference to men, many prominent reporters of hadith were female well into the medieval era; the Prophet's wife Aishah was perhaps the most important transmitter of either sex for information about him.) If two named transmitters could not have met, for instance, or if a reporter was known to have a bad memory, then the hadith was not accepted or was noted as weak. Contrary to some Western scholarly assertions, hadith collectors did consider content as well.

The two most important **Sunni** hadith collections are the "Sahih" works of Bukhari and Muslim, the former having slightly more prestige than the latter. The title term *sahih* means "authentic," and the standards of inclusion used by these authors are the most rigorous (although later authors such as al-Daraqutni did not deem them exempt from critique as some modern Muslims have done). These two works are the best known of a group known as the "six books"—the others are by Abu Dawud, Ibn Majah, al-Nasa'i, and al-Tirmidhi— that are usually considered canonical. There is considerable overlap between the collections, at least in terms of subject matter when not chains of transmission. There are famous hadith, however, that enjoy wide circulation and general acceptance despite not being found in these compilations.

The six books are organized by topic, as were other early collections such as the *Muwatta'* (part hadith collection, part legal handbook) of

Malik ibn Anas and the *Musannaf* works of 'Abd al-Razzaq al-San'ani and Ibn Abi Shaybah. Other scholars organized their works according to transmitters; these works are called *"musnad"*.

Shi'i hadith collections generally cover ground similar to those of the Sunnis, and have some transmitters in common, but many important Companions and Followers who figure prominently in Sunni *isnads* were deemed unreliable by Shi'i scholars, based on their loyalties in the first *fitnah* that shook the Muslim community in the seventh century and resulted in the Shi'i/Sunni split. Major Shi'i hadith compilations are those by al-Kulayni, al-Qummi, and Tusi.

While the hadith have always been vital as a source of material for moral exhortation and legal reasoning by jurists, the prominence of **salafi** and **Wahhabi** methodologies in the contemporary period has meant that lay Muslims are turning to hadith as direct guidance for behavior in a way that was less common in past centuries. A contrary tendency has some modern Muslims rejecting hadith in favor of exclusive reliance upon the Qur'an, something which has always existed on the margins of Muslim societies in the past. Muslim feminists, for instance, disdain hadith reports about the **creation** of woman from a crooked rib in favor of adhering closely to the less gendered Qur'anic account of creation (4:1) which does not single the first woman out as secondary or deficient.

Further reading: Graham 1977; Lucas 2004; Motzki 2004

HAJJ see **pilgrimage**

HALAL see **lawful and forbidden**

HANAFI, HANAFIYA see *madhhab*

HANBALI, HANBALIYA see *madhhab*

HARAM, HARRAMA

The contrast between the "forbidden" (*haram, harrama*) and the "permitted" or "lawful" (*halal, ahalla*) goes right through the Qur'an. The root of the word *haram* is used eighty-three times in the Qur'an. Generally it means those things that God disapproves of, and the basis of what is forbidden is always the will of God. The term can also sometimes mean "sanctify," especially in relation to sacred space. God's house is called holy (*al-bayt al-haram*) in 5:97, a secure sanctuary (*haram amin*) in 28:57 and 29:67, sacred territory in 27:91, and, most of all, the sacred mosque (*al-masjid al-haram*) on fifteen occasions. This phrase is taken to be a reference to the **Ka'bah** in Mecca (e.g., 2:144, 149, 150 in the context of the *qiblah* (niche marking **prayer** direction); 2:196, 48:27 in the context of the hajj, and *al-bayt al-muharram* (the sacred house); 14:37). *Haram* in all of these passages describes a link with God and represents something that God provides for humanity. The believer is the individual who follows these instructions. Those things that are *haram* in its meaning of sacred are free from impurity. The *haram* is secure and inviolable—and it is here that the two senses of the term merge: the area around the Ka'bah is sacred in part because entry is forbidden to those who are non-Muslim.

Haram in the sense of "forbidden" includes certain types of food but extends beyond dietary regulations. Usury is *haram* (2:275), land can be forbidden for people to enter (for instance, the Jews and the holy land in 5:26), and the breast of a foster mother can be held back (as in the case of Moses in 28:12). Certain other actions are also forbidden, for the Jews in 2:85 and the pagans in 6:138, with the ultimate outcome that "God shall prohibit [*harrama*] him entrance to **paradise** and his refuge shall be the fire" in 5:72.

In later Muslim ethical theory, *haram* refers to a prohibited act which, if performed, renders one liable to punishment in the hereafter, as opposed to the obligatory (*wajib*) act which, if omitted, leads to punishment in the hereafter. Intermediate categories of "recommended" (*mandub*), "repugnant" (*makruh*) and a neutral "permissible" (*mubah*) completed the five-part scale (*al-ahkam al-khamsah*). In addition to this five-part scale, a twofold distinction between **lawful and forbidden** also operated: everything was *halal* which was not specifically prohibited. The word *halal* was also used for permissible ritually slaughtered food.

Al-Haramayn are the two holy cities, Mecca and Medina, and *harim* (from which we get the term harem) is the seclusion in which women sometimes live separated from men not of their families. The term *mahram*, derived from the same root, refers to relatives within the "forbidden degrees" such as brothers, fathers, or uncles; requirements for visual and spatial segregation are relaxed in these cases because these men are not potential marriage partners.

See also: **hell, morality, obligation, pilgrimage, purdah**

Further reading: Izutsu 1966; Marmon 1993; al-Qaradawi 1994

AL-HARAMAYN see *haram*

HARIM see *haram*

HELL

Hell is the home of the damned after the **day of judgment**. It is a place of endless punishment, physical torture, mental anguish, and despair. One of the crucial functions of **prophethood** is to warn humanity of what lies before them and yet is not at present visible: the everlasting consequences of one's earthly deeds.

There are several Qur'anic words for "hell." The most frequent is "fire" (*nar*). The second in frequency is a place name, *jahanam* (Gehenna). Hell is the opposite of the garden of **paradise**, a place of shade and well-being with rivers and trees. Hell is characterized by fire, heat, thirst, and pain. 9:68 states: "God has promised the hypocrites, men and women, and the unbelievers, the fire of Gehenna, in which to live forever. That is enough for them; God has cursed them; and there is in store for them a lasting chastisement." By contrast, in 9:72 paradise is described: "God has promised the believers, men and women, gardens underneath which rivers flow, in which to live forever, and goodly dwelling places in the Gardens of Eden; and even more, God's good pleasure; that is the mighty triumph."

Much happens in hell: human skin is burned (4:56); the sinners are tortured with hooked iron rods (22:21); their garments are of fire (22:19); their faces are burnt black (39:60); horrible food has to be swallowed; pus (44:16) or boiling water (18:29) is drunk; and the inhabitants will sob ceaselessly (21:100). "It shall be proclaimed to the unbelievers: 'Surely God's hatred is greater than your hatred of one another'" (40:10). God in a dramatic dialogue asks hell: "Upon the day We shall say to Gehenna: 'are you filled?' And it [i.e. Gehenna] shall say: 'Are there any more to come?'" (50:30). In 69:30–33 an unidentified voice that could be divine commands the **angels** of hell: "'Take him, and fetter him and then roast him in hell, then put him on a chain of seventy cubits length'." The Qur'an emphasizes on several occasions that God personally prepares Gehenna for humankind (71:18), that God supervises the torment and tells the sinners: "Taste! We will only give you more chastisement" (78:30).

The fuel of hell include stones and idols (21:98), but consists mainly of men and women (2:24). Some of the *jinn* are in hell (11:119), and even the **devil** will also be punished by hellfire (17:62). In general, unbelievers (3:10) and polytheists, and idolaters who associate partners with God (*mushrikun*), as well as hypocrites (*munafiqun*), will suffer damnation. Also mentioned as among the damned is the person who slays a believer willfully (4:93), the coward fighting the unbelievers (8:15–16), whoever mocks God's prophets and God's *ayat* or signs (18:102), and whoever calls the Qur'an sorcery or human speech (74:24). A wide variety of other sinners merits punishment in hell, including those who squander the property of orphans (4:10), usurers (2:275), and rumor mongers and slanderers (104:1).

Human fate in the hereafter is decided upon by God on the day of judgment. God judges each individual according to his or her record. "Then he whose deeds weigh heavy in the balance shall inherit a pleasing life, but he whose deeds weigh light in the balance shall plunge into the womb of the pit. And what shall teach you what the pit is? A blazing fire" (101:6–11). The question of whether hell and paradise exist already before the day of judgment is not raised in the Qur'an, although it was discussed at length in Islamic **theology**. In some verses the Qur'an speaks as if hell and paradise already existed. This problem is linked to the question of what happens to the human soul in the time between death and resurrection, a question which is not touched upon by the Qur'an either, but was extensively discussed in the later literature.

Whether damnation is eternal is another interesting issue discussed extensively by the theologians. It is often stressed that the evildoers will dwell in hell forever (e.g., 3:87–88). However, 11:107 states of those in hell: "They live there forever, as long as heaven and earth last, except as the Lord wishes." This verse potentially limits the eternity of damnation. Mu'tazili commentators interpret it in this way, and they are followed by some modern thinkers who see hell as more like purgatory.

The function of hell is punishment (*'adhab*). The point of punishment in hell is to frighten the listeners and to win them over to the message of the Prophet. On several occasions the Qur'an threatens with hell those who refuse to believe in hell: "and We shall say to the evildoers, 'Taste the chastisement of fire, which you lied about'" (34:42).

For mystics like Rabi'a (c. 95–185/714–801) hell is "a veil," and al-Ghazali (d. 505/1111) also suggests that much of the language dealing with the **afterlife** should be taken as metaphorical. He also said that it should be accepted as literally true as well, but for those who were above material suasion the sort of language in the Qur'an should be taken as referring more to spiritual than to material conditions.

See also: *qadr*

Further reading: al-Ghazali 1995b

HERESY

Heresy (*zandaqah*) encompasses several forms of incorrect belief and practice, including *bid'ah*, derived from *bada'a* (to introduce something new), meaning a condemned and rejected **innovation**. Heretics should be distinguished from atheists or unbelievers (sing. *kafir*), a term also used for polytheists, which means "denier" or "concealer."

In Arabic, "atheism" is often translated *ilhad*, which can also mean "heresy." The Qur'an is silent on the earthly punishment for heresy and apostasy, though not on the subject itself. The Qur'an is highly critical of people who return to unbelief after believing, labeling them hypocrites (*munafiqun*) and marking them as enemies and as people who will be punished by God (9:73–74). The **hadith** literature is explicit on the death sentence for **apostasy**, and heresy is severely criticized also.

It was not unusual for thinkers to be charged with freethinking or heresy or even unbelief (**kufr**) by their opponents. Al-Ghazali (d. 505/1111), in his *Incoherence of the Philosophers*, charged Peripatetics like al-Farabi and Ibn Sina (Avicenna) with seventeen counts of heretical innovation (*bid'ah*) and three counts of unbelief. The three major philosophical conclusions that al-Ghazali characterized as incompatible with Islam were the eternity of the universe, the claim that God knows things only insofar as they are universals and not as particulars, and the denial of the resurrection of the body—that is, conceiving of the "return" (*ma'ad*) in purely spiritual or intellectual terms.

See also: **philosophy**

Further reading: Hallaq 1997; 2001; Ibn Rushd 1976

HIJAB

Although the term *hijab*—which connotes hiding something or screening it from view—is used almost exclusively today for Muslim women's distinctive headcovering, it originally referred to a physical partition or, less concretely, a metaphysical one.

In one Qur'anic use, it refers to a curtain that served as a barrier between Muhammad's wife or wives and other (male) Muslims; the Qur'an commands that Muslims "ask them from behind a *hijab*" or curtain (33:53). Several scholars have suggested that the phrase "she donned the *hijab*" was originally used to mean "she became Muhammad's wife."

The Qur'an's discussions of female dress (24:31 and 33:59) do not use the term *hijab*, instead referring to *khumur* (sing. *khimar*, a head-covering that appears to have been worn by women and sometimes men in seventh-century Arabia) and *jalabib* (sing. *jilbab*, an outer robe or cloak). The Qur'an makes no mention of veiling the face. Early **hadith** references to the uncovering of the face by Muhammad's wives when on pilgrimage suggest that they did cover it at other times.

The references to "veiling" in earlier sources, as with Egyptian feminists' removal of the veil in the early twentieth century, refer to the face veil, not the headcovering, which usually remained. Nazira Zein al-Din's 1928 book *Al-Hijab wa'l-Sufur* (Veiling and Unveiling) caused controversy in Syria. But the removal of headcovering eventually happened throughout many twentieth-century urban Muslim communities.

The *hijab* or "Islamic dress" has become deeply embedded in twentieth-century identity politics. It has been forbidden to varying degrees at times in Muslim societies such as Iran and Turkey and required in others, including Iran (again), Saudi Arabia, and Afghanistan. In nations which allow women choice, the spectrum of female dress may run from revealing Western-style clothes to fully covered in the "new" Islamic dress. In between, one may find modest pants or skirt and a headscarf or forms of modest dress, such as shalwar kameez with a long narrow scarf known as a dupatta, that are understood to be traditional rather than "Islamic." The adoption of standardized forms of Islamic dress has been a key symbolic issue in **fundamentalist** movements; bearded men and covered women have been seen by some as equivalent. However, while some extremist groups such as the Taliban chastised men for failing to conform to these norms, female dress has been much more central.

Controversies over the use of Islamic covering—the headscarf and, less often, the face veil—have emerged in Europe, especially France, in the last decade of the twentieth century and the first decade of the twenty-first century. A ban on headscarves in government institutions in Turkey has meant that women who choose to cover cannot attend universities—a challenge by a medical student was rejected by the European Court of Justice in 2005, which upheld the prohibition as an appropriate expression of European values—or be employed in government institutions such as offices and hospitals. A Turkish woman elected to parliament was prevented from taking her seat because she refused to remove her headscarf.

Many women view *hijab* as a non-negotiable religious **obligation**.

In the United States as well as in Europe, Muslim women may face discrimination or harassment for choosing to cover their hair; in some instances civil rights organizations have intervened on their behalf. Yet a significant number of Muslims believe that modesty is situational and that headcovering is not always required. American Muslim scholar Amina Wadud, incensed by the disproportionate attention granted to women's dress by many contemporary thinkers, has referred to *hijab* sardonically as "the sixth pillar of Islam." American student and poet Su'ad Abdul-Khabeer has written poems exploring her experiences wearing *hijab* that highlight the complex negotiations over the terrain of women's bodies.

Modern discussions over veiling and unveiling ignore the deeper mystical and theological uses of this symbolism in the Qur'anic text and exegetical literature. The terms "veil" and "veiled" may refer to a partition separating one who recites the Qur'an from "those who do not believe in the world to come" (17:45), or to a separation between human beings and God. Indeed, even for a prophet, it is not fitting that "God should speak to him except by **revelation** or from behind a veil" (42:51).

See also: *'awrah*, **morality**

Further reading: Abdul-Ghafur 2005; Ahmed 1992; Shirazi 2001; Wadud 2006

HIJRAH

Hijrah, or emigration, refers to the relocation of the first Muslims from the urban center of Mecca, Muhammad's birthplace, to the oasis town of Yathrib, which eventually became known as "the city," Medina (short for *Medinat al-Nabi*, or City of the Prophet). The "hijri" calendar in use among Muslims dates from this emigration, which occurred in 622 CE.

The *hijrah* looms large in the Muslim imagination because it is through this emigration that the first Muslim community was truly established. The **mosque** became the center of community life and political leadership was in the hands of God's Prophet.

The emigrants (*muhajirun*) had prestige among early Muslims for having accepted Islam and shown their commitment by following Muhammad to Medina. Once there, they were paired with residents who assisted them in establishing themselves in their new town; these individuals became known as "helpers" (*ansar*). There were some areas of conflict between the groups, relating to customary practices.

It is said, for instance, that Medinan women were freer than Meccan women, which could lead to friction in mixed marriages.

The notion of emigration has become an important metaphor for some Muslim thinkers who, adopting for themselves the mantle of authenticity of the first Muslim community, have advocated flight from "un-Islamic" society. One influential radical group, al-Takfir wa'l-hijrah (Excommunication and Emigration) was an offshoot of the Egyptian Muslim Brotherhood in the middle decades of the twentieth century.

HIKMAH see **knowledge**

'ID see **Eid**

IJTIHAD see **reform**

IKHLAS

Ikhlas means purity or sincerity. Islam is based on belief in one God and declaring this is taken to be a sign of sincerity and purity of spirit, both key religious virtues. The link between sincerity of faith and purity of theological doctrine appears in the Qur'anic **surah** entitled Ikhlas.

Surah 112 is often regarded as especially significant despite or perhaps because of its brevity; it contains only three short *ayat*. This surah, one of the surahs first taught to Muslim children as they learn to pray, proclaims the oneness (*tawhid*) and absolute nature of the divine essence. This concept is presented in the first verse which commands: "Say: He, God, is one." The second declares that God is eternal (*samad*), that is, beyond the bounds of time and space. The third states that God does not give birth, nor is he born, and declares that he is beyond comparison: "There is no one like Him."

This final verse figures heavily in distinguishing Muslim doctrine from Christian **theology**. In particular, the affirmation that God does not participate in procreation is used to refute claims of Jesus' divinity or divine sonship. As a whole, surah Ikhlas directly supports the Muslim profession of faith (*shahadah*), the first of Islam's **five pillars**: "There is no god but God."

See also: **worship**

Further reading: Izutsu 1966

IMAM

Imam, a title of respect, in its simplest sense means the one who leads. It is used for giants of scholarship (Imam Shafi'i, d. 204/820) or those considered specially qualified religious authorities, as with the **Shi'i** line of Imams to whom rightful rulership of the Muslim community is held to belong. Most frequently, it refers to the person who leads others in **prayer**.

In congregational prayer, one person leads the others. Selection criteria for imams include knowledge of Qur'an, awareness of the elements of ritual prayer, and piety. It is generally agreed that a man may lead a congregation comprising men, a mixed congregation, or a congregation comprising women. Most scholars have held that a woman can lead an entirely female congregation in prayer but cannot under any circumstances lead men. A few have held that a group solely comprising women cannot pray in congregation but only individually, since a woman cannot serve as *imam*. At the other end of the spectrum, a small number of jurists have held that a woman may lead a male or mixed group in prayer, particularly during non-obligatory prayers such as the customary devotional evening prayers (*tarawih*) in Ramadan.

The issue of who can be an *imam* is complicated in minority modern Muslim communities by new expectations associated with the role. In the United States, for instance, the *imam* of a **mosque** has functions well beyond those of leading prayers and delivering Friday sermons or **khutbah**s. He may be called upon to engage in interfaith dialogue, to mediate family disputes, to serve as an expert witness in court cases involving Muslims, and to oversee other programming at a mosque or Islamic center. Indeed the "congregational" model which characterizes many North American Muslim communities, with membership dues and elected boards of directors, is a departure from the way mosques function in majority-Muslim societies. Some Muslim leaders such as Ingrid Mattson, a professor elected to be the first female president of the Islamic Society of North America in 2006, have suggested the need for increased professional training to prepare *imams* for these new responsibilities.

Mattson and others have called for increased dialogue and reflection on which of these roles—apart from leadership of mixed-sex prayer—can be filled by women. Women as well as men are trained in the Hartford Seminary's unique Muslim chaplaincy program, which Mattson heads. These issues of gender and religious authority are not unique to the United States. In the early years of the twenty-first century, Morocco trained a group of female scholars and religious leaders. These women were originally to be called *imams*, but controversy forced selection of a new title: *mourshidat*, or "guides."

See also: **fatwa, feminism, heresy, innovation, ulama, worship**

IMAN see **faith**

INNOVATION

Innovation, *bid'ah*, is a conceptual battleground where issues of authenticity and authority are contested by modern Muslims. When used without qualification, the term usually carries a negative meaning; some translate it simply as "reprehensible innovation." Avoiding *bid'ah* —understood in extremely broad terms to encompass nearly everything that was not specifically a part of the practice of the Prophet Muhammad and the first Muslims—is central to **salafi** and **Wahhabi** thought. The guiding sentiment is summed up in the **hadith**: "Every innovation is "misguidance" and every misguidance leads to the Fire [i.e., **hell**]."

Most Muslim scholars, though, including many classical jurists, have viewed innovation with more nuance. While maintaining a generally reserved or negative stance towards many types of innovation, they recognize some innovations as good (*bid'ah hasanah*). One example is the Companion whose spontaneous response to the Prophet's affirmation in **prayer** that "God hears those who praise Him," was "Oh Our Lord, to You belongs the praise." This statement pleased the Prophet, who incorporated it into the standard prayer ritual. A tradition in Bukhari reports 'Umar using the term with regard to optional congregational prayers during Ramadan. (Some would not see these incidents as *bid'ah*, since they occurred during the Prophet's lifetime or that of his Companions and were approved at that time.)

According to a tradition in *Sahih Muslim*, whoever innovates in a good way will get rewarded for everyone who follows the innovation just like the one who innovates in a bad way. Of course, there are matters, such as the celebration of Muhammad's birthday (*mawlid*), where Muslims disagree as to whether the innovation in question is good or bad.

See also: **heresy**, *kufr*

INSAN

Insan may be translated as human being, and there is a surah in the Qur'an (76) with this name. Understanding "the human being" as *insan* can be taken as an indication of the basic equality that exists in the heart of Islam, since it makes no distinction as far as humanity is concerned between men and women, free and slave, or Arab and non-Arab. By contrast, human beings are differentiated from animals as well as from *jinn* and **angels**.

In **Sufi** literature, the Prophet is often called *al-insan al-kamil*, "the perfect human," and his life is taken to exemplify the heights that those who follow him later in time may seek to attain. The "perfect human being" is the person who manifests God's attributes in a completely harmonious fashion, an ideal of balance that Ibn al-'Arabi links with the Prophet Muhammad and less perfectly with other major saints and prophets. The more perfect a human being is, the closer he comes to the real or the true (*haqq*). Most people share to a degree in this level of reality, although at a much lower level than the Prophet himself, who typifies perfection in so far as a human being can.

See also: **truth**

Further reading: Chittick 1989

INSPIRATION see **revelation**

'ISHQ see **love**

ISLAM

Islam is an Arabic word meaning submission or surrender, understood to mean to the will of God specifically. Related to the word for peace (*salaam*), Islam has come to be the name of the **religion** that received its **revelation** through the Prophet Muhammad (570–632) in the form of the Qur'an. Its followers are called Muslims—though the Qur'an usually refers to Muhammad's followers simply as "believers"—and it has been one of the world's major religions ever since its explosive growth starting in the seventh century CE.

Islam is repeated in the Qur'an eight times in the form of a verbal noun. Of the eight, in three places (6:125, 39:22, 61:7) it is used as *Islam* alone and in two places with a pronoun as *islamakum*, "your submission" (49:18), and *islamihim*, "their submission" (9:74). The connotation of the remaining three appearances (3:19, 3:85, and 5:3) is very important for they occur together with the noun **religion** (*din*).

First and foremost among the basic beliefs of Islam as set forth in various creeds (sing. *'aqidah*) is the unity of God (*tawhid*), which is also emphasized as the first of **five pillars** of Islam in the form of the *shahadah*. God is one and has no associates. All people should form a united group (*ummah*) both in belief and practice. Second is the belief in **angels**, heavenly creatures in the service of God. There are four archangels: Jibril (Gabriel), Mika'il (Michael), Israfil and 'Izra'il. Shaytan (Satan, the **devil**) or Iblis is thought by some to have been an archangel before being eternally condemned due to his refusal to bow down before Adam. Third comes the holy scriptures, which are said to have been initiated with the first revelation to Adam and completed with the last to the Prophet Muhammad. The Qur'an is the last definitive true revelation that contains and affirms what we can know of eternal reality while amending the inaccuracies and falsehoods that crept into previous revelations to humanity. Fourth is the prophets, whose exact numbers cannot be known for certain, except that the first was Adam and the last was Muhammad. There are other significant beliefs that vary with the particular doctrinal group, but these noted here are commonly accepted among all Muslims.

Further reading: Denny 1994; Hodgson 1974; Iqbal 1965

ISLAM IN AFRICA

During the time of the Prophet (615 CE) a group of Muslims were temporarily exiled from persecution in Mecca to Ethiopia, where the Christian ruler protected them. This was the first contact, we are told, between Islam and Africa. Under the Ummayad dynasty, which came to rule in the second half of the seventh century, there was a rapid expansion of Muslims into the coastal regions of East and North Africa, followed by gradual incursions into the interior from those starting points. After the first sweep of territorial conquest, the forces of **conversion** were often the traders and sailors who moved from place to place and became influential in the African locales they visited. In the ninth and tenth centuries CE, Arabs founded permanent colonies on the islands off the east coast of Africa, especially on Zanzibar, where Arab mariners had for many years journeyed to trade.

Land and sea trade routes shaped the growing Islamic influence in Africa. For instance, the Islamization of Egypt was followed by a slow progress of the religion along the Nile until it came to dominate in what is today Sudan. Islam spread inwards from the coast in East Africa also. In West Africa, whole kingdoms converted and sought to influence others, though the depth of even the ruling class's adherence to Islamic doctrine and teachings remains subject to debate. In some areas, more formal Muslim practice was largely limited to the elite while the populace continued to practice indigenous religions, even if they adhered nominally to Islam.

Before European colonial rule in most of Africa during the nineteenth and twentieth centuries, Islam was in a position of strength on the continent. Although the effect of later European imperialism was to introduce forms of Christianity into the continent, it did not succeed in uprooting Islam. Both religions remain powerful in Africa, and are frequently the source of intercommunal dissension and conflict. Evidence suggests that Islam is likely to be the major **religion** on the continent.

One major challenge currently confronting Muslims in Africa is the AIDS epidemic which has ravaged parts of the continent. Although in some nations Muslims are less likely than others to be infected (perhaps in part because, as recent studies show, male circumcision—virtually universal among Muslims—reduces viral transmission rates), the threat is real and growing. Religious sensibilities may constitute a hindrance to effective prevention measures, since Muslims may be reluctant to acknowledge risky behavior; exhortations to chastity alone are insufficient to combat the spread of the virus, particularly if combined with an aversion to condom usage. Polygamy and cultural double standards surrounding extramarital **sex** combined with religio-cultural norms enforcing wifely sexual availability also place wives at risk for infection from husbands who stray.

Further reading: Gray 2004; Esack 2005b; Trimingham 1959; 1964; 1965a; 1965b; 1968; Wadud 2006

ISLAM IN AMERICA

The first significant group of Muslims in the Americas was enslaved. Today, descendants of those slaves vie with immigrants from Muslim areas and their descendants for presence and influence in American Muslim communities. Smaller percentages of white and Latino/a converts complete the picture.

Diouf suggests that 15–20 percent of the African slaves in the

United States were Muslim, somewhere between two and three million people; a slightly smaller percentage of Africans enslaved in Latin America and the Caribbean may well have been Muslim also, coming from a variety of West African regions. Because of the nature of **slavery** in the Americas, it is difficult to gather substantial personal information about enslaved individuals. Some were educated in their African communities of origin, though this **education** could range from rudimentary literacy in Arabic to a high level of scholarly competence. A variety of Arabic documents survive, from amulets with Qur'anic verses possessed by the Brazilian *malês* who rebelled in 1835 to the autobiography of 'Umar ibn Sayyid, enslaved in the southern United States.

Some Muslim practices survived through slavery. African American groups such as the Ishmaelites of Illinois, Indiana, and Kentucky in the late nineteenth century were known to abstain from alcohol, conduct **pilgrimage** rituals to towns named Mecca, Mohamet, and Morocco, and adopt Muslim names.

A significant institution was the Moorish Science Temple, founded in the early twentieth century by Noble Drew Ali (d. 1929). While the Moorish Science Temple had their own "Circle Seven Koran" and were largely a proto-black-nationalist movement similar to Marcus Garvey's United Negro Improvement Association, the "Moors" had several distinctive practices that probably had an Islamic origin. They had similar dietary restrictions to Muslims, considered Friday as their holy day, practiced gender segregation in religious ritual, wore the fez, and called God "Allah."

It remains a matter of contention whether the later Nation of Islam had links through W. Fard Muhammad with Noble Drew Ali and the Moorish Science Temple. There is no doubt that racial issues and black empowerment provided the background for both. The Nation was founded in 1933 by Wallace Fard Muhammad (who allegedly came from Mecca, Saudi Arabia) and Elijah Muhammad. The movement began to flourish in the late 1940s. Malcolm X, a charismatic leader, became the movement's spokesperson. Malcolm, who was assassinated in 1965, broke from Elijah Muhammad in 1963 and adopted more mainstream **Sunni** practices. He drew on a long legacy of using Islam to articulate anti-colonial and anti-racist liberation ideology, and through his ability to reach a broad audience he played a major role in encouraging **conversion** and the entry of Islam into the mainstream of African-American culture.

When Elijah Muhammad died in 1975, his son W.D. Muhammad inherited leadership of the Nation. Wallace (later Warith) Deen promptly began to dismantle the Nation and move his followers closer to mainstream Islam, founding an organization called the World Community of Islam in the West (later the American Society of Muslims, then Mosque Cares). A few years later, a former leader in the Nation, Louis Farrakhan, revived the Nation of Islam, saying that there was still a need for an Islamic movement specifically oriented towards the black community. As the twenty-first century begins, Farrakhan has tempered his separatist rhetoric and stressed commonalties with other Muslims.

Liberalization of immigration policies in the 1960s brought unprecedented numbers of foreign Muslims to America. While African-American Muslims outnumber any other Muslim ethnic group in the United States, in terms of Islamic education and income they often suffer in comparison with those from immigrant groups. The latter tend to adhere more or less closely to the cultural and religious practices of their countries of origin, and have established a solid infrastructure of **mosques** and Islamic centers throughout the United States. Many of these mosques remain largely segregated by ethnicity, with attendees being primarily South Asian or Arab.

There are also substantial and well-established Muslim communities in Latin America and the Caribbean, but not primarily among those of African descent. In nations such as Trinidad and Guyana, the Muslim population is largely South Asian; among the indentured laborers imported by the British from India in the wake of abolition, the majority were Hindu but a sufficient minority were Muslim. In Brazil and elsewhere in Latin America, immigrants from Syria and Lebanon in the nineteenth and twentieth centuries built new Muslim institutions when they arrived. In keeping with their origins in the Ottoman Empire, the descendants of these immigrants may still be referred to as Turks.

Further reading: Austin 1984, 1997; Curtis 2002; 2006; Dannin 2002; Diouf 1998; Gomez 2005; Haddad 2002; Khan 2000; Hunwick 2003–4; Jackson 2005; Reis 1993; Rouse 2004

ISLAM IN ASIA

Islam has a long and important history in Asia, from China's Hui minority to the Central Asian states where medieval **Sufi** orders flourished. The world's largest Muslim populations today are found in South and Southeast Asia. The four nations with the largest

Muslim populations as measured around the turn of the twenty-first century are Asian: Indonesia (194 million), India (150 million), Pakistan (145 million), and Bangladesh (130 million). China also has a population of forty million Muslims. Muslims are a majority in Kirgizstan, Uzbekistan, Tadjikistan, and Turkmenistan in Central Asia; Afghanistan, Pakistan, and Bangladesh in South Asia; and Malaysia, Brunei, and Indonesia in Southeast Asia. There are also significant minority populations in Kazakhstan, India, Thailand, and the Philippines. Sizable Muslim communities are also found in Sri Lanka, Burma, and Singapore.

Just as Asia itself is large and diverse, so is Muslim experience in the region. In some places, Islam spread through military conquest, in others by missionaries or traders. In Southeast Asia, some suggest that Islam first came through trading links with the Middle East, while others credit direct missionary contact. The dynamics of trade clearly contributed to Islam's rapid spread and popularity. The vast increase in trade led to more and more contacts with dynamic and relatively successful Muslim traders, no doubt increasing the status of Islam in local eyes. However Islam was established in the region, Malaysia, southern Thailand, Indonesia, Brunei, and the southern Philippines all have significant Muslim populations. As in certain regions of Africa, existing beliefs were incorporated into local manifestations of Islam.

Asian Muslims are mostly **Sunni**; **Shi'ah** only make up a significant portion of the population in Afghanistan and Pakistan.

Further reading: Bulliet 1995; Esposito 1987

ISLAM IN EUROPE

Islam and Europe have a long history that begins with the Arab and North African Muslim conquest of Iberia at the beginning of the eighth century and encompasses the "golden age" of Andalusian culture. It also spans the Crusades; the "reconquest" of the Iberian peninsula by Christian leaders and final expulsion of Muslims in the fifteenth century; and European colonialism in Africa, the Middle East, and Asia. Contemporary debates over Muslim identity in Europe are grounded in this complex history of conflict and cooperation.

Muslim numbers in contemporary Europe are significant. Setting aside Turkey, which spans the continents of Europe and Asia, two

European countries, Bosnia-Herzegovina and Albania, have Muslim majorities. One in seven Russians—over twenty million people—is Muslim. In contrast to Europe's non-Muslim population, the Muslim population is young and growing fast. The non-Muslim population of Europe is calculated to shrink by 3.5 percent by 2015 while Muslims will double, due to both immigration and higher birth rates. There are three million Turks in Germany and another twelve million Muslims—Algerians, Moroccans, Pakistanis, Bangladeshis, Egyptians, Senegalese, Malis, or Tunisians—in the rest of the European Union. Furthermore, recent retroactive changes to German law have naturalized over a million immigrants and automatically granted citizenship to the approximately 160,000 Muslims born in Germany every year. Between two and three million Muslims in France—half their number—are eligible to vote. Another million—one out of two—vote in Britain, where several Muslims, including one recently elected woman, serve in Parliament.

During the late stages of the Soviet Union, Islam was the second-largest religion in the country with about forty-five to fifty million people, mainly in Central Asia, identifying themselves as Muslims. Even after the independence of most of those republics, the proportion of Muslims in Russia is about 15 percent, mainly concentrated among the minority nationalities residing between the Black Sea and the Caspian Sea: the Adyghs, Balkars, Bashkirs, Chechens, Cherkess, Ingush, Kabardins, Karachay, and numerous Dagestani nationalities. In the middle Volga Basin are large populations of Tatars, Udmurts, and Chuvash, most of whom are Muslims. Many Muslims live in the big cities also. The population is very much **Sunni**. Some identify as **Sufi**s also, especially in areas like Chechnya.

The growing presence of Muslims in Western Europe has become controversial at the start of the twenty-first century, when riots in France and terrorism in Britain and the Netherlands has raised the issue of whether they will become properly integrated into those societies. It was assumed initially that as with other religious minorities emigrating to Europe there would eventually be assimilation of the locally born population that the immigrants produced, but there are concerns that this will not happen and that a radical underclass will continue to be a problematic feature of European life. In many urban areas Muslims are poised to become majorities.

The increasing demographic and cultural prominence of Muslims has been perceived by some as threatening to European values. Importantly, there are conflicts among European thinkers and public figures about what actually constitutes the most important elements of European identity. Is European society essentially Christian or is it primarily based on secular human rights norms? The debates over the headscarf (*hijab*) in France as well as elsewhere demonstrate the ways in which racial, ethnic, and even class discriminations merge with religious ideas.

Complicating the question of Islam and European identity are converts. **Conversion**—sometimes, but by no means exclusively, through Sufi contacts—has become a notable phenomenon, although rates of conversion are much lower than in the United States.

Further reading: Köse 1996; Malik 2004; Nielsen with Allievi 2003; Nielsen with Maréchal, Allievi, and Dassetto 2003; Nielsen 2004; Roald 2001

ISLAM IN THE MIDDLE EAST

Islam as a religion in its present form first arose in the Middle East, in particular the Arabian peninsula, and rapidly spread throughout that part of the world, and then much further, as a result of a very successful series of military campaigns. By 632 CE, the date of the Prophet's death, most of the Arabian peninsula was dominated by Islam. In the next few years Syria was captured from the Byzantines and the Persian Empire was defeated. In 642 Egypt was conquered, and Arab armies moved on west across North Africa and into Spain in 711. Others moved east toward China. Over time the region's original religions were replaced by Islam, although some small groups of adherents to older traditions such as Zoroastrianism have persisted, to varying degrees of toleration and persecution.

With the exception of Israel, today all the countries of the Middle East have Muslim majorities—quite large majorities, in most cases—and many declare Islam as the state religion. Despite this apparent uniformity, conflict between nations, and within nations between different communities, have been prevalent. These difficult relations over issues of borders and allocation of natural resources result in part from the way states were created during the European colonization that followed Ottoman imperial rule. Other persistent sources of conflict include the relationships between **Sunni** and **Shi'i** communities in many countries, and also between secular and religious citizens. In recent years the Islamic part of the region has become even more homogeneous with the rapid reduction in its minorities. The difficult economic and political circumstances in which many live have encouraged the development of extreme forms of religious expression on occasion.

The guardian of the holy places (*al-Haramayn*) is now the government of Saudi Arabia, which has used some of its oil wealth to invest heavily in infrastructure for the **pilgrimage** or hajj, involving the annual movement of millions of Muslims in and out of the Kingdom. Despite its official **Wahhabi** interpretation of Islam it does allow pilgrims from a wide variety of backgrounds to enter the country for pilgrimage. Yet the hostility of the Saudi leadership to tombs and other sites of veneration has led to the destruction of many ancient buildings, particularly those respected by the Shi'i world.

ISLAMIC LAW see *fiqh*, *shari'ah*

ISLAMIC RENAISSANCE see *nahdah*

ISLAMISM see **fundamentalism**

ISLAMOPHOBIA

In Islamophobia Islam and Muslims are subject to special scrutiny because they are understood as a threat to Western civilization. Islamophobes usually consider violence an essential component of Islam, and **fundamentalism** and terrorism are equated with Islam. Many Islamophobes assert that they are not equating all Muslims with Islamic radicalism, but in practice they focus on extremist elements to the neglect of more mainstream Muslim voices. Some will acknowledge that not all Muslims are terrorists or sympathizers, but may then claim that this is because they are not truly religious Muslims. In this way, Islamophobes echo certain Muslim fundamentalists who consider only their own understanding of Islam to be correct.

Islamophobia is found in the United States among neoconservatives, some Christian evangelicals, and some pro-Israel groups. Islamophobia is also deeply influential in some segments of the United States media—Fox News is particularly noteworthy—and among right-wing lobbyists and politicians who understand Islam as a potent threat to America, Christianity, and "the West" more broadly. Massachusetts governor, Mitt Romney, for instance, in 2005 advocated surveillance of **mosques** as a means of combating terrorism.

The best analogy for Islamophobia is the Cold War "red scare." Now, Islam has replaced communism as the enemy, but the portrayal of both as inherently insidious, threatening, and with the ultimate aim of world domination remains the same.

See also: **orientalism**

Further reading: Safi 2007

ISM see *al-asma' al-husna'*

JIHAD

The Arabic verb *jahada*, from which the noun "jihad" is derived, means to struggle or exert oneself. The Qur'an often uses the phrase *jihad fi sabil Allah*, "exerting oneself in the path of God" (4:96, 9:20). Believers are said to be those "who strive with their wealth and themselves" (*jahadu bi amwalihim wa anfusihim*, 8:72). This struggle need not always refer to fighting.

> Oh you who believe—shall I point out to you a bargain which will save you from a painful punishment? That you believe in God and His Messenger and strive in the cause of God with your wealth and yourselves. That is better for you if you did not know.
>
> (61:12–13)

Jihad can include the giving of **charity**, freeing slaves, and challenges to oppression. Its primary sense, though, both in the Qur'an and in later Muslim discourses, is armed struggle, which may comprise resistance to perceived injustice or the creation of space for Islam and Muslims to flourish.

In the wake of the 9/11 attacks, Muslims and others who wanted to dissociate Islam from terrorism frequently cited a **hadith** according to which jihad in the form of fighting is the "lesser jihad" while the "greater jihad" is the struggle believers must wage against their own baser instincts. Although many Muslims undoubtedly agree with the sentiment, this way of framing the issue downplays the centrality of jihad to the Qur'an and the classical Muslim tradition more generally. In the Medinan **surah**s, generally later than the Meccan surahs, mentions of fighting, killing, and jihad are common. But these verses express competing sentiments on the scope of permitted fighting.

The Qur'an mentions at 22:40–41 defensive fighting: "permission to fight is given to those against whom war is made . . . Those who have been driven out from their homes unjustly" because they affirm belief in God. Killing is said to be better than oppression. However, not all unbelievers need to be fought; groups such as the **dhimmi**s, who do not fight against the Muslims, are not to be combated militarily. Treaties, likewise, are to be honored so long as the other party upholds their end of the bargain.

In opposition to these verses approving limited forms of fighting are seemingly unrestricted statements such as "O Prophet! Do jihad against the unbelievers and the hypocrites and be harsh to them. Their abode is **hell**, an evil destination" (9:73; also 66:9).

Are these verses contradictory, symptomatic of a Qur'anic confusion, or do they show an evolutionary pattern? What is clear is that where fighting is required, able-bodied male believers are expected to fight. (Though there are recorded instances of female Muslims fighting on the battlefield, the Qur'an anticipates that women as a collectivity will remain behind.) Those who do not fight "are not equal in the sight of God" to those who do so with the intention of obeying and pleasing God. This striving is linked to "believing in God and the last day" (9:19). Jihad, even though done "in the way of God," is in fact to the benefit of the believer's own self (29:6). And the rewards for those who do fight are both earthly and heavenly (4:95). On the other hand, when the believers go off to fight, a party should stay behind to become educated in matters of **religion**.

Beyond the Qur'an, jihad is the subject of extensive reflection by later Muslim scholars. Within the reports about Muhammad's battles, it can be difficult to distinguish between fighting in defense of the Muslim community, fighting to expand the geographical boundaries of the community (e.g., to conquer Mecca or, eventually, Syria and beyond), and fighting to accumulate wealth (raiding was common Arab practice at the time). Early chronicles refer to Muhammad's fighting with the term *maghazi* (raids).

Muhammad's conduct in war serves as both justification and example for later Muslims, but their practices in many respects differed from his. Later generations of jurists did discuss the conditions permitting or requiring fighting. However, as Abou El Fadl points out, most of their attention went to discussing appropriate conduct *in* war, including matters such as whether civilians could be targeted (almost always the answer was no); how one identified combatants; when and whether one should kill, ransom, or enslave captives; and how to deal with destruction of property.

See also: *sirah*

Further reading: Abou El Fadl 2001c; Bonner 2006; Cook 2005; Peters 1996; Turner 1997

JINN

The *jinn*, to whom the Qur'an devotes a surah (72), were created before human beings. They originate in fire (15:26–27). They live in a world invisible to us. They eat, drink, and procreate. Like us, some are righteous while others are not. They are a part of divine **creation** separate from humanity and the **angels**. They share certain qualities with humanity including intelligence and free choice. They have the power to choose between true and false, right and wrong, and they are expected to behave accordingly. Like the human being (*insan*) they have duties, since "I only created the *jinn* and humanity to **worship** me" (51:56). Those who fail will be punished in **hell**.

JUSTICE

Justice is a critical concept in the Qur'an ("My Lord has commanded justice," 7:29) and in Muslim thought generally, and is related to broader concepts of equity (*al-ma'ruf*), honesty, and, for feminist thinkers in particular, equality. Legal thinkers stressed the importance of justice in interpersonal relations, though what justice could mean has differed dramatically. In **marriage**, classical jurists agreed that just treatment did not require full equality in all areas (**love** and **sex**, in particular), but only in the measurable dimensions such as allocation of time and financial support. Even here, a wife from a wealthier background might be due greater maintenance than a poorer one. The jurists' rulings on these matters are not drawn directly from the Qur'an, which does not provide these specifics, but they reflect the notion of appropriate hierarchies that *is* present in the sacred text.

As with most pre-Enlightenment thought, the Qur'anic text assumes inequalities of status between human beings. These may be based on innate qualities such as **gender**, accidental facts of life such as wealth, or outcomes of social processes such as **slavery**. Justice did not demand precisely equal treatment of each of these individuals but rather fair or equitable treatment.

Mu'tazilite thinkers placed such importance on justice that they were known as the "people of justice and unity, *tawhid*." The view that God was necessarily just—and that the just and the good could be known through rationality as well as **revelation**—was a key element of their **theology**. The Shi'ah likewise consider justice absolutely central.

See also: **morality**, *qadr*, **suffering**

Further reading: Khadduri 1984; Mir-Hosseini 2006

KA'BAH

Ka'bah in Arabic is derived from the root meaning "cube." In the Qur'an, the Ka'bah is God's house of **worship**. God twice refers to it as "My House" (2:125, 22:26), and Abraham calls it "Your sacred house" when talking to God (14:37). It is referred to eighteen times in the Qur'an in one form or another, while the specific term Ka'bah itself occurs only twice, in the surah The Table (5:95, 5:97). The location of the Ka'bah is also given, according to many interpretations, as at Bakkah (3:96), in a valley with no cultivation (14:37). The sacred shrine was instituted to create a sanctuary for worshipers and to establish **prayer**s (*salat*). The Ka'bah is the ritual and symbolic center of Muslim worship; it is the direction in which Muslims the world over face during prayer. **Mosque** architecture usually includes a prayer niche or *qiblah* that allows worshipers to turn to Mecca.

The sacred black stone now located in the southeast corner of the Ka'bah is said to be part of what came down from heaven to provide light for Adam and Eve. However, after the great flood, the position of the Ka'bah was hidden. The **angel** Gabriel revealed its site to Abraham and Ishmael and they were instructed to rebuild it on its original site. The *maqam Ibrahim*, the "place of Abraham" (2:125), is still today indicated there, together with the footprints of Abraham. The area for one mile around the Ka'bah was sacred and no warfare was to take place there nor was any blood to be spilled. Abraham and Ishmael were also instructed in the ceremonies of the **pilgrimage** (hajj), which now included not only circumambulation of the Ka'bah (2:125) but also the ritual of the *sa'*, the movement back and forth seven times between al-Marwa and al-Safa, in reenactment of Hajar's movement as she searched for water in the valley of Bakkah. When pilgrims today drink from the spring of Zamzam, which is located in the sacred precincts, they are celebrating the miraculous appearance of the angel Gabriel who brought forth water for the thirsty Hajar and her son.

The Ka'bah is also intricately connected with the ritual of the hajj. It is said that the call for the hajj, first initiated by Abraham after he had built the Ka'bah, was itself a kind of miracle. According to the hadith, Abraham asked the angel Gabriel how people from all the regions of Arabia could possibly hear his proclamation. God's answer is Q. 22:27: "And proclaim to people the hajj. They will come to you on foot and on every lean beast; they shall come from every deep and distant ravine." The ritual words *labayk allahuma labayk* ("I hear Your calls, Our God"), which tradition says have been repeated by pilgrims since the time of Abraham, respond to the divine command.

The Ka'bah is itself covered by a cloth, the *kiswah*, which is periodically replaced. It is black with intricate gold embroidery.

See also: *tawhid*

KALAM see theology

KHUTBAH

A *khutbah*, or sermon, is an essential part of congregational Friday **prayer**s; it also figures in the services marking each of the two yearly festivals or **Eid**s. In the weekly congregational prayer it comes before the ritual prayer while on the Eids it comes after. A less formal *khutbah* often forms part of weddings.

A *khutbah* is traditionally delivered from a standing position on the *minbar* in the **mosque** at the front of the main prayer space, although some mosques use a lectern or podium instead. The *khutbah* is divided into two portions, and the *khatib* pauses briefly, sitting, in between. The *khutbah* usually opens with a series of formulae praising God and seeking God's forgiveness and protection followed by verses from the Qur'an which stress the need to revere God. The sermon itself may be devoted to exploring a particular Qur'anic theme, often with references to the *sunnah*. Depending on the preacher's interests, it may focus on a particular (desirable or undesirable) behavior, an edifying historical event, or a narrative drawn from a story related in the Qur'an.

Delivering the *khutbah* is often but not always the task of the person who leads prayers. Preachers historically have been important figures and the content of Friday *khutbah*s can be influential in swaying public opinion on political as well as religious topics. Certain fiery preachers in the Middle East have become famous, and cassettes of their sermons have been circulated since the late twentieth century; in the twenty-first century, many are available online for downloading for those with internet access.

The Qur'an does not use the term *khutbah* for sermon or preaching (the closest equivalent being the granting of "decisive speech," *khitab*, to the Prophet David in 38:20). The term *khitbah* appears in Q. 2:235 for a marriage proposal or betrothal. Instead, the Qur'an uses the term *wa'aza*—to admonish, exhort, or warn—both for God's admonitions to humanity (2:231, 4:58, 16:90, 24:17), and for the exhortations of human moral leaders including Muhammad and other prophets (e.g., 31:13). Unusually, it appears as a command to men with regard to women whose *nushuz*—rebelliousness, recalcitrance, or antipathy—they fear (4:34).

See also: ***imam*, worship**

KNOWLEDGE

The Arabic root verb "to know" (*'alima*) and its derivates occur in the Qur'an about 750 times to refer to both divine and human knowledge. The Qur'an often states that God's knowledge is superior to human knowledge, and that he knows secrets we cannot (6:59, 11:31). Human beings and **angels** both owe anything they know to God, from whom knowledge, like everything else, eventually originates.

Real knowledge is linked to religious insight. Prophets possess knowledge that comes to them from God, and they are an important source of human knowledge. This is not ordinary human knowledge, though (7:62). **Revelation** contains knowledge, so the Qur'an describes itself as a book which God has sent based on knowledge (7:52). Knowledge may be acquired by human action, but it is God who, as source of everything, grants knowledge in the first place. When we speak of human knowledge we should note its difference from divine knowledge, although even human knowledge ultimately comes from God. In this sense, knowledge is related to wisdom, *hikmah*, a term which later came to be used for gnostic or esoteric **philosophy** and philosophers (*hakim*, pl. *hukama'*).

From a religious point of view, the point of knowledge is to understand the world that God has created. Unless one appreciates the larger divine context, knowledge is piecemeal and unconnected with anything higher. Since the whole of reality is subordinate to God, we need to be aware that our knowledge has a unifying theme. One cannot lose sight of ***tawhid***, the basic unity that characterizes the world as a reflection of its creator.

Ignorance (*jahal*) is the opposite of knowledge, and implies bad behavior also. The term *jahiliyyah* appears four times in the Qur'an, and refers to the ignorance of the pagan Arabs who reject God. The point is that it is not difficult to come to the conclusion that the world has a divine creator. This is a very basic idea that we can derive from looking at the world itself, whose signs (*ayat*) are just like the signs of nature in pointing to the existence, influence, and attributes of God. "And if you ask them: 'Who created the heavens and the earth?' they will certainly say 'God'" (31:25). On the other hand, despite the obviousness of **religion** many people still do not get it: "So, set your face positively towards religion. It is the original nature according to which God fashioned humanity. There is no altering of God's **creation**. That is the true religion; but most people do not know" (30:30). To a certain extent, knowledge of God's existence is self-evident. It seems to require no **education**, reflection, or even evidence. It is contained in the innate nature of the human being (*fitrah*), which is constant. The wrong sort of training and upbringing can temporarily take away this natural belief in God, and then we should use knowledge to reacquire it.

See also: **prophethood, hadith**

Further reading: Goldziher 1967; Mohamed 1996; Nasr and Leaman 1996; Rosenthal 1970

KUFR

Kufr, usually rendered "disbelief" or "unbelief," is one of the most important concepts in the Qur'an. In one of the chronologically early surahs of the Qur'an, "The Disbelievers" (109), Muhammad is ordered to speak to the *kafirun*, clearly setting out his disagreements with them. The *kafirun*, the surah states, do not and will not **worship** the same deity as Muhammad, who is to conclude: "to you your **religion** and to me the religion,"—that is, the correct path of belief and practice.

Lack of belief or faith (*iman*) is intimately related to the other meaning of *kufr*, ingratitude. Ingratitude is something that one must be careful not to slip into: "It is a fact that the human being is ungrateful to his lord" (100:6, 43:14–15). Aware of the human tendency to forgetfulness, believers will cultivate gratitude (*shukr*) as a response to God's benevolence, while unbelievers will remain ungrateful. Lack of gratitude implies not believing in God, as it means one does not recognize God as the creator whose favors are bestowed on the universe. The reverse is also true: if one does not believe in God, one is by definition not showing appropriate gratitude.

Kufr is subject to gradations. One can be outwardly Muslim and inwardly hypocritical.

The issue of *takfir*, declaring someone who self-identifies as Muslim to be a *kafir*, or disbeliever, has emerged on numerous occasions throughout Muslim history, beginning with the secessionist Kharijites, an extremist sectarian movement that emerged in the years after

Muhammad's death. Labeling opponents as unbelievers has been criticized in the past as it is today; one who practices *takfir* assumes to
know the fate of another human being, which is a prerogative that
belongs solely to God. A **hadith** stating that if a Muslim calls another
Muslim a *kafir* then it is true about one of them represents the disdain
for *takfir* by the generality of scholars. Al-Ghazali's cogent plea for
greater theological tolerance in the eleventh century CE represents
one entry into an ongoing debate. However, charges of *kufr* or **apostasy** were a potent way of dealing with individuals and opinions of
which one disapproved.

Today, the **Wahhabi**s are known for this practice of excommunication; they draw in part on the opinions of Ibn Taymiyyah (d. 728/
1328) who declared certain common practices of his era such as visiting and praying at tombs of significant religious authorities to be
innovation and *kufr*. Ironically, Ibn Taymiyyah himself was charged
with unbelief for his **fatwa** on this issue, resulting in his imprisonment and execution.

See also: **knowledge**, *ziyarah*

Further reading: Izutsu 1966; Jackson 2002

LAWFUL AND FORBIDDEN

The categories of lawful and forbidden (*halal* and **haram**) have been
vitally important through Muslim history, though their use was
often limited to the scholarly elites. In the modern era, due in large
part to the influence of **Wahhabi** and **salafi** thinkers, the *halal/haram*
distinction is pervasive among even lay Muslims. Premodern scholars warned against "making lawful what is forbidden and forbidding
what is lawful." They did not usually stop there, however, using the
fivefold scale of values known as the *ahkam al-khamsah*. At one end of
this scale are forbidden actions; at the other, those that are obligatory.
In between are reprehensible and recommended actions as well as, in
the middle of the scale, morally neutral acts. In this sense, everything
above forbidden on the fivefold scale was "lawful" but not necessarily ethical or proper.

Halal as a term is also used for ritually slaughtered (*dhabiha*) meat
and, more generally, for food that is lawful for Muslims to eat.

Further reading: Abou El Fadl 2001b; Cook 2000b

AL-LAWH AL-MAHFUZ see **Preserved Tablet**

LOVE

Love takes myriad forms. Passionate unrequited human desire and deep filial or parental affection share certain characteristics with the love of the worshiper toward God and the love of God for the believer. Various words for love are used to describe both love between humans and love between creator and **creation**. In Q. 30:21, the "love and **mercy**" (*muwaddah wa rahmah*) that God has put between spouses draws from God's attribute of being *al-Wadud*, "the Loving." *Hubb* and *mahabbah* are sometimes understood as lukewarm emotions, and sometimes as quite strong. In 3:31, those who love (with *hubb*) God are commanded to follow the Prophet; then "God will love [them] and forgive [them their] sins." Lastly, *'ishq* suggests lack of control as a result of strong passion. It is often regarded as a kind of madness, and is treated as such in the popular tale of Layla and Majnun, but is also the defining concept for a school of Persian **Sufism**.

In surat Yusuf (Joseph), the chapter of the Qur'an that tells the story of the prophet by that name, love and desire figure prominently as themes. The wife of an Egyptian nobleman (the 'Aziz) and Joseph's father Jacob both passionately love Joseph. However, the character of their love is very different: Jacob's love is deep, wise, and unself-ish, basically spiritual; the love of the wife of the 'Aziz, who comes to be known as Zulaykha, is intense and violent, but it lacks depth and wisdom. Jacob achieves these characteristics through suffering and self-renunciation.

The accounts of Jacob and 'Aziz's wife contain passages of the Qur'an which have been given symbolic interpretation from early on in the interpretive tradition. In a sense, the wife of the 'Aziz imitates God, albeit in the material realm; God is described as "beautiful" and "loving beauty," and Joseph's **beauty** makes him desirable to Zulaykha. This divine role is also taken on by Joseph himself, to a degree, since Zulaykha wanted to unite with the object of her love, just as a person in love wants to unite with the object of her love. She is attracted to that object, while the object is itself unmoved by those that are in love with it. One of the interesting aspects of the story of Yusuf is that he never appears to change during all the things which happen to him on the Qur'anic account. Even when he is in prison and he has the opportunity to leave it, he remains where he is until he is entirely satisfied that the ruler is certain about his innocence.

He concentrates on preserving his integrity, and the rest of the world revolves around him, like the planets around Aristotle's unmoved mover. Aristotle characterizes that relationship as one where those who are in love with the mover do things in response to that love while the mover remains unmoved; everything else just moves around him in response to his being, not to anything he does.

Jacob loves Joseph more deeply—and in a different way—than the wife of 'Aziz, who was mainly captivated by him physically. Joseph is said to be *ahabb* (more loved) (12:8) by Jacob than were his other sons. After Joseph's disappearance, Jacob loses his eyesight out of grief. Jacob takes Joseph's disappearance as a test to evaluate his patience (*sabr*) and **trust** in God, and never believes in his son's death. In return for his patience, God provides him with a deep spiritual intuition which can be described as *'irfani* or mystical: when Jacob's sons leave Egypt, carrying with them Joseph's shirt, Jacob immediately feels the aroma of Joseph, although the caravan is still hundreds of miles away. When the messenger bringing the shirt arrives and casts it over Jacob's face (12:96), he regains his eyesight. Yet his love had in a way given him greater powers of perception before this event; the pangs brought on by separation give the lover a spiritual wisdom that cannot be acquired by mere **worship** of beauty.

Sufi thinkers regard the concept of love as particularly crucial. Dhu'l Nun al-Misri (d. 246/861); Junayd (d. 298/910); Shibli (d. 334/946); and, in particular, Nuri (d. 295/907), who called himself *'ashiq Allah* or the lover of Allah; and Hallaj (d. 309/922) employed the word *'ishq* in their writings. The extreme nature of *'ishq* interested Persian thinkers, including for example Ahmad Ghazali's (d. 520/1126) *Sawanih* (Inspirations), 'Ayn al-Qudat Hamadani's (d. 525/1131) *Tamhidat* (Prolegomena), and Ruzbihan Baqli's (522–606/1128–1209) *'Abhar al-'ashiqin* (The Yellow Narcissus of Lovers). Together with the poetical works of Farid al-Din 'Attar (d. 618/1221) and Jalal al-Din Rumi (d. 672/1273) and perhaps the *Flashes* (*Lama'at*) of Fakhr al-Din 'Iraqi (d. 688/1289) these writings constitute the main texts of the *madhhab-e 'ishq* (the school of love). This moved on from Persian culture to influence the direction of Sufism in Turkish thought also. The term *'ishq* is also used by Ibn al-'Arabi (d. 638/1240), but scholars often argue that the concept never took on the significance in Arab Sufi thought that it did in the Persian tradition.

Three Sufi works from the school of love analyze the Qur'an entirely in terms of *'ishq*: Rashid al-Din Maybudi's (d. after 520/1126) *Kashf al-asrar wa 'uddat al-abrar* (Unveiling of the Secrets and Resources of the Devout), Ruzbihan Baqli's *'Ara'is al-bayan fi haqa'iq al-Qur'an* (The Brides of Explication Concerning the Hidden Realities of the Qur'an) and Ahmad Ghazali's *Bahr al-muhabbah fi asrar al-mawaddah* (The Sea of Love Concerning the Secrets of Friendship). These commentators concentrated on words and phrases which were either direct statements of the importance of love (for example, *fa sawfa ya'ti Allah bi qawm yuhibbuhum wa yuhibbunahu*, "God will bring forth a people whom He loves as they will love Him," 5:54) or which they saw as code for the hidden meanings dealing with love. In many cases the word *habba* was taken to be much stronger than "like" and interpreted as representing the intensity of *'ashiqa* and passionate love.

Further reading: Ghazali 1986; Mahmutćehijić, 2006; Murata and Chittick 1994; Nizami 1997; Schimmel 1975

MADHHAB

The term *madhhab* (pl. *madhahib*) is derived from the root for the verb "to go" and refers to a school of thought. It may be used for groups of scholars, as with the Persian mystical "*madhhab* of **love**" or a tendency in **theology**. Most commonly, it refers to a school of jurisprudence or *fiqh*. Although there have been many that are now defunct, four main schools of **Sunni** jurisprudence have dominated Muslim history, along with one major and several minor schools of **Shi'i** jurisprudence.

The Sunni *madhhab* system arose after a period of less formal scholarly ties, where students learned with a variety of teachers. By the early fourth/tenth century, these groups of more or less loosely affiliated scholars were clustered into definable schools of thought, with fairly regular curricula – at a minimum, the works attributed to the school's eponym or his main disciples—and increasingly formal methodologies and doctrines. The rise of *madhahib* did not eliminate internal dissent but rather circumscribed its boundaries.

The Sunni schools, Hanafi, Maliki, Shafi'i, and Hanbali, are named after, respectively, Abu Hanifa (d. 150/767), Malik ibn Anas (d. 179/796), Muhammad ibn Idris al-Shafi'i (d. 204/820), and Ahmad ibn Hanbal (d. 241/855). Although these men are sometimes referred to as the founders of the schools, they did not actually found them though they did originate many of their distinctive doctrines. Their life histories are intertwined: one of Abu Hanifa's main disciples, Muhammad al-Shaybani, also studied with Malik; al-Shafi'i studied with Malik and al-Shaybani and was himself Ibn Hanbal's teacher. The schools became recognizable as such in the generations after these figures lived, as students transmitted their doctrines and redacted their works. There are interconnections as well between early Sunni and Shi'i scholars; Ja'far al-Sadiq (d. 765), sixth Shi'i **imam** and eponym of the main Twelver Shi'i legal school, the Ja'fari *madhhab*, was one of Abu Hanifa's teachers.

Some now-defunct schools have interesting legacies. The Zahiri *madhhab*, so named for its reliance on the explicit and apparent (*zahir*) meaning of texts, are not quite literalists in the sense that some have thought but rationalists who remained committed to avoiding analogy, a key element of Sunni *fiqh* methodology. Ibn Hanbal himself distrusted analogy, which figured little in his own thought, but the Hanbali *madhhab* eventually adopted a methodology similar to that of the other Sunni schools.

It is an important principle of Islamic jurisprudence that competing or contradictory rulings can be equally valid. Juristic doctrines were, because they were the product of human reasoning, potentially fallible. It was possible for the jurist to be rewarded for his effort in formulating a rule even if he was ultimately wrong. These principles help explain the coexistence of the doctrine of mutual orthodoxy of the Sunni legal schools with very real, and occasionally quite heated, disagreements between them on numerous matters of doctrine. The validity of a doctrine rested on the diligence and sincerity with which a jurist decided the matter, but its "correctness" was ultimately knowable only to God. There were serious and ongoing debates and disputes among the scholars about particular legal positions. Vehement polemical treatises circulated and debates occasionally turned violent (though these last were usually over speculative theology, rather than details of legal regulations). While there were occasional freethinkers who continued to reason very broadly—the Andalusian Maliki Ibn Rushd (520–595/1126–1198) was one such figure—most jurists remained within the methodological and doctrinal boundaries of their own *madhahib*.

Although most premodern Muslim societies allowed individuals to choose which school to follow, and judges adjudicated among claimants according to their own *madhhab* allegiances, different schools came to predominate in various areas of the Muslim world. The Hanafi *madhhab* gained much of its influence as the official school of the Ottoman Empire and currently predominates in South Asia, with many Middle Eastern adherents as well. Indonesia is largely Shafi'i, due to the fact that the traders who introduced Islam to the area were Shafi'i. Malikis, who originated in Medina, where the first Muslim community was formed, today predominate in North Africa and are influential in some other African areas as well. The Hanbali school, historically the least significant in numbers of adherents, has gained prominence with Saudi Arabia's oil wealth and its support of the **Wahhabi** movement, which draws on key Hanbali thinkers, such as Ibn Taymiyyah (d. 728/1328).

In the postcolonial period, nearly all Muslim nation-states have adopted legal codes that replace the *madhhab* court system, although many individuals still look to *madhhab* authorities for guidance. Other pressures militate against continued *madhhab* relevance, including **salafi** rejection of the established schools of jurisprudence. Salafis argue that one ought to rely on Qur'an and sunnah alone. Their critics argue that some methodology is necessary to derive rules from the textual sources when they do not explicitly address the issues at stake, precisely the situation which led to the formation of *madhhab*s in the first place. There is a counter-movement, in fact, arguing that following an established *madhhab* is necessary; those who fail to follow a school risk contravening Islamic law and even falling into disbelief or **kufr**. Likewise, American Muslim scholar Sherman Jackson has argued that black American Muslims in the contemporary era should draw from the learning of the *madhhab* scholars.

Further reading: Ibn Rushd 1994–96; Jackson 2005; Melchert 2000

MADRASAH see **education**

MARRIAGE

The Qur'an (4:21) refers to marriage as a "solemn covenant," using a term, *mithaq*, otherwise used primarily to describe compacts between God and prophets or communities (2:63, 2:83, 3:81, 5:7, 33:7, 57:8). It is used on occasion for binding compacts between communities, as in 4:90, 4:92 and 8:72.

The Qur'an uses the metaphor of garments to describe the relationship between spouses (2:187). Q. 30:21 declares that God "created for you mates from among yourselves that you may dwell tranquilly with them and He put **love** and **mercy** between you."

In addition to these general statements on marriage, which situate marriage firmly within a broader context of divine oversight of the created universe, the Qur'an sets forth certain specific provisions regulating marriage, **divorce**, and **sex**. It stipulates the payment of dower: wives are owed "compensation" or "reward" for what men "enjoy from them" (4:24). The dower is to be given to women as "a free gift" (4:4) and is not to be taken back in case of divorce unless the woman is guilty of "flagrant indecency" (4:19). (If the marriage is dissolved before consummation, only half an agreed dower is due; if no dower was settled, then a compensatory gift is prescribed, 2:236–37). Pre-Islamic divorce practices, including now-obscure oaths (24:6–9, 29:25), are modified.

The Qur'an recommends marriage for the unmarried and also clarifies who is permissible as a marriage partner. Idolators are forbidden as spouses for both male and female Muslims (2:221) and women who convert and seek refuge with the Muslims may not be returned to their disbelieving husbands, who are no longer lawful spouses for them (60:10). Q. 5:5, however, specifically grants permission for Muslim men to marry women from the **People of the Book**. Marriages between enslaved persons and of slaves with free people are also permissible, unlike in most other traditions (2:221, 4:25, 24:32). Of course, some relations are too close for marriage, such as a man's mother, grandmother, daughter, sister, or aunt; others are prohibited by "milk-fosterage," an issue arising from the common nature of wet-nursing in Arabia of Muhammad's time. Prohibitions may also arise from marriage; a man cannot ever marry his mother-in-law or a woman her father-in-law. Additional women may be forbidden due to circumstance: a man cannot be married to two sisters at the same time (4:22–24).

The basic permissibility of a man's marrying more than one woman at a time is taken for granted in Q. 4:23, but outlined in 4:3, which refers specifically to the situation of fatherless children (though whether it is orphaned females who are to be married, or widows with children, is the subject of debate). The verse prescribes marriage to "two, three, or four" women, though if one fears one will commit injustice, then "one" only. Q. 4:129 acknowledges the impossibility of being exactly fair ("you cannot do **justice** between your wives"), but requires that a man refrain from "complete partiality." Some reformers have argued that this latter verse cancels the permission in the former. They reason that if polygamy always causes injustice, and doing justice is a condition for the permissibility of polygamy, then polygamy is effectively forbidden. Premodern scholars did not see the matter in this way, taking for granted the permissibility of polygamy. They did, however, devote significant attention to a man's obligations to each wife and what precisely was required for justice.

In a famous **hadith**, the Prophet Muhammad states, "Marriage is my *sunnah*." In another, he declares that one who has married has completed half of **faith**, and warns one to be careful with the other half. Muhammad himself was a much-married man. He remained monogamously married to his first wife, Khadijah, from the time he was twenty-five until her death twenty-five years later, shortly before the *hijrah*. In the remaining years of his life, he married multiple women; at his death in 632 CE he had nine wives and, according to the hadith sources, maintained marital relations with eight of them.

Al-Ghazali (d. 505/1111) wrote extensively about marriage in his massive compilation *The Revival of the Religious Sciences*. He did not view marriage as an absolute **obligation** for human beings, and discouraged marriage for those who doubted being able to fulfill its obligations. However, for those who could fulfill their duties it was highly recommended as a lawful means of channeling the sexual impulse and also of procreating, which had the merit of increasing the Muslim populace.

Beyond its role in legitimating sexual relations—the legal term for marriage, *nikah*, literally means "intercourse"—marriage established interdependent but **gender**-differentiated rights and obligations between spouses. For medieval thinkers, in addition to the husband's general ethical duty of "good treatment" of his wife, his marital duties (and her rights) were mostly financial. She had the right to food and clothing or money to purchase them. The amount and quality depended on the parties' social status; among all but the poorest strata, it was also expected that he would provide a servant for her.

A wife's obligations, which were her husband's rights, were mostly behavioral. It was assumed by jurists that wives would obey their husbands—though, they took care to note, only in religiously permissible matters—but jurists devoted little attention to obedience per se. Rather, they focused on wives' duties to be available to their husbands, remaining in the marital home unless permitted to go out and not refusing a husband's sexual advances. Wives did not, according to most authorities, have legally enforceable duties to cook, perform housework, or care for children, though where this was customary it might be considered appropriate. However, a man could not withhold his support for a wife's refusal to perform these tasks.

The extent to which couples' actual married life followed this legal blueprint is impossible to determine with any precision, but only women from the elite usually followed rules for seclusion very carefully. Among the lower classes women have always performed the bulk of work within the household, including childcare; many have also engaged in economic activity in productive tasks such as agriculture or commerce.

Shifts in modern laws have altered the legal landscape dramatically, and social shifts have done the same for customary practices. Polygamy, historically rare outside of Africa except for among elites, has become increasingly uncommon. A number of nations have passed laws restricting or outlawing it. Yet the **Shi 'i** institution of *mut'a*, or temporary marriage, has, after largely falling into disuse, been somewhat revived in Iran since the 1979 Islamic revolution.

See also: *fiqh*, *shari'ah*

Further reading: Ali 2006; An-Na'im 2002a; Esposito with DeLong-Bas 2001; Murata 1987; Haeri 1989; Rapoport 2005; al-Shafi'i 1993; Sonbol 1996a; Spectorsky 1992; Tucker 1998; Wynn 1996

MARTYRDOM

The Arabic word *shahadah* is often understood to mean "martyrdom," and *shahid* means "martyr." The word *shahid* and its derivatives in the Qur'an means "eyewitness," but the term is linked in both classical and modern Muslim discourses to **jihad** or struggle. Martyrdom comes to someone who struggles in a just cause, being aware of the **truth** and endeavoring to carry out the divine will in whatever way is available to him or, occasionally, her. It is a concept particularly stressed by **Shi'ism**, harking back to the death of Imam Husayn at Karbala and the putative unjust sufferings of other major figures in its history.

The term "martyrdom" carries tremendous resonance and what Western media refer to as suicide bombings are called by those who support them "martyrdom operations."

See also: *sabr*

Further reading: Ayoub 1987; Bonner 2006; Cook 2007; Lewinstein 2002

MASJID see **mosque**

MECCA AND MEDINA see *haram*

MERCY

Mercy, *rahmah*, is one of God's most important characteristics. Muslim **theology** and especially **Sufism** have been concerned with the relationship between competing aspects of divine nature. God is both merciful and wrathful, but in what proportion? A *hadith qudsi*, a saying taken to be divine speech separate from the Qur'an, resolves the matter, stating: "My mercy has outstripped my wrath." This precedence of mercy is reflected in the **basmalah** which precedes each Qur'anic surah except the ninth; it refers to God as both al-Rahman and al-Rahim. Al-Rahman, one of God's all-encompassing names, is unique to God, but mercy is not limited to God. The prophet Muhammad is said to be "a mercy for the worlds."

Terms for mercy are related etymologically to the word for womb (*rahm*, used in 4:1), and God's care for humanity has been likened to the tenderness that a nursing mother shows for her baby.

See also: ***al-asma' al-husna'***

MORALITY

The Qur'an addressed itself to the Arabs who were its first audience. It seeks to change their behavior from violent and passionate to serene. Concerning this impetuous quality the Qur'an states: "When the unbelievers instilled in their hearts fierceness, the fierceness of ignorance, God then sent down His serenity upon His messenger and upon the believers, and imposed on them the word of piety, since they deserved and earned it. God has **knowledge** of everything" (48:26). The expression "fierceness of ignorance" (*hamiyyat al-jahiliyyah*) in the Qur'an refers to the proud spirit of tribal life, which led to many blood feuds in pre-Islamic Arabia.

By contrast, the Book advocates the calm, relaxed, and humble path of **religion**, summed up in the quality of *hilm*, which became a dominant virtue in the Qur'an. The word *hilm* is absent from the Qur'an, but the adjective *halim* is mentioned as a divine attribute and also a quality of Abraham (9:115), Isaac (37:99), and Shu'ayb (9:89). It is generally rendered as "slowly suffering," "patient," and "gifted with toleration." This property, together with patience or steadfastness (*sabr*), is a significant aspect of the moral revolution brought about by Islam.

Goodness (*khayr*) and Righteousness (*birr*)

The term *khayr* has both material and religious meanings. When a rich man asked the Prophet about how to use his wealth, the answer linked doing good with material generosity and **charity**: "They ask you what they should spend. Say: 'Whatever bounty (*khayr*) you give is for the parents, the near of kin, the orphans, the needy and the wayfarer. And whatever good [*khayr*] you do, God is completely aware of it'" (2:211). The term also refers to paying prayer-tax and the alms or *zakat*. God will observe and punish and reward accordingly (2:104).

The word *birr* (righteousness) is linked with social justice and **love** for God which inspires charity and good behavior:

> Righteousness is not to turn your faces towards the East and the West; the righteous is he who believes in God, the Last Day, the **angels**, the Book and the Prophets; who gives of his money, out of love for Him, to his kin, the orphans, the needy, the wayfarers and the beggars, and for the freeing of slaves; who performs the prayers and pays the alms-tax. They stick to their agreements, and endure patiently adversity, difficulties, and violent times.
>
> (2:177)

Justice and Responsibility

Justice is a supreme virtue in Islam, often linked with belief in the Oneness of God and the truthfulness of the Prophet. There are many verses in the Qur'an that command believers to adopt this as a moral ideal: "God commands you to deliver trusts to their owners, and if you judge between people, to judge justly" (4:58); "O believers, be upholders of justice, witnesses for God, even if it be against yourselves, your parents, or kinsmen. Whether rich or poor, God takes better care of both. Do not follow your desire to refrain from justice" (4:135).

The Qur'an does not only call to **faith**, but also to moral action. Believers are required to obey God and his Prophet, who is the standard of moral conduct and piety, a "beautiful example" (33:21) for others to emulate.

Modesty

Modesty is promoted in the Qur'an for both men and women, but discussion has tended to concentrate mainly on the latter. Some express requirements for modesty in terms of what must be covered (hair, legs, arms) while others list instead what may be uncovered (eyes, hands, feet).

Q. 24:30–31 lay out certain requirements for modesty and chaste behavior. Both men (24:30) and women (24:31) are commanded to lower their gazes and protect their chastity. What does "lower their gazes" mean? The linking of lowering the gaze with guarding chastity suggests for some that the prohibition is not directly about the act of looking but about the quality of the gaze. The sense of the passage is to restrain the intensity of what takes place when we look at each other (31:19, 49:2); an intense or lusty gaze is prohibited.

The text goes on to give additional guidance for female dress and comportment. Women are told to draw their "veils" (*khumur*, a customary headcovering) over their breasts or cleavage. They are also required to conceal their adornments. The verse makes an exception for "what [ordinarily] appears." Authorities have disagreed as to how to interpret this phrase and indeed as to whether the adornments are external beautifiers, such as jewelry, or instead comprise part of a woman's natural attractiveness, such as her face. A second exception is made for certain individuals in front of whom a woman does not have to cover herself so fully: "their husbands, their fathers, their husbands' fathers, their sons, their stepsons, their brothers, their brother's sons, their sister's sons, their women, or those whom their right hands own [i.e., in **slavery**], or their male attendants lacking in sexual vigor, or small children who have no awareness of women's nakedness [*'awrah*]."

At least one of the verses regulating modesty (33:53) gives special instructions for the wives of the Prophet; some have suggested that it might not have wider extension. Muhammad Ashmawi has challenged the necessity for Muslim women to be veiled at all, something defended by the mufti of Egypt at the time, Sayyid Tantawi. Ashmawi argues that veiling is a pre-Islamic custom that has been mistakenly taken up by legal thinkers in Islam. This dispute in 1994 was only one instance of a lively debate on what precisely is involved in the Qur'anic injunction for the preservation of modesty.

Objectivity of morality

A protracted debate developed between the Mu'tazilites and the Ash'arites on the issue of whether morality was established by divine fiat or order, or whether it is objective and God established it to help us fit in with what is natural for us to do. The Mu'tazilites argued for the objective view while their opponents defended the position that became generally accepted in Islamic **theology**, that nothing constrains God in his determination of divine law.

See also: *fitrah, sabr, taqwah, hijab*

Further reading: Denny 1985; Fakhry 1991; Goldziher 1967; Hourani 1985; Izutsu 1959; Mohamed 2004

MOSQUE

The Arabic term for mosque, *masjid*, refers literally to a place of prostration, which is one element of the ritual **prayer**. Mosques vary across the world in size, style, and, to a certain extent, function. Each contains, at a minimum, a large open area for prayer known as a *musallah*; in many places it is customary to prevent non-Muslims from entering this space. Inside the prayer area, a niche in the wall (*mihrab*) customarily indicates the direction of prayer (*qiblah*) which is always facing toward the **Ka'bah** in Mecca.

Traditionally, mosques also have a *minbar* or pulpit, usually made of ornately carved wood from which the **imam** delivers the sermon (**khutbah**) at Friday congregational prayers. (The day of congregational prayer, *yawm al-jumu'ah*, is mentioned in 62:9.) Towns and cities in majority-Muslim nations usually have numerous smaller neighborhood mosques along with one major mosque (*jami' masjid*) which hosts the Friday midday service.

The original mosque in Medina served as a social center and meeting place for Muslims. Not only was it the location for prayers and meetings, it was also the compound where the Prophet's wives, known collectively as the Mothers of the Believers, lived. Through the premodern era, mosques continued to function as more than prayer spaces. Scholars of various types hosted teaching circles in mosques—sometimes several would meet concurrently, each by a different pillar. Other types of compound might be attached to mosques, including educational institutions, tombs, or **Sufi** lodges. Isma'ili Muslims, a sect of the **Shi'ah**, refer to their places of worship as *jama'at khana*.

Women's presence in mosque spaces has long been controversial. Jurists have generally agreed that women are not *required* to attend Friday congregational prayers but disagree over whether they are *permitted* to do so. In one **hadith** frequently cited against women's mosque attendance, Muhammad declares that the best mosque for the woman who came seeking his advice is the innermost part of her home. Yet there is clear evidence that women attended the mosque regularly while Muhammad was alive; the disagreement likely dates from during or shortly after his lifetime. The Prophet's reported saying, "Do not prevent God's female servants from [going to] God's **mosque**" demonstrates one side of the debate; another, attributed to Aishah, presents the other: had Muhammad known how bad morals would become, he would himself have prevented women from attending the mosque. Ironically, those who would prevent women from appearing in public space take a woman's opinion above the Prophet's explicit command.

During Muhammad's lifetime, Muslims practiced **gender** segregation in the main mosque of Medina during the prayer; women entered through a separate door and prayed in separate rows behind men in an undivided *musallah*. In the modern world, practices of gender segregation in mosques vary. In some places, including much of South Asia, women are effectively barred from mosques. Even where women are not barred—as in many American mosques—they may be made to feel subtly or not so subtly unwelcome, through inferior facilities. In Egypt, "conservative" women have become very active in claiming places for women in the mosques. The movement of women attending mosques regularly not only challenges the status quo but also calls into question definitions of gendered activism and notions of what transformation in female roles might look like.

Like social practices regarding mosque use, mosque architecture has varied greatly over space and time. Larger early mosques have a central courtyard with fountains for (men's) ablutions. Today, mosques may be built with well-appointed bathrooms including specially built low sinks for washing feet during ablutions.

Mosque construction reflects local architectural influences. In some places, such as North America, many mosques or Islamic centers are adapted commercial or even residential buildings. Those that are designed and built as mosques often aim to include distinctive architectural elements even when they no longer fulfill their original purposes. For instance, the Toledo, Ohio, mosque's minarets are not used to project the muezzin's voice as he calls for prayer, but clearly echo Andalusian style with a domed cupola. These may, of course, not be recognized by everyone as Islamic; one trucker viewing the Ohio site from the highway before the mosque was completed in 1983 reportedly thought he was seeing a new Taco Bell in the works. The Islamic Center of Toledo is notable, as well, for its side-by-side segregation of male and female worshipers in the prayer hall with a waist-high partition.

Islam is no exception to the practice of taking over other religious sites and transforming them into places of worship for the conquering religion, either through adaptation of the existing structure or reconstruction at or near the same site. The reclamation of the Ka'bah does not really count, as Muslim tradition holds that it was originally built by Abraham and Ishmael, but other famous mosques include the Aya Sofia in Istanbul and the Masjid al-Aqsa on Temple Mount in Jerusalem (see 17:1).

Through Muslim history, mosque-building projects have showcased the power of rulers or the patronage of important persons.

Women of the Ottoman imperial household were notable patrons of key mosque construction projects. In addition to the prestige gained through patronage, there could be less worldly motives. In a famous hadith reported by Bukhari, Muhammad stated, "Whoever builds a mosque, intending God's pleasure, God will build for him a house in **paradise**." These words, which can appear as decorations inside mosques, also often feature in appeals for donations to pay for mosque construction projects in Western Muslim communities.

See also: **pilgrimage**

Further reading: Khalidi 2000; Macaulay 2003; Peirce 1993

MOTHER OF THE BOOK

The expression *umm al-kitab* ("the Mother of the Book," also "source" or "foundation" of the book) appears three times in the Qur'an. It appears in the context of a distinction between verses that are **mutashabih** (ambiguous) and those that are **muhkam** (clear), identifying itself with the clear portions of the text. In Q. 3:7, "It is He who sent down upon you the Book, in which are clear verses that are the *umm al-kitab*, and others are ambiguous." Those who are keen on dissension select the ambiguous interpretation in preference to those that are clear and should serve as the foundation, the *umm al-kitab*.

Not only is the *umm al-kitab* clear, but it is with God. Q. 43:2–4 says: "By the clear book, behold, We have made it an Arabic Qur'an so that you will understand; and behold, it is the *umm al-kitab*, with Us; sublime and wise." Similarly, 13:39 states: "God blots out, and He establishes whatever He wishes; and with Him is the *umm al-kitab*." The preceding verse refers to God's giving his messengers signs (*ayat*).

The *umm al-kitab* could be a heavenly prototype, the essence of all holy books including Jewish and Christian scripture and the Qur'an. The particular expression *umm al-kitab* is how the Qur'an describes itself. As with the distinction between clear and ambiguous verses, the Qur'an represents the **truth** clearly while other scriptures are, to a lesser or greater extent, obscure. Muslim scholars often identify the *umm al-kitab* with the **Preserved Tablet** (*al-lawh al-mahfuz*, e.g., 85:21), considered the heavenly record of destiny (*qadr*) in which all human deeds together with the Qur'an are recorded. It is not obvious whether both the prototype of scripture and the slate of destiny are referred to by these terms.

See also: **abrogation**

MUFTI see **fatwa**

MUHKAM AND MUTASHABIH

The Qur'an refers to some verses as "clear" or established (*muhkam*) and others as "ambiguous" (*mutashabih*) (3:7). It commands that people follow what is clear and not get overly caught up in arguments over the meaning of ambiguous or allegorical phrases. The fact that some verses in the Qur'an were *muhkam* or clear in meaning while others were *mutashabih* and less clear did not oblige Muslims to spend extra effort to make the *mutashabih* verses comprehensible; rather, 3:7 warns that those who are interested in sowing confusion will concentrate on the less clear verses. They could after all be made to prove all sorts of things that deviate from God's intended message.

Muslim theologians discussed the precise nature of the *muhkam/ mutashabih* dichotomy extensively. It remained an issue of conceptual and practical import for scholars engaged in commentary (**tafsir**), who debated which verses were which. One approach holds that the clearer verses are those that deal with actions incumbent on Muslims. As an example, 47:20 refers to a surah that is "clear" and obviously intended to have regulatory import. By contrast, the *mutashabih* verses refer to metaphysical issues such as the nature of the divine attributes and other very difficult matters that arise for interpreters of the Qur'an but cannot be decisively resolved.

See also: **Mother of the Book, theology**

NABI see **prophethood**

NAFS

Nafs and its plurals *anfus* and *nufus* usually mean the human self or person, and are associated with us as material creatures. One's *nafs* should be restrained and hence the significance of patience (**sabr**). **Nafs** is sometimes also translated as "soul," though the Qur'anic term *ruh*—"spirit" or "breath"—is also used with spiritual connotations, to refer to both people and especially **angels**. It describes a close relationship to the deity.

The self is perfected (*al-nafs al-kamila*) by divine grace. A distinction often made by **Sufis** is between *al-nafs al-insani* (human soul), which refers to our emotional and rational nature, and *al-nafs al-hayawani* (animal soul), which refers to our bodies. The animal soul is the source according to them of our passions and desires like hunger, anger, and desire for **sex**.

The *nafs* is linked with the *ruh* or spirit when it is still in its pure state prior to **creation**. Once the *ruh* enters the body and gives it life it acquires a new character. We start off with a *ruh* and it becomes a *nafs*. When we are dominated by our passions we are at the level of the *al-nafs al-ammara bi al-su'* or "the self that commands to evil." This is what the Prophet refers to when he famously said that we should distinguish between the greater and the lesser **jihad**, and the former is the struggle against the self. The self makes us think we are very important and takes us away from God, and he was suggesting here that it is harder to fight the self than it is to take up arms and physically confront an enemy.

Some Sufi scholars developed a tripartite system of spiritual development. The lowest stage is that of the "commanding self," which inclines toward one's animal passions. Next, one arrives at the stage of self-blaming, the *nafs al-lawwama*. It is with arrival at the "peaceful self," *al-nafs al-mutma'inna*, that one achieves spiritual balance and is able to recognize the proper location of the human being in the cosmos, particularly in relation to God.

When the **angels** were told to bow before Adam they objected. It was because they were concerned at the role he had as God's representative or caliph on earth when he could easily destroy the earth, given the variability and strength of his passions. God, though, knew what the angels did not know. He instilled in the human animal a secret, the *ruh*. After all, we are told: "Then He fashioned him in due proportion, and breathed into him from His spirit [*ruh*]. And He made for you hearing, seeing, and feeling; little thanks do you give!" (32:9).

See also: **caliphate**, **philosophy**

NAHDAH

One of the most important events in the nineteenth century in the Islamic intellectual world was the *Nahdah* (rebirth, renaissance). The *Nahdah* movement represented an attempt to introduce some of the main achievements of Western culture into the Muslim world. It also sought to defend and protect the major positive features of Arab and Islamic culture and revive them despite the assaults of Western imperialism. What makes the **reforms** of the movement so influential was that they sought to confront modernity not by rejecting it nor by rejecting Islam, but by bringing about some kind of synthesis.

Muslim societies have often sought to revitalize themselves in response to the criticisms of other systems of thought that appear capable of presenting a more attractive or modern view of the world. Some areas of the Islamic world have on occasion totally rejected the importation of foreign ideas, and also sometimes completely given themselves up to them. The *Nahdah* movement argued that Islam is itself a profoundly rational system of thought, and has no problem in accepting science and technology. So there is no reason for Muslims to abandon their **faith** if they want, as they should, to accept the benefits of Western forms of modernity. The approaches to understanding the Qur'an that the *Nahdah* fostered were relatively open to a range of ideas and possibilities from outside of the traditional background, although they saw their work also as fitting in with the prevailing traditions in the Islamic world.

Among the most important intellectual figures in this movement were the Muslim modernists Sayyid Jamal al-Din Afghani (1838–1897), Rashid Rida (1865–1935), Rifa'a Rafi' al-Tahtawi (1801–1873), and Muhammad 'Abduh (1849–1905). They all supported the principle of the reform of the institutions of the Muslim world, while preserving the timeless truths of Islam. Since they were generally themselves part of the establishment, or close to the establishment, they managed frequently to influence the direction of policy in the waning years of colonialism and in emerging nation-states. More recent reformist thinkers have had a hostile attitude to aspects of modernity, displaying greater confidence in the survival skills of Islam as a world **religion**. Debates among political, religious, and economic elites about the appropriate relationship between Muslims and non-Muslims, about adopting Western technology and adopting Western social norms, continue to occur, and the working solutions differ vastly from region to region.

Further reading: Hourani 1982; Kedourie 1966; Kurzman 2002

NAMES see *al-asma' al-husna'*

NASKH see **abrogation**

NINETY-NINE NAMES OF GOD see *al-asma' al-husna'*

OBLIGATION

It has been said that in contrast to some modern Western societies where the focus is on individual rights, Muslim societies have focused on obligations. These obligations include those to God and to other human beings. In fact, there is a crucial interconnection between these spheres of responsibility.

The concept of obligation includes the intertwined concepts of *fard* and *taklif*. The term *fard* refers to an obligation. Many religious obligations are a matter for the individual (*fard 'ayni*). The **five pillars** fall within this category. Other obligations are collective (*fard kifaya*), meaning that the performance of the obligation by a sufficient number of individuals releases others from the obligation to perform it. Thus, while an individual Muslim must say her own daily **prayer**s, funeral (*janaza*) prayers for an individual Muslim need not be said by every inhabitant of a town.

The term *fard* is also used to describe a religious obligation in the same sense as *wajib*, at the top of the fivefold scale valuing human actions from required to forbidden (though some jurists distinguish between the two based on what type of source text made them obligatory).

Taklif refers to moral and legal responsibility—the point at which an individual becomes legally responsible for his or her deliberate actions. Someone who is *mukallaf* is capable of making contracts and is required to pray and fast.

Obligation is one meaning of the word *haqq*, which also means "right." How can something be both an obligation and a right? Something that is a right or claim for one individual is the duty of another. Thus, for classical jurists, a wife has a *haqq laha* (for her) to be supported by her husband, for whom her support is an obligation upon him, *haqq 'alayhi*. More broadly, when one speaks of God's rights, including to be properly worshiped, these are duties for human beings.

See also: **fasting**, *haram*, **truth**

ORIENTALISM

Orientalism is a theory from postcolonial thought according to which the West established its own identity by manufacturing a fictitious entity, the "Other," in opposition to which it constructed its own identity. This "Other" was the east and everything that emanated from it. The orientalist attitudes of European intellectuals cannot be divorced from the colonial interactions of Europeans with the Ottoman Empire especially, which was a particular source of interest for the British as well as the French and others.

Although orientalism is apparently focused on the east, it is in fact more interested in the nature of the West; its study of the east is an (unconscious) attempt at getting clearer about the nature of the observer, not the observed. While Edward Said's famous *Orientalism* was most concerned with literary texts, his thesis has had an impact on how Islam is studied by many scholars. Those who do not share his view have continued to pursue work on Islam and the Qur'an in the traditional manner. When studying the Qur'an, Westerners often fail to respect it as a major text in its own right, but link it with earlier texts (the Hebrew Bible and the Gospels) and question the account of early Islamic history that is provided by Muslims as part of the Islamic sciences. This condescending attitude applied to Muslims, and Arabs in particular, is very much an offshoot of colonial attitudes.

What Said usefully contributed in his work is the observation that scholarly research is not disinterested. Those studying a subject should be aware of how their approach to it is influenced by who they are and how their attitude to their work is shaped by the culture within which they operate. His specific arguments have been refined and in some cases rejected in the decades since he wrote but his central insights have persisted. Other scholars have recently begun to study the mirror phenomenon of Muslim understandings of "the West" or occidentalism, showing that the gaze—which could both see and misperceive—was not unidirectional.

Further reading: Irwin 2006; Said 1978

PARADISE

Paradise is literally a garden, *al-jannah*. It was created for Adam and his mate. It is also the destination of the righteous believers after the **day of judgment** as a reward for their good deeds. The garden is originally the place where God tells the **angels** of his intention to create Adam as his representative (*khalifah*) on earth (2:30, 38:71). A much rarer Qur'anic word for "paradise" is *firdaws* (18:107, 23:11)—presumably of Persian origin.

The garden of paradise is described in lush terms. It has a moderate climate (76:13); the shade is everlasting; grapes and pomegranates are common; and rivers of wine, milk, honey, and fresh water flow through it (47:15). The inhabitants can ask for every kind of fruit (44:55), and they receive "what their souls desire" (43:71). They are clad in silk and brocade, and wear golden bracelets and recline upon couches (56:15). Immortal youths offer flesh and fowl and serve wine out of "goblets, ewers, and a cup from the spring" (56:18).

The believers in reward for their righteousness will be wed to houris: "We [i.e. God] shall marry them to wide-eyed houris" (44:54). "Perfectly We formed them [plur. fem.], perfect, and We made them spotless virgins, chastely amorous" (56:35–38). They are "like hidden pearls" (65:23), "maidens restraining their glances, untouched before them by any person or *jinn*" (55:56).

God greets those in paradise with the word "peace" (36:58). They live in God's atmosphere, which is more significant than gardens and rivers (9:72). The passage "Upon that day faces shall be radiant, gazing upon their Lord" (75:22–23) led to a long controversy about whether the blessed would actually see God in paradise. Opponents of such a possibility point to the verse "The eyes attain Him not" (6:103). In general there is a protracted discussion about how literally the **afterlife** should be taken in the Book.

See also: **caliphate, hell**

PATIENCE see *sabr*

PEACE

The Arabic word for peace, *salaam*, shares its root with the word "Islam." American Muslim scholar T.B. Irving (1914–2002) insisted that rather than simply translate "Islam" into English as "submission," one should explain it as the peace that is found through subordinating one's own will to the will of God. Peace is a central value within Islamic thought and Muslim life. At the most basic level, Muslims greet each other with the statement "*assalaamu 'alaykum*, Peace be upon you," and wishes of peace are thus a constant refrain in Muslim communities. Mentions of the Prophet Muhammad's name are often accompanied by a formula asking that he be granted blessings and peace by God and a similar though less elaborate formula tradition-ally follows the mention of any of God's warners.

Peace is not only a rhetorical flourish, however. Muslim history, like that of all civilizations, has been marked by major and minor mil-itary conflicts, both internal and external. The achievement of stable, lasting, social tranquility has been a major aim of Islamic political thought, to the extent that some thinkers suggested that the populace had the duty of tolerating an oppressive ruler so long as he kept order. Others, however, thought the benefits of stability to be outweighed by certain harms. Ultimately, peace cannot be purchased at the price of **justice**; therefore, there will be occasions where fighting is justified even within the *dar al-Islam*, theoretically the abode of peace in contrast to *dar al-harb*, the abode of war.

In addition to potential conflicts within Muslim-ruled polities, classical Muslim thinkers weighed the value of peace against the religious requirement of undertaking **jihad** under certain circumstances. In the wake of the 2001 attacks by Muslim terrorists on the United States, many public figures, both Muslim and non-Muslim, insisted that "Islam is a **religion** of peace." The statement, though obviously well intentioned, did not gain in credibility through its frequent repetition. Although most Muslims want to live peaceful lives free of violent conflict, one cannot plausibly make such a grandiose claim for any religious tradition.

PEOPLE OF THE BOOK

Islam is, for its adherents, both the first revealed **religion** and the last. It is first in the sense that "submission to God" is the natural state of humanity. The first human being, Adam, was also the first prophet. Muhammad, "seal of the Prophets" (33:40), is the last, and the Qur'an is the final **revelation** from God to humanity, perfecting God's religion. In between Adam and Muhammad, there were numerous other communities to whom God sent guidance. This guidance was sometimes in the form of warners. At other times, it was in scriptures revealed to messengers. When the Qur'an refers to "those who received the book before," it is understood to be referring to Christians and Jews, with the books being (primarily) the Torah, revealed to Moses, and the Gospels (*Injil*), revealed to Jesus. (The Qur'an also makes reference to the "pages" of Abraham and the Zabur, the Psalms of David.)

The People of the Book as a category are given a special status in the Qur'an. Certain types of interactions with them are permissible that are not permissible with "disbelievers" or those who associate partners with God (*mushrikun*—polytheists, pagans). Q. 5:5 permits Muslims to eat the food of, and marry women from, the People of the Book. The Qur'an makes no explicit reference to Muslim women's **marriage** to men from the People of the Book, but scholars have forbidden it; they have, however, considered the permission of eating food to apply to both males and females.

There is room for variation of belief and practice among the People of the Book. The Qur'an refers to "those who believe from among the People of the Book" (3:199), suggesting that some may believe while others do not. Generations of scholars debated whether belief and ultimate reward in the **afterlife** were contingent on People of the Book coming to accept the **Prophethood** of Muhammad, or whether it was legitimate for them to continue following their own faith. For some, surah 109, "The Disbelievers," which states "to you, your religion and to me, the religion," is sufficient to describe the fate of any non-Muslim. Others hold that those who believe in previous revealed religions must come to believe in the prophethood of Muhammad if they are to achieve everlasting success.

Setting aside the theological issues, jurists dealt with the realities of minority Christian and Jewish populations. In legal terms, People of the Book living in the **dar** al-Islam were accorded the status of **dhimmi**, a protected but subordinate minority. Though originally conceived as limited to Christians and Jews and often, but not always, Zoroastrians, in practice most large populations were effectively treated as *dhimmi* rather than being viewed as subject to forced **conversion** or **jihad**.

With regard to Christians (and Jews, though this was of less import given the scarcity of conversions), some made a distinction between those communities that had already been adherents at the time of Muhammad versus those who only converted later, with the latter being illegitimate. Likewise, freedom of **faith** for a Christian only meant to remain a Christian or become a Muslim, not to convert to Judaism (or vice versa). A convert to Islam who wished to revert to her or his original religion would be considered an apostate.

See also: **afterlife**, **apostasy**, *fitrah*, **marriage**

Further reading: Friedmann 2003

PHILOSOPHY

Classical Islamic philosophy is deeply intertwined with both the Qur'an and mystical thought, and in conversation with the Greek philosophical tradition. Most Islamic philosophers in the classical period were mystics. Often the approach they followed was to criticize Peripatetic (*mashsha'i*) or Aristotelian philosophy as far too limited in scope, since it only deals with the natural world, the world of *zahir* (the open), and avoids the world of the *batin* or the hidden. Mystical philosophy often directs itself to the exoteric understanding of the Qur'an. Logical thought divides a concept into its parts, and analytical philosophy separates arguments into smaller constituents. This way of reasoning fails to represent accurately the basic unity that exists in reality as a result of God's **tawhid** (unity). For these opponents of analytical philosophy, then, any accurate philosophy had to be based on unity, not division. Many philosophers linked mysticism with Peripatetic philosophy, arguing that they were just different ways of working theoretically, and that mysticism went deeper into the nature of reality.

Illuminationist (*ishraqi*) thought comes from the term *ishraq* or "east," where the sun appears, and sets out to replace Peripatetic thought by abandoning the notion of definition and substituting immediate or intuitive knowledge. The Peripatetic view is that reasoning starts with definition in terms of genus and differentia, a process of explaining something by breaking it down into its smaller parts, very much what we mean by analysis. Illuminationist thinkers such as al-Suhrawardi (549–587/1154–1191) argue that attempting to explain the unknown in terms of something even less known than itself is vacuous. They also replace deductive knowledge, the sort of knowledge we get from using the principles of Aristotelian reasoning, with knowledge by presence, which they describe as knowledge that is so immediate that it cannot be doubted. It is here that the notion of light comes in as part of the term *ishraq*: such knowledge is lit up in a way which makes it impossible to doubt, as result of the way in which light flows through the universe and brings to existence and awareness different levels of being. God is often identified with the Light of Lights, the light that is the source of all other light and that does not itself require illumination. As one might imagine, the Light Verse (24:35) is popular with Illuminationist thinkers, who frequently write about it.

The soul

The nature of the soul, linked with the **nafs** and the *ruh*, the thinking part of human beings, gave rise to great controversy. Many Peripatetic thinkers followed Aristotle in regarding the soul as the form of a person, which implies that once the body or matter dies, its soul or form disappears also. Yet the Qur'an has a well-developed notion of an **afterlife**, and the soul together with the body would then seem to be eternal. Some philosophers suggested that this religious notion should be taken as allegorical. Our actions in this life have consequences which are not limited to only this life, and the notion of eternal souls is merely a good way of illustrating that reality. Other thinkers developed a Platonic account of the soul as something eternal and immaterial, which also seems to contradict the Qur'anic account of the afterlife as a very physical sort of place. They argued that the religious account places emphasis on the physical because for most people that is what is important. Given the importance of imagination in our lives, we need to form a material idea of things if they are to make real sense to us, and imagination involves our sensory equipment, i.e. our bodies. It is a way of making vivid to us why it is important for us to behave well, since the more spiritual understanding of the links between this world and the afterlife is available only to a limited number of intellectuals. This spiritual view should not be forced onto everyone, as not all will be capable of seeing the future in non-material terms.

Philosophy's relationship with the Qur'an

Philosophy came into conflict and harmony with the Qur'an in a variety of ways. Conflict is easier to notice. Some of the theories that the philosophers developed did not fit neatly within the structure of Qur'anic doctrines, seeming to go against Islamic ideas. For example, few philosophers believed literally in resurrection of the body and soul, which seems to be asserted by the Qur'an. Few philosophers could take literally the idea that God, who lacks sensory equipment, knows everything. Not only could he not know everything, they often argued that the only things he could know are abstract and eternal things. This would mean, contrary to common Muslim belief, that God is essentially disengaged from the daily life of the world and our everyday experience.

Perhaps the most damaging claim that philosophers made is about their approach to the nature of **religion**. They suggested that they alone could understand what religion is really about while professional religious people like theologians are actually floundering in intellectual darkness. Since they viewed religious language as logically inferior to philosophical language, when issues of controversy arise philosophers have the upper hand. Ibn Rushd, in his *Fasl al-maqal*, emphasizes this point when he claims that in cases of difficulty of interpretation only the philosophers can be called upon to resolve the difficulty. The theologians, whom one might think are the right people for the job, are lost in dialectical and **rhetorical** language and cannot come up with a demonstratively established conclusion.

Quite apart from any doctrinal dispute on a particular issue, this last claim is very damaging to the universal aspirations of religion. It might well seem that the last word on a religious topic should be a religious word, not something from some other theory, and the idea that a higher level of theory needs to be introduced to resolve religious issues is potentially threatening to the confidence of the ordinary believer in the religious sciences. This is not just an issue for Peripatetic philosophy, but for all the varieties of philosophy in the Islamic world, including **Sufi** and Illuminationist or *ishraqi*. In attempting to carve out a role for themselves in the Islamic cultural environment they each claim that they are an essential part of any proper understanding of the nature of reality, and therefore of the Qur'an which serves as the blueprint for the structure of that reality.

The role of the Qur'an in Islamic philosophy

Although various schools of philosophers claimed their approaches were essential for properly understanding the Qur'an, the Qur'an was not used in the same way by the different thinkers. Some made only superficial use of the Book while others engaged seriously with its language, doctrines, and themes.

On many occasions a **surah** or *ayah* is thrown into a philosophical argument for rhetorical purposes but plays no real part in it. The point is perhaps to establish the Islamic credentials of the argument itself or the thinker; in some cases, the quotation is merely decorative. For example, Ibn Rushd refers to 21:19 when he is criticizing al-Ghazali for discussing allegorical interpretations (*tafsir*) of scripture in works that are accessible by ordinary believers. The *ayah* states: "And no one knows their interpretation except God." One should not discuss such difficult verses with people who are not qualified to understand them, but instead they should be described as ambiguous and left alone. What the *ayah* seems to be saying, though, is that only God should tackle such topics; it does not say that only those qualified to do so should, thus bringing in the philosophers. In fact what Ibn Rushd does in his book is seek to explain such difficult verses, albeit in a way he says is limited only to an appropriate audience. There is a logical problem, though. If God is the only person who can tackle them, then Ibn Rushd is directly contravening the *ayah*. Yet he uses the *ayah* to criticize someone else's attempt at interpretation. It has to be said that the ayah is being used merely as decoration, as it does nothing for the argument and in fact if taken seriously works against it. It plays the same role as the traditional flourish at the start and end of books during this period where there is a reference to God as the only one who knows (in which case, why write the book?) or to the divine attributes.

Other philosophers use the Qur'an more centrally in their work. For example, al-Ghazali spends a lot of time in his many-volume work *Ihya' 'ulum al-din* (*The Revival of the Religious Sciences*) discussing the various stages of changing our character in order to bring us closer to God. Al-Ghazali criticized Miskawayh's view that our dispositions were adapted by God when he settled on rituals in the Qur'an. According to Miskawayh, many of the rules in the Book are based on our natural dispositions, so they work on the basis of things we already enjoy doing. We like associating with other people, so communal **prayer** is emphasized; we enjoy going on trips, hence the hajj; we appreciate having rules in general that regulate our behavior, and so the Qur'an and *sunnah* specify various restrictions on human behavior. God then uses our natural likes and dislikes to embed religion more firmly in our hearts. Quite the reverse is the case, argued al-Ghazali: these religious practices make such an impact on us because we would not naturally want to do them. By subduing our will to the word of God we put ourselves in the right frame of mind for approaching our creator, al-Ghazali suggested; the passages in the Qur'an which instruct us in the moral qualities we need to acquire are a spiritual guide to how we should change our characters. This is a good example of the Qur'an becoming part of the philosophical discussion itself. The Qur'an plays a real role in the argument, with its moral prescriptions seen as stages of refining our characters in the appropriate way. The notion of a character and what it involves certainly comes in its sophisticated form from Aristotle and his followers, but when al-Ghazali came to discuss it, the Qur'an served as his basis for drawing examples and illustrating essential notions of human moral development.

Mulla Sadra (c. 979–1050/1571–1640), the outstanding *ishraqi* thinker, also takes the Qur'an very directly to be the object of his work. The Qur'an, like reality, has a syntax and a semantics, a language and a system of meaning; it is the blueprint behind the **creation** of the world. Mulla Sadra's thought in general can easily be considered a profound meditation on particular aspects of the Qur'an, and it has as its basis a theory of how the understanding of reality is mirrored in the Qur'an itself. In fact the Qur'an is involved in any and every aspect of *ishraqi* metaphysics regardless of the direct topic.

The effect of philosophy on the Qur'an

Could philosophy ever challenge the Qur'an? It certainly could if it came to conclusions that went in a direction contrary to the Book, and if those conclusions appeared to be rigorously established. Much of the opposition to different kinds of philosophy came from Muslims who believed that philosophy was *bid'ah* (**innovation** or **heresy**) and produced ideas that did not cohere with the Islamic creed.

Perhaps an even greater threat to the Qur'an is the use of philosophy at all to produce an alternative way of analyzing and understanding reality. Could it come to replace the Qur'an as a route to **knowledge**? It could if its conclusions and principles are contrary to Islam, but otherwise there is no reason to think that it is any more opposed to Islam than any other form of knowledge such as mathematics or medicine. Of course, it will be said that the conclusions of philosophy often are opposed to religion, and these arguments have to be dealt with by any religion that wishes to rest on secure intellectual foundations. But there is no reason in general to think that in the encounter of faith and philosophy Islam is any worse off than any other religion.

See also: *muhkam* **and** *mutashabih*

Further reading: al-Ghazali 1980; 1985; Ibn Khaldun 1958; Ibn Rushd 1976; Leaman 1999; 2001; Nasr and Leaman 1996

PILGRIMAGE

Making pilgrimage or hajj to Mecca once in a lifetime is a duty for every Muslim who is physically and financially capable of doing so. This pilgrimage is one of the **five pillars** of Islam. Q. 3:97 refers to this obligation as it declares: "It is the duty of people to God to make pilgrimage to the House." The house mentioned here is the **Ka'bah**.

The Ka'bah was the center of pilgrimage rites among pre-Islamic Arabs, but Muslim tradition holds that it was originally built by Abraham and his son Ishmael. Its significance appears in Q. 3:96–97, where a location in Bakkah (Mecca) near the "first House established for people" is referred to as the station of Abraham (*maqam Ibrahim*), literally the place where Abraham stood.

The rites of the pilgrimage reenact certain foundational stories. Pilgrims run seven times between the hills of Safa and Marwa, for instance, as **hadith** literature says Hajar did in an increasingly frantic search for water after Abraham had left her in the desert with the infant Ishmael. Ishmael, meanwhile, kicked his feet in the sand, resulting in a pool of water surfacing which by the grace of God took the form of a well. It was named Zamzam. Today there is a dome on top of the well and its water, highly valued by Muslims, is often given to those at home by returning pilgrims. Other rites include circumambulation of the Ka'bah and the symbolic stoning of the devil.

The Qur'an discusses the pilgrimage primarily in surah 2, "The Cow." People are ordered to make the pilgrimage to the House (2:158) at appointed times (2:189). In addition to pilgrimage, they should complete "visitation" (*'umra*), which has similar rites but can be performed at other times of the year (2:196–97).

Throughout the centuries Muslims engaged in the journeys in search of **knowledge** that prepared them to join the scholarly class of **ulama** often made pilgrimage as part of their travels, which, in the era before airplane travel, might last years. In the modern world, the hajj is not only a religious **obligation** but also big business; more than two million pilgrims from countries across the globe make the journey each year. Longstanding rules prohibit non-Muslims from entering the sacred precincts but in previous generations a number of Western adventurers disguised themselves in order to experience the pilgrimage. More recently, several Western Muslims, both converts and those born into Islam, have written about their experiences of the hajj. For Malcolm X, a prominent member of the Nation of Islam, the experience of pilgrimage was transformative. Seeing Muslims of all skin colors and national origins engaged in the same **worship** provided an impetus for him to reject the Nation's racialized view of Islam. For Asra Nomani, on the other hand, her experience of hajj as a woman of Indian origin raised in America was simultaneously powerfully liberating and painfully evocative of the discrimination women and girls face in certain Muslim settings.

See also: *'aqidah*, *ziyarah*, **Eid**, *haram*

Further reading: Bianchi 2004; Nomani 2005a; Peters 1994

PRAYER

The call to prayer (*adhan*) is one of the most easily recognized signs of a majority-Muslim society. Traditionally performed by a muezzin from the minaret of a **mosque**, the call alerts nearby Muslims that the time for one of the five daily prayers has arrived. In the contemporary world, it may be broadcast over the radio or television. Entrepreneurs have designed an "*adhan* alarm clock" that emits the call at the proper times; one can download computer programs to do the same thing. Prayer is a vital part of Muslims' **worship** practices; the ritual *salat*, obligatory five times daily, constitutes the second of Islam's **five pillars**. The Qur'an refers often to "those who keep the prayer" as worthy of reward.

Salat occurs daily at dawn, midday, afternoon, sunset, and evening. After an ablution to establish ritual purity, the worshiper declares his or her intention to perform the specific prayer at hand. Muhammad reportedly said that "Acts are judged according to their intentions," and a formal declaration of intention (*niyyah*) is a required component of prayer. Each prayer comprises required and supererogatory portions and each portion consists of two, three, or four cycles (*raka'at*). Each cycle of prayer consists of a series of fixed movements (standing, bowing, prostrating, kneeling) and recitations from the Qur'an and of other formulae. The short first chapter of the Qur'an, al-Fatihah, is always recited as part of each cycle; its verses are thus known as the "seven oft-repeated."

Muhammad's statement "Pray as you have seen me praying" encapsulates the importance of his example for the development of the prayer ritual. While jurists from each **madhhab** may disagree on specific elements—such as whether the entire head must be wiped with wet hands during ablution, and whether the hands are to be folded on the chest during recitation or remain by one's sides—all agree that the **sunnah** is necessary as a supplement to the Qur'an as a source for guidance in this matter. One could not derive the practice of *salat* simply from the sparse Qur'anic references on the subject (2:238, 4:103, 11:114, 20:130, and 24:58). This is also the example commonly cited in debates over the relevance of the **sunnah** today.

In addition to the *salat*, there is the less formal *du'a* or supplication. While the ritual prayer is virtually always performed in Arabic—the jurist Abu Hanifa's (d. 150/767) reported view that prayers could be performed in Persian notwithstanding—supplication may be performed in the worshiper's own language. Supplications may be taken from the text of the Qur'an, the example of Muhammad, or the writings of famous scholars and figures through Muslim history.

Both men and women are obligated to pray the same prayers. The differences, apart from the fact that women do not pray while menstruating, are mostly minor, such as different placement of the hands or how loud the voice is to be raised. (Similar differences also exist from one legal school or *madhhab* to another.) One key area of difference, however, is in women's participation in, and leadership of, congregational **prayer**.

Congregational prayer is not limited to the Friday communal prayers. Rather, collective prayers may be performed, in or out of a mosque, whenever two or more Muslims pray jointly. Various **hadith** suggest that prayers performed in congregation are more highly rewarded than those performed individually. In any congregational prayer, one worshiper serves as *imam* while the others follow. Nearly all Muslim scholars agree that only a man may lead men, and that a man may lead a male–female group or a group of women only. Most agree that a woman can lead other women in prayer, though some hold that women alone do not constitute a congregation but must pray individually.

Women's leadership of mixed-**gender** prayers has become controversial. Though throughout Muslim history a few scholars—including Ibn Hanbal (d. 241/855)—have held that women can lead supererogatory prayers, such as *tarawih* prayers during Ramadan, either in their households or with broader groups, the issue came to the forefront of Muslim discussions in 2005, when African-American Islamic studies professor Amina Wadud led a Friday prayer service in New York. Although the overwhelming majority of Muslim authorities worldwide were critical and proclaimed that female leadership rendered the men's prayers invalid, a few, including one Spanish imam, supported the action which, contrary to Wadud's expressed desire, garnered intense media attention. Some lay Muslims were less opposed. While holding that leadership of prayer was by no means the most important issue facing Muslim women, they objected to the virulence with which male authorities responded.

There is one other famous linkage between women and prayer: a saying of the Prophet, found most often in the work of **Sufi** scholars such as Ibn al-'Arabi (560–638/1164–1240). In his *Bezels of Wisdom*, he quotes Muhammad's declaration that "I have been made to love three things from your world: women, perfume, and the comfort of my eye in prayer." Reports on his wife Aishah's authority tell that he rose and prayed in the small hours of the night. However, other hadith report that he admonished men who spent the entire night at prayer that they needed to emulate his example of balance, including using part of the night for sleep and part for lovemaking.

PRESERVED TABLET

"Tablet" appears in the Qur'an five times: three times in reference to the tablets revealed to Moses, once in reference to a celestial "preserved" tablet (*al-lawh al-mahfuz*), and once in reference to Noah's Ark (54:13).

The story of Moses and his tablets on the mountain mentions a **revelation**, and its incorporation on a tablet. The passage 7:145 states: "We wrote for him [Moses], upon the tablets, from all matters, exhorting and explaining all things."

The Preserved Tablet is mentioned only once, and is linked explicitly to the Qur'an: "But this is a glorious Qur'an, upon a Preserved Tablet" (85:21–22). A **hadith** provides more detail: "God created the preserved tablet from a white pearl with a ruby surface; its pen and its writing being of light—upon which all worldly affairs are laid out." Thus it functions as a book of fate, or the medium through which God's will is effected in the world. The link between the Qur'anic revelation and the Preserved Tablet is an important one. Regarding the revelation to Muhammad, we are told: "We sent it down to him on the night of destiny [*qadr*]" (97:1). Ibn Kathir again elaborates with a hadith from Ibn 'Abbas to the effect that "God sent down the Qur'an all at once from the Preserved Tablet to the place of glory in the lowest heaven. Then He sent it down on various occasions, stretching over thirteen years, to the prophet." Elsewhere in the Qur'an, this Preserved Tablet is referred to as the **Mother of the Book**. The passage runs, "We have made it an Arabic Qur'an, that you may understand. Truly it is the Mother of the Book, in Our presence, lofty and full of wisdom" (43:3–4). The third/ninth century **Sufi** Sahl al-Tustari calls the Preserved Tablet the heart of the mystic believer, while al-Qushayri (d. 465/1074), evoking a Neoplatonic cosmology, describes the Tablet as extending from God's Throne down to the realm of the **angels**.

Further reading: Ibn Kathir (n.d.)

PROPHETHOOD

Prophethood is an essential element of human history and the key to the way the creator relates to **creation**. From Adam through Muhammad, God has periodically sent prophets or warners (*anbiya'*, sing. *nabi*) to remind human beings of their ultimate fate and the need for them to behave with appropriate reverence for God and awareness that they will eventually be judged for their actions and face the consequences in the **afterlife**.

The Qur'anic vision of history is both cyclical and linear. The Qur'an describes a cycle where God repeatedly provides warners to human communities to confront them about their unjust practices and lack of **faith** in and reverence for God. These communities, or at least most of their members, fail to accept the warners' guidance and remain mired in their disbelief and heedlessness, whereupon God punishes them. The pattern then continues with another prophet and another community. This cycle, however, does not continue indefinitely. Rather, God has chosen Muhammad as the final warner and messenger. The Qur'an refers to Muhammad as the "seal of the prophets" (33:40), a phrase understood to mean that there can be no further prophets and that the Qur'an is God's final, complete, and perfect message to humanity.

Within the group of those entrusted by God with preaching to humanity, some recipients of divine inspiration (*wahy*) or **revelation** are considered to be "messengers" (*rusul*, sing. *rasul*). Although the Qur'an itself is less precise in its use of these categories, later Muslim scholarship often treats messengers as a subset of the larger category of prophets: every *rasul* is a *nabi* but not vice versa. Messengers are distinguished from other prophets because they are entrusted with a scripture or Book, or a law, to found or govern a community. Jesus and Moses, for instance, are said to be messengers, the former having brought the *injil* or Gospels and the latter having brought the *tawrah* or Torah. In Muslim contexts, the term *rasul Allah*, "God's messenger," always refers to Muhammad.

The cessation of revelation from God in the wake of Muhammad's death necessitated decisions about how to allocate authority, both communal and interpretive. The institutions of the **Sunni caliphate** and **Shi'i** imamate were partial answers to this question, and the role of the **ulama** has been central in the ongoing project of applying revelatory guidance to human life in the absence of a living emissary. In the millennium and a half since Muhammad's death, a number of Muslim religious leaders have claimed authority more like that granted a prophet than a mere scholar; some of these figures have been identified as "renewers" (*mujaddid*) or even the *mahdi*, "the guided one," whom various **hadith** suggest will eventually appear from among Muhammad's descendants to institute a reign of **justice**.

PURDAH

Although the term purdah has been mostly used in a South Asian context, it describes a cluster of practices, designed to keep women secluded from unrelated men, that have resonance across the Muslim world. Variant systems of seclusion have been implemented in differ-ent societies throughout Muslim history, many with antecedents in pre-Islamic systems of the ancient and medieval world.

Rigid practices of seclusion usually only apply to elite women. In the lower classes, rural women often work in the fields or care for ani-mals outside the walls of the home. In urban areas, non-elite women have practiced a variety of trades. Some provided goods and services to secluded elite women; thus elite women's seclusion depended on the free movement of women from the lower classes as well as, in the premodern period, enslaved servants. But seclusion and commerce need not always be incompatible; some Nigerian Muslim women today manage to work while secluded, sending their children to sell their home-produced goods.

Female seclusion for urban upper classes was practiced in Cairo through the first half of the twentieth century. Naguib Mahfouz's (d. 2006) famous *Palace Walk* novel, part of his Cairo Trilogy, recounts the story of such a household, including the tragedy that occurs when the secluded wife deigns to exit the family home for an innocent outing accompanied by her children. Egyptian feminist Huda Sha'rawi recalls, in her memoir *Harem Years*, her early family life in a similar system as well as her eventual rejection of the constraints imposed. Moroccan sociologist Fatima Mernissi's fictionalized memoir *Tales of a Harem Girlhood* likewise recounts her experiences growing up in a female home environment. The overwhelmingly homosocial nature of much private life cross-culturally is not limited to those areas that practice seclusion, however.

In Western contexts, the term "harem" has sexy connotations, con-juring up images of odalisques reclining on couches awaiting their master's pleasure. Only in a few royal households did this stereo-type even come close to being met. In the Ottoman Topkapi palace, for instance, the sultan did have numerous concubines whose chas-tity was guarded by eunuchs. Even there, however, the mother of the reigning sultan (*sultan valide*, "queen mother") effectively governed the harem, including both concubines and the far more numer-ous slave-servants who took care of the extensive domestic tasks of the royal household. The term "harem" more usually described the family quarters of a dwelling where unrelated men could not enter. The senior woman—the wife of the head of household—would supervise daughters-in-law and servants in carrying out household duties.

Although strict seclusion is seldom practiced anywhere in the Muslim world today, **gender** segregation in both public and private space continues to a greater or lesser extent in family homes, social gatherings, educational and business institutions, and **mosque**s.

See also: *haram*, *hijab*, **morality**, **orientalism**

Further reading: Peirce 1993; Sha'rawi 1986; Mahfouz 1990; Marmon 1993; Mernissi 1995

QADI

A *qadi* is a judge, appointed by the state, who issues binding rulings. He is differentiated, in this regard, from a *mufti*, whose **fatwa**s are non-binding. *Qadi*s in the premodern period were invariably male, although a few scholars including al-Tabari accepted in principle women's ability to serve as judges. A number of contemporary Muslim nations, however, have women serving on the bench.

In the medieval period, a judgeship was a political appointment and thus potentially perilous. First, one served subject at the whim of the ruler, so shifts in political tides—or in the ruler's favor—could lead swiftly to unemployment or worse. Second—and well represented in the numerous advice manuals for judges authored by legal scholars, bearing titles such as *Adab al-qadi*, meaning approximately "Comportment Befitting a Judge,"—were the moral risks inherent in taking up such a position. It is a common trope in these works that a jurist offered the position of *qadi* resists out of fear for what will happen if he fails to faithfully carry out the weighty responsibilities of the office.

In the premodern Muslim world, most cities would have *qadi*s from each **madhhab** or legal school, available to rule for adherents of that school. Although this could create its own problems when disputants belonged to different schools, it also allowed judicial flexibility in dealing with a variety of matters.

Further reading: Masud, Messick, and Powers 1996

QADR

Qadr—destiny, power, fate—is a meaningful concept Qur'anically, theologically, and philosophically. *Taqdir* means to make something according to a plan. Some derivatives are *qadir* (someone who has power) and *qadr* (the standard or plan in accordance with which action is taken). There are many passages in the Book which refer to God following a plan in his construction of the world, and in his organization of its everyday events. This plan represents the best way of doing it and takes into account our abilities and potential. It represents God's power and at the same time the sort of balance that he establishes in his **creation** (6:96, 13:8, 15:21, 25:2, 41:39, 56:60, 65:3, 87:1–3).

Does this suggest that God has done everything so that there is nothing anyone else can do to affect the outcome? This is not the case for human beings, for we have the ability to act freely and may choose to reject what God has done for us (18:29). We should seek to understand the divine plan, perhaps through science, since then we can best align what we do with the rest of the universe. The night of destiny (*laylat al-qadr*) is the night in Ramadan where God "sent down" the Qur'an to humanity (97:1). Since the Qur'an is the plan in accordance with which the world was created, it is appropriate to refer to that night as *qadr*, given the link between destiny and the notion of such a plan.

"He created everything and meted out for it a measure" (2:25) uses the concept of *taqdir* and suggests that everything has been arranged once and for all by God. If that is the case, though, then how can we be held responsible on the **day of judgment** for our actions, which we certainly are according to numerous other passages in the Qur'an? Perhaps we are free to decide what to do, but God knows how those decisions will work out, so that his foreknowledge does not interfere with our freedom. This problem of free will and predestination led to a controversy in early **theology**, between the Jabarites or fatalists and the Qadarites who believed in the possibility of human freedom.

Jahm ibn Safwan (d. 128/745) and his followers were impressed with verses that stressed divine power, such as "To Him belongs the dominion of the heavens and the earth. He brings to life and causes to die, and He has power over everything"(57:2), and, "Say: 'Nothing will befall Us except what God has decreed for Us'" (9:51). Jahmites tended to link the processes of the natural world with human actions, seeing the latter as no more independent of influence and predetermination than the former. The opposing Qadarites distinguished between natural processes and human actions, claiming that humans have the power to establish their own direction, within limits. They viewed this power as necessary, given divine **justice**: it would be unfair to punish people for doing what they could not help.

A popular way of resolving the stalemate between advocates of determinism and free will was the doctrine of *kasb* (acquisition). According to this view, we acquire the act which God alone can bring into existence when we do things. This appropriation of the act created by

God represents free will and makes us responsible for our actions. The other side of the doctrine is the denial of natural causality. Everything that happens in nature is willed by God, and his power is actively to be seen in everyday events, not just in establishing the general plan of the world. This doctrine was developed in evocative ways by the **Sufis,** who base all action on God, not in the sense of denying free will, but due to real power lying nowhere except in the deity.

Further reading: Watt 1973; Wolfson 1976

QUR'AN

The Qur'an refers to itself as the word of God. It was, in Muslim belief, revealed through the **angel** Gabriel to the prophet Muhammad. Muslim tradition holds that the **revelation** began in Muhammad's fortieth year (610 CE), and continued until shortly before his death in 632 CE. The Qur'an consists of 114 **surah**s (chapters) which vary in length from just three verses or *ayah*s (108 and 110) to 286 *ayah*s (2). The surahs of the Qur'an are generally classified as either Meccan because they were revealed in or around Mecca or Medinan because they were revealed in or around Medina. Some surahs incorporate verses from both places.

The Qur'an argues that it includes everything genuine from previous scriptures, which include the Torah (*Tawrah*) given to Moses and the Gospel (*Injil*) entrusted to Jesus; that it has brought these texts to perfection; and that it has abrogated their legal messages. For Muslims, the Qur'an is a miracle that could not have been created by human beings.

The word "Qur'an" means "**recitation**" or "reading" and the aural experience of the text is central to Muslim experience of it in learning, ritual use, and devotional piety.

There are four main themes in the Book. Monotheism (*tawhid*) describes the unity of God. It is opposed to polytheism (*shirk*), by which is meant the association of others with God. **Prophethood** (*al-nubuwwah*) confirms the prophethood of Muhammad and his predecessors and that the Qur'an is the word of God. Eschatology deals with the **afterlife** and the **day of judgment**, while reward and punishment results in human beings going to either **paradise** or **hell**.

The Qur'anic text has been central not only to Muslim ritual **worship** and devotion but also to Muslim intellectual life. It is a central source for jurisprudence and Qur'an interpretation—*tafsir* or exegesis—has been one of the most important disciplines of the **ulama**. Qur'anic motifs are highly significant in both Muslim literatures and daily life.

While non-Muslim scholars have usually accepted the basic chronology of the text as originating in its entirety, or nearly so, during Muhammad's lifetime and in his conscious or perhaps unconscious mind, an increasing number of scholars have suggested that the Book was created piecemeal and put together over a long period by a variety of different individuals. This revisionist scholarship draws from manuscript fragments, philological evidence, and other sources to suggest a much longer redaction history and far less secure origins for the Qur'anic text than has usually been accepted. The debates over the Qur'an's history seem likely to continue increasing in complexity and sophistication over the decades to come.

Muslims, by contrast, believe that the Qur'an was directly transmitted as it now stands to God's final prophet, Muhammad, and has been preserved perfectly as God's final revelation to humanity. The **beauty**, uniqueness, and inimitability of the Book—doubters are challenged to produce its like—are proofs of its miraculous and divine status.

Non-Muslims approaching the Qur'an are often at a loss to understand just what Muslims find so compelling about it. They may consider it repetitive, disorganized, and derivative of texts such as the Bible. Two strategies can help overcome this gap in understanding. First, it is important for non-Muslims to recognize the central role of recitation in the Muslim experience of the Qur'an, even for those— the majority of the world's Muslims—who do not understand Arabic. Second, the front-to-back approach to reading the Qur'an is not likely to prove nearly as satisfactory as approaching the text differently.

Any reading should begin with the first surah, al-Fatihah. Rather than proceeding to surah 2, "The Cow," one can then turn to the last surahs, either working backwards from 114 to 30, or proceeding in three groups: 81–114, 51–80, 30–50. The surahs which appear closest to the end of the Qur'an represent the chronologically earliest portions of the book and are concerned with major themes of divine power, the day of judgment, eschatology, and human accountability. The middle surahs (10–29), which have a lot of the stories of the prophets in addition to other materials, ought to come next. The story of Joseph (which deals with **love**), found in its entirety in surah 12, is the most coherent single narrative in the Qur'an and an interesting one for comparison to the biblical account. Lastly, surahs 2–9 contain prophetic stories (Mary, Jesus, Moses) as well as significant legislative content covering matters including **marriage**, **divorce**, and inheritance. Surahs 8 and 9, which should be read together, discuss military conflicts and are thought by some to have once been a single surah, accounting for the unique lack of the *basmalah* at the beginning of surah 9.

See also: **orientalism, prayer**

Further reading: Abdul-Rauf 2001; Algar 1998; Esack 2005a; Hawting and Shareef 1993; Leaman 2004; Robinson 1996; Sells 1999

RAMADAN see **fasting**

RASUL see **prophethood**

RECITATION

From its inception, the Qur'an has been an aural and oral text. Muslim tradition holds that in the first instance of **revelation**, the **angel** Gabriel appeared to Muhammad as he was meditating in a cave on Mt. Hira, on the outskirts of Mecca. The angel commanded him: "Iqra," a word which means both "read" and "recite." Muhammad's repeated denials that he did not know what or how to recite were of no avail, and he did eventually repeat the first verses of the Qur'an (96:1–5): "Recite, in the name of your Lord, who created, created the human being from a clot; Recite, and your Lord is most Generous, the One who taught by the pen, taught the human being what he did not know."

Unsurprisingly in a society where the recited word held great power, the Qur'anic text was both assimilated to and distinguished from other forms of potent speech, particularly poetry.

Eventually, rules for the recitation of the Qur'an were developed. Two main types of recitation exist: *tartil* or *murattal*, a straightforward style emphasizing clarity and precision, and *tajwid* or *mujawwad*, which seeks embellishment or beautification of the text without sacrificing clarity of pronunciation. Although many Muslims, in order to pray or for personal devotion, learn to sight-read Arabic without learning the meaning of the words they pronounce—the mere recitation of the words is thought to convey blessing to the reciter—it takes formal training as well as inherent talent to become a skilled reciter. As in past centuries, students can still seek instruction from an acknowledged master and, upon successful completion of tests of their recitation ability, be granted an *ijaza* or diploma that affirms their mastery of the subject and also authorizes them to teach other students.

Associated with but distinct from the science of recitation is the memorization of the Qur'an. One who succeeds in this task—once the foundation of any **education** in the sciences of **religion**, the basis of training for the **ulama**—will be known as *hafiz(a)*, one who "protects" or "guards" the Qur'an.

See also: **aesthetics**, *barakah*

REFORM

The issue of reform has arisen in Islam ever since the **religion** started, and it can take various forms. It could involve a revival of the religion, on the lines suggested by al-Ghazali in his *Ihya' 'ulum al-din*, which implies a reframing of religious language as a way of making religion more relevant to the modern generation. It has in the past also inspired movements such as **Sufism**, which seeks to interpret Islam in a mystical way, and in some of its schools gives priority to certain kinds of inner experience over traditional religious practices. Other reforms have sought to take Islam back to what are seen as the views of the original participants, rejecting supposed accretions to the essence of Islam. The **Wahhabi** movement in what is today Saudi Arabia followed this strategy, for instance, in arguing against **worship** at tombs or the veneration of particular places, as inauthentic practices incompatible with the Islamic critique of *shirk* or idolatry. The *Nahdah* movement also saw itself as *salafi*, harking back to the original principles of religion, while at the same time arguing for reform of current practices.

One obstacle to the reform enterprise is the view that after a certain period long in the past the door to interpretation or *ijtihad* was closed and should never be reopened. That implies that the varieties of interpretation that were then on the table remain available to us today, but nothing else. Yet as with all successful religions Islam has succeeded in changing direction with social and political developments. This is only possible if Muslims are able to take on new ideas and use them within the framework of the basic principles of Islam. In line with this there are today, for example, Muslim feminists who find within the Qur'an and the rest of the Islamic sciences material supporting their positions. They take references to *insan* to be about humanity in general and to point to the need to value everyone equally They view references to men being a degree above women (2:228) to have a limited scope, and suggest that male leadership or responsibility in family life (*qiwama*, 4:34) is linked to the different roles that men and women play due to their biological differences. These differences, they argue, have no necessary consequences for their social roles. The fact that the Qur'an has largely been interpreted within the context of patriarchal cultures has nothing essentially Islamic about it, but is merely an unfortunate fact of history.

Other groups also adopt a similar approach and argue for the reform of Islam along the lines of accepting that previously disadvantaged groups are treated equally and regarded as full-fledged members of the *ummah*. Whether these attempts at reform, and less radical varieties, will become part of the mainstream remains to be seen and will depend in part on developments within the diverse societies where Muslims live. Reforms within Islam are not likely to take the same path as in the case of Christianity and Judaism. The Qur'an is very different as a text from the Bible, and its miraculous and perfect nature is so much part of the basic beliefs of Islam that any successful reform has to take this into account before having any prospect of success. The widespread demythologization of the Bible looks an unlikely proposition when applied to the Qur'an, in the minds of many Muslims. But Islam has throughout its history been reformed on many occasions and there is every reason to believe that this process will in one form or another continue.

See also: **feminism**, *ziyarah*

Further reading: Esack 1997; Safi 2003

RELIGION

The term *din* is multivalent. In the Qur'an, it can mean "reckoning"—thus on the *yawm al-din*, **day of judgment**, one's acts will be weighed. In other places, *din* means something approaching but not precisely the same as the modern category of "religion." Whether it ought to be understood narrowly as constituting a religious identity or broadly as a way of approaching life is subject to debate. The verses "whoever desires a *din* other than **islam**, it will not be accepted from him" (3:85) and "the *din* before God is *islam*" (3:19) have varying implications depending on how one understands the key terms *din* and *islam*:

"a religion other than Islam" means something quite different from "a way of life other than submission [to God]." The Qur'an uses the terms Islam and Muslims in ways that do not necessarily denote the community of adherents associated with Muhammad; his followers are often simply called believers (*mu'minun*) and *islam* is the primordial state of **creation** as well as of those entrusted with **prophethood** before Muhammad.

However, there was an understanding of conversion and religiocommunal identity within the first community—people could become Muslims. This process of **conversion** had a variety of ramifications. Religious identities did exist and resulted in varying relationships to other Muslims and to the Islamic state. The **hadith** "whoever changes his *din*, kill him" suggests an understanding of *din* as equivalent to religious affiliation. This saying exists in tension with the Qur'anic declaration: "There is no compulsion in (*din*)" (2:256).

See also: **apostasy**, *dhimmi*, **faith**.

REPENTANCE

Repentance (in Arabic *tawbah*) is a critical religious concept. Human repentance for **sin** allows for the possibility of divine forgiveness. The Qur'an refers to God as "the *Tawwab*, the Merciful." God's **mercy** is expressed through the forgiveness of human sins and the acceptance of repentance. However, while God readily accepts human repentance, those who persist in sinning do not truly repent. Those who follow the pattern of committing sins, then repenting, then returning to their sins are not truly repentant but merely opportunistic. Deathbed repentance, when one has spent a lifetime refusing to repent sincerely, is likewise disallowed.

One surah of the Qur'an (9) is called "Repentance"; it deals extensively with matters of war and fighting and is noteworthy for being the only surah not to be prefaced by the *basmalah.*

RESURRECTION see **day of judgment**

REVELATION

The Arabic term *wahy* means revelation or inspiration. In its more technical sense, *wahy* is understood as the word of God which is communicated to his prophets and messengers. It can also mean the scripture revealed to particular prophets: the Torah to Moses, the Gospel to Jesus and the Qur'an to Muhammad. In this last case, the revelation continued for twenty-three years, from the first instance in 610 CE through Muhammad's death in 632.

Many verses in the Qur'an have a direct bearing on the concept of revelation (*wahy*), be it the revelation received by the Prophet Muhammad or by other prophets. The Qur'an uses the word *wahy* and its variants on a number of occasions from both the Meccan and Medinan periods. *Wahy* often means transmitting a message from God; *wahy* is not limited to a relationship between God and his prophets, but includes inspiration to inanimate objects (41:12, 99:4–5); to animals (16:68–9); to human beings as a whole, such as the mother of Moses (28:7—although a few Muslim scholars consider her receipt of *wahy* to indicate that she was a prophet, most do not); to prophets in particular, such as Jesus (4:163, 5:111); and to **angels** (8:12).

The Qur'an provides some detail as to the way in which revelation comes from God to human beings: "It is not fitting for a human being that God should speak to him except through inspiration, or from behind a veil, or by the sending of a messenger to reveal, with God's permission, what God wills" (42:51).

As to any human element in the revelation of the Qur'an, the Qur'an stresses that the Prophet was required only to receive the sacred text and that he had no authority to change it (10:15). The Qur'an strongly denies that it is the speech or the ideas of the Prophet or of any human author. Revelation, according to the Qur'an, comes from God, who reveals his will to the human prophet. The prophet Muhammad, however, was not reduced to a passive bystander; although a recipient, he was active. This is not to say that he composed the content of the revelation, but that he received it in full consciousness, witnessing in his heart the magnificence of the voice of God. Muslim theologians were less concerned with the experience of revelation than with what was said or communicated in the experience. God did not make his being known through revelation, only his will. There is nothing in the Qur'an to suggest that the Prophet "saw" God in the experience of "revelation."

The Qur'an declares itself to be God's speech, and this idea is repeated many times as representing the Qur'anic view of revelation. In the Book it is taken for granted that God speaks and has spoken from the beginning of **creation** and to a whole variety of different communities and in a range of languages. Muslim theologians had some difficulty in deciding how to classify God's speech, particularly as it related to the Qur'an. The question was whether the speech of God, as represented in the Qur'an, was "created" (like any other being) or "uncreated" (an attribute of God). Some theologians, in particular the Mu'tazilites, argued that the Qur'an, even though it is God's speech, is created. Their opponents, the Ash'arite theologians, argued that the Qur'an as the speech of God should not be considered "created." However, even to the Ash'arites, the "uncreatedness" of the Qur'an was not to be accepted without qualification. As they suggested, there are three ways of looking at speech in relation to the Qur'an: language and expression (*lughah wa nutq*); letters and writing (*huruf wa kitabah*); spirit and meaning (*ruh wa ma'nah*). It is only with respect to the latter notion that the Qur'an, the speech of God, could be said to be "uncreated" or co-eternal with God. All theologians accept that the Qur'an is the word of God; that the Prophet did not compose the Qur'an; and that the words, ideas and composition of the Qur'an were attributable to God alone.

In the modern period, a number of Muslim scholars have attempted to reformulate the dictation theory of revelation as generally accepted in Islamic **theology**. Fazlur Rahman (d. 1988) believed that early Muslim theologians did not have the capacity to confront the issue of the close relationship between the Prophet Muhammad and the Qur'an. For Rahman, it was important to emphasize the role of the Prophet in the genesis of the revelation; he saw a close connection between the Qur'an as word of God, the Prophet and his mission, on the one hand, and the socio-historical context in which the Qur'an was revealed on the other. However, Rahman did not argue that the Qur'an was the word of the Prophet, although he did see some role for Muhammad's consciousness in the revelatory process; his concern was the lack of emphasis, in the widely accepted view of revelation, on the close relationship between the Qur'an and the socio-historical context of the revelation. This relationship, if developed appropriately, would allow Muslim scholars to reinterpret some sections of the Qur'an in the light of contemporary realities and challenges. This interest in rethinking the dictation theory of revelation is expected to continue as increasing emphasis is placed on the socio-historical context of the Qur'an in understanding its message. Most advocates of **reform**, including those influenced by **feminism**, have used contextualized interpretation of the Qur'an without turning to Rahman's views about the nature of revelation.

See also: *insan*

Further reading: Abu Zayd 1998; Esack 1997; Izutsu 1964; Rahman 1966; 1982; Reinhart 1995; Tabataba'i 1987

RHETORIC

Qur'anic commentators recognized the significance of rhetoric (*bala-ghah*; also "eloquence"). They often argued that the Book's content was miraculous not in the sense that it reported on miracles or claimed them for its main characters, but because the structure and language of the Book were so perfectly constructed. The role of rhetoric enabled the Qur'an to frame arguments and ideas in precisely the right way to captivate and convince a particular audience. The Qur'an does exactly this in fitting its language so neatly to the needs and intellectual capacities of both its original audience in the Arabian peninsula and to all the world today. This perfection came to be called the miracle of the Qur'an (*i'jaz al-Qur'an*) and has remained ever since a potent idea in Islamic **theology**.

Perhaps the most recognizable use of the term *balaghah* is in the title *The Peak of Eloquence*, a compilation of advice and admonition in various genres (prayers, sayings, speeches) attributed to 'Ali ibn Abi Talib, the first *imam* of the **Shi'ah** and fourth holder of the **Sunni** office of the **caliphate**. It is widely circulated and quoted by scholars in both groups and is an influential spiritual guide for many individual Muslims.

RIBA

Riba is usually understood to constitute any interest paid on capital and is forbidden by Islamic law. This prohibition is based in part on Qur'anic verses (2:275–79, 3:130, 4:161) and in part on prophetic statements warning of dire consequences for those who consume *riba*.

Jurisprudence regulating commercial transactions takes special care to avoid running foul of prohibitions against *riba*. Certain commodities—including gold, silver, and dates—are susceptible to rules prohibiting the exchange of unequal amounts (by weight) of the same substance. Thus, one could not exchange a smaller amount of fine gold jewelry for a larger amount of gold coin. Jurists arrived at several acceptable solutions to this problem. One could pay for the gold with silver. Alternately, one could provide gold and then pay a craftsperson (with whatever currency one wished) for the work involved in making the jewelry.

Other prohibited transactions involved immediate delivery with delayed payment, something acceptable under certain circumstances. Hanafi jurists were known for their use of legal stratagems (*hiyal*) to make lawful, according to Islamic rules, specific transactions that might otherwise involve interest. Hanbali jurists, among others, objected strenuously to such stratagems.

In the modern world, Islamic banking has become a lucrative enterprise because of its claim to avoid *riba*. In order to avoid interest, transactions are often structured as partnerships, which are quite flexible in Islamic legal thought. A similar philosophy governs the "Islamic mortgages" that have become an industry in many countries such as the United States where Muslims live as minorities.

Some Muslim scholars have argued that rules against *riba* apply only to usurious—that is, outrageous—interest rates and that it is not possible to function in contemporary economies without accepting or paying interest. Others have suggested that paying interest may be fiscally unwise but it is not religiously objectionable; it is only receiving interest, in this view, that puts one's ultimate fate in jeopardy.

Further reading: Maurer 2006; Vogel and Hayes 1999

RUH see *nafs*

SABR

True believers are those who "when angered are willing to forgive" (42:37). As a consequence *sabr* (patience) is described in the Qur'an as one of the greatest virtues. The root *sabara*, with its many different forms, is used 103 times in the Qur'an. It is commonly associated with those who have **faith**. One verse (39:10) speaks of the "reward without measure" that will come to those who persevere patiently. Another (13:24) speaks of the greeting to those entering **paradise** because they "persevered in patience." **Peace** is prescribed by the Qur'an even in the face of hostility and injustice; 41:34 suggests that believers "repel evil with goodness," and as a result even a hateful person will become a friend. Patience is linked with peace, and as such might be regarded as the defining sign of how a Muslim ought to live.

The reward that awaits the patient constitutes recognition that perseverance is required not when things are going well but rather when one is confronted with troubles in life: "And whatever misfortune befalls you it is because of what your hands have earned. And He pardons much" (42:30). Also "And We tested them with good and evil in order that they might turn back" (7:168). Tests of faith and patience are not only for those who do not believe but even or perhaps especially for those who do: "Alif Laam Mim. Do people think that they will be left alone because they say, 'We believe,' and will not be tested? Indeed We tested those before them" (29:1–3).

Prayer and patience are often linked: "O you who believe! Seek help in patience and prayer. Truly, God is with those that are patient" (2:153). Prayer is recommended in difficult circumstances. Consider the positioning of this *ayah*: "Guard strictly the prayers, especially the middle prayer and stand before Allah in obedience" (2:238). While the verses before it and after it deal with **divorce**, this verse itself has nothing obvious to do with divorce. Yet in the difficult times that a person goes through when divorce is at issue prayer can serve as a reminder of God and a means of attaining the patience that is so highly valued.

See also: **morality**, *taqwah*

Further reading: al-Qaradawi 1989

SAINTHOOD see *walayah, wali, wilayah*

SALAFISM

Salafism is a Muslim reform movement that has influenced numerous intellectuals and served as the basis for a number of social movements. It is related to **Wahhabism**, in the sense that Ibn 'Abd al-Wahhab shared certain key concerns with salafi thinkers, but is much broader. Further, it is not specifically linked to the history of the Saudi regime in the way that Wahhabism is.

The term "salafi" refers to the "pious forebears" or *salaf al-salih*—that is, Muhammad's Companions. The key theme for salafis is the return to the pristine Islam lived by the first Muslims. To that end, they reject most **innovation** (*bid'ah*) as reprehensible. Often included in the sweeping condemnation of developments since Muhammad's lifetime is the intellectual heritage of centuries of Muslim thinkers. Rejecting not only **philosophy** and **theology** as well as most forms of **Sufism**, many salafi thinkers also reject the legacy of the *madhhab*s or legal schools. In the legal arena as in others, the salafis are distinguished by their insistence on making decisions only with recourse to the Qur'an and *sunnah*, discarding what are perceived to be accretions of later centuries of jurisprudence or exegesis.

Many salafis also attempt to emulate the early Arabs in their personal presentation, with men wearing beards of a certain style and clothing that resembles what Muhammad is said to have worn. In this way, they participate in an ongoing tradition of emulation of the prophet which has been part of many forms of Muslim personal piety for centuries.

See also: *Nahdah*

Further reading: Abou El Fadl 2005; McDonough 1984; Safi 2003

SALAT see **prayer**

SATAN see **devil**

SAWM see **fasting**

SCHOLARS see **ulama**

SEX

Sexual desire is a natural and important aspect of the human condition. Both bawdy tales and jokes can be found in classical belles lettres works and numerous Muslim poets use erotic imagery to profound effect. The Qur'an, **hadith**, and law do not diminish the scope of desire but emphasize that it must be sated lawfully. A famous hadith about the Prophet, found in *Sahih Muslim*, makes this point. Muhammad "saw a woman, and so he came to his wife, Zaynab, as she was tanning a leather and had sexual intercourse with her." The Prophet subsequently advised his Companions that any man who becomes aroused by seeing a woman to whom he has no lawful access should follow his example and return home to have sex with his wife. According to Muhammad, just as a man would be punished by God for satisfying his desire in an unlawful manner, in satisfying his natural desire lawfully, he earns reward, even beyond the pleasure in the act itself.

Sexual pleasure, lawfully obtained, is also valued for its own sake. Contraception is almost universally permitted by Muslim scholars. Some consider it reprehensible, however, if used to avoid procreation entirely without a legitimate motive. Fear for a woman's health or spacing of children have been considered solid reasons for avoiding conception.

One drawback of the most common method of contraception—coitus interruptus or withdrawal—is that it can interfere with a wife's sexual pleasure. Although much discussion related to men's desires—

as with the example of a man becoming aroused by a stranger and returning to his wife—scholars including al-Ghazali (d. 505/1111) stressed a man's duty to keep his wife sexually sated. This duty was both for the sake of a harmonious marriage and in order to prevent the social chaos or *fitnah* that might ensue if an unsatisfied woman decided to seek her satisfaction outside of marriage.

A man might – theoretically – have more than one lawful partner at a time while a woman is always only allowed one partner, making his duty to satisfy her even more vital. Based on Q. 4:3 and prophetic precedent, classical law allowed a man up to four concurrent wives. **Shiʻi** jurisprudence adds an unlimited number of temporary (*mutʻah* or *sigheh*) wives. When **slavery** was practiced, a man could also take his own female slaves as concubines; with abolition, this is no longer lawful. While a double standard existed with regard to the number of lawful partners an individual might have, outside these bounds the punishment for illicit sex, or *zina'*, applied equally to males and females, as did the basic requirement of protecting one's chastity.

The Qur'an defines good conduct as chastity and warns against transgressions, which are indecency. The virtue of *hifz al-farj*, chaste conduct, literally "protecting (or guarding) the genitals," does not require complete sexual abstinence, but rather limiting oneself to permitted partners (23:5, 70:29). Q. 33:35 mentions both men and women while elaborating the reward due to believers who display particular qualities. Chastity, here, is a virtue like other virtues; guarding one's genitals is like believing, submitting, being humble, having **patience, fasting,** and remembering God often, in earning divine reward. Another set of verses links chastity with other acts of bodily and behavioral modesty; the Qur'an refers to men (24:30) and women (24:31) who cast down their gazes and guard their genitals; in the case of women, the text gives additional rules for appropriate dress and comportment.

Indecency or obscenity (*fahishah*) must also be avoided by both men and women. Just as guarding one's chastity appears in tandem with other virtues on occasion, so indecency—which can also be non-sexual corruption—may appear with other vices and **sin**s (2:169, 4:22, 12:24, 16:90, 24:21, 29:45, 42:37). Indecency can be "outward or inward" (6:151, 7:33) and even "flagrant" (4:19, 33:30, 65:1); the phrase "flagrant indecency" is reserved for sexual misconduct. The clearest linkage of "indecency" with the specific sin-crime of *zina'* is Q. 17:32, which commands "approach not *zina'*; surely it is an indecency."

Elsewhere, the Qur'an details both the punishment of one hundred lashes for *zina'*—making it a **hadd** crime—and the required proof (24:2), both of which are elaborated and modified in the *sunnah*. The Qur'an specifies four witnesses, whom jurists insist must be male; hadith reports also attest to punishment on the basis of confession, which was accepted in *fiqh*. The Maliki **madhhab** went on to consider pregnancy in an unattached woman prima facie evidence of *zina'*, but most jurists insisted it was not sufficient proof. Accusation of *zina'* was a serious matter; the Qur'an (24:4–5) also sets forth a penalty of eighty lashes for the *hadd* crime of slander (*qadhf*), meted out to anyone who accuses a woman of *zina'* without substantiating the claim with three additional witnesses.

Lashes are the Qur'anic penalty for *zina'*, but the *sunnah* reports stoning to death in some cases. The jurists reconcile these precedents by considering lashes the penalty for those offenders who have never been married. Those who have been married are considered *muhsan* and are subject to stoning. These punishments do not vary on the basis of gender but only on the individual status of the accused. A married man who has extramarital sex with an unmarried woman would be subject to stoning while his paramour would be lashed; the reverse would be the case if it were a married woman and an unmarried man.

Despite the fact that there is no legal gender difference with regard to illicit sex in classical law, social norms disproportionately focus on women's behavior and some modern national laws place a heavier burden on women accused of *zina'*, as with Pakistan's notorious 1979 Hudud Ordinances, modified to remove some of the most unjust provisions in 2006. In a few nations, such as Nigeria, the implementation of *hadd* punishments—without the usual associated medieval safeguards—has become a key demand of Islamists, and a number of women have been prosecuted. Social custom in many nations still places a great deal more weight on female compliance with chastity norms. Female virginity, in particular, is highly valued, although it may be less important among educated urban elites. So-called honor killings, which violate Islamic law and prophetic *sunnah*, are by no means universal in the Muslim world, but where they exist, as in Afghanistan, they may pose a risk to women or girls whose behavior violates, or is merely thought to violate, chastity norms. These extrajudicial killings are carried out by family members to cleanse the family honor; some national laws, such as Jordan's, grant impunity to killers in certain circumstances.

See also: *'awrah*, *hijab*, **marriage**, **morality**.

Further reading: Ali 2006; Bowen 1981; Dunne 1998; Khan 2006; Kugle 2003; Hidayatullah 2003; Murray and Roscoe 1997; Musallam 1983; al-Rouhayeb 2005

SHAFI'IS, SHAFI'IYA see *madhhab*

SHAHADAH

The *shahadah*, or profession of faith, is the first of the **five pillars** of Islam followed by **prayer**, **charity**, **fasting**, and **pilgrimage**. One becomes Muslim by "taking the *shahadah*," declaring that "there is no God but God and Muhammad is the Messenger of God." This formula neatly encapsulates the central premise of Islam—*tawhid*, absolute unity of the divine—and the historical implications of that premise, the **prophethood** of Muhammad and the **revelation** of the Qur'an. Although the *shahadah* is an act, like the other pillars of Islam, it is the only one that is primarily doctrinal; it is the basis of belief on which the other **worship** obligations of a Muslim rest. Some formulations of a Muslim's duties, such as that used by most **Shi'ah**, take the *shahadah* for granted; it is only once one subscribes to it that one is a Muslim, after all.

The elements of the *shahadah* figure prominently in the call to prayer and the *shahadah* is uttered during prayer.

See also: **conversion**

SHARI'AH

The *shari'ah* has always held a central place in Muslim life and Islamic thought. As God's revealed law to guide humanity on the proper path, it is meant to govern both individual and communal life, from matters of **worship** to commerce to warfare to family relationships. Yet despite the undeniable importance of *shari'ah*, determining precisely what constitutes its ruling on a given point is not always as straightforward as it seems. And although appeals to *shari'ah* are a vital component of contemporary **fundamentalist** political demands in numerous countries, it is not clear what precisely *shari'ah* means in the context of modern democratic nation-states with elected legislatures and civil codes. Further, appeals to *shari'ah* as the governing law for Muslims ignore the fact that religious and secular legal systems have coexisted in various arrangements throughout Muslim history.

Calls for implementation of *shari'ah* usually focus on family law and *hadd* punishments. It is in matters of **marriage**, **divorce**, and **sex** (as well as, less prominently, inheritance and theft) that modern governments have retained any semblance of Islamic content. In most other criminal matters as well as commercial and civil regulations governments do not claim adherence to religious law. In those matters of personal status based on Islamic doctrine, the specific rules applied may be drawn directly from the Qur'an or, more often, the doctrine prevailing in the area's dominant *madhhab* or legal school. In a number of legal **reforms** throughout the twentieth century, a ruling from another legal school was adopted and written into law in a process of selection (*takhayyur*) or patching together (*talfiq*) doctrines to achieve an acceptable law. Egypt and India both followed this pattern in making reforms that granted women greater rights to divorce for cause. In the more recent campaign to reform the Moroccan Moudawwana (2003), rather than look to import specific rules from other nations or schools of jurisprudence, the reformers appealed to principles of fairness and **justice** which they argued were essential to the *shari'ah*.

The Qur'an and *sunnah* are the primary ways in which humans come to know God's *shari'ah*, but the *shari'ah* is conceptually broader than either. Muslim jurists have always been careful to distinguish their activities—the science of *fiqh* or jurisprudence—from the divine law itself. God's law is perfect, as God is, while human understandings of the law are imperfect, as human beings are. And while there is only one *shari'ah*, there can be multiple competing and sometimes contradictory interpretations by jurists from different *madhhabs*. The jurists' easy acceptance of divergent opinions (*ikhtilaf*) emerges from their understanding that *fiqh* is only an attempt to grasp the *shari'ah*.

The **ulama** have considered interpretation necessary in order for *shari'ah* to be applied in society but modern Muslim scholars and lay thinkers disagree dramatically over the scope of interpretation possible. Some call for a reenergized *fiqh* while others such as the Sudanese scholar and law professor Abdullahi An-Na'im argue that governments should not promote ostensibly religious laws; rather, secular law should prevail while individuals can follow the advice of muftis on matters of personal ethics and conduct.

See also: **fatwa**

Further reading: An-Na'im 2002a, 2002b; Abou El Fadl 2001b; Esposito with DeLong-Bas 2001; Ibn Rushd 1994–96; Kamali 2006; Keller 1994; Reinhart 1983

SHI'AH, SHI'I, SHI'ISM

In the Qur'an, the expression *shi'ah* and its two plural forms occur eleven times. The primary meaning that comes across in these verses is that of factions, ancient communities of **faith**, people with similar views, or followers and supporters. For instance, in 37:83, "Indeed Abraham was among [Noah's] followers" (*wa inna min shi'atihi la-Ibrahim*). Today the Shi'ah constitute a major branch of Islam with several subdivisions, including the Zaydiyya or Zaydis, the Isma'iliyya or Ismailis, and the Ithna'ashariyya or Twelvers. The latter constitute the numerically largest group. All of these groups defend the special status of the Prophet's family (*ahl al-bayt*), yet differ from each other on quite specific doctrinal issues. Collectively, they differ even more from the **Sunni** majority on many, although not all, issues.

The history of the Shi'ah begins with political disagreements over who was to succeed the Prophet Muhammad as leader of the Muslim community. Some held that 'Ali should have been first and that the first three caliphs were usurpers. 'Uthman, the third caliph, was assassinated and 'Ali elected as the fourth caliph in the year 35/656. 'Ali's followers, known as the *shi'at 'Ali* or "partisans of 'Ali" as opposed to the *shi'at 'Uthman*, heralded him as the most excellent of Muslims. But 'Ali had to immediately face a rebellion from two of the Prophet's Companions who were joined by the Prophet's widow Aishah, the daughter of the first caliph, Abu Bakr. The three were defeated by 'Ali at the Battle of the Camel, so named for the camel on which Aishah was carried. The violence which had erupted sporadically eventually gave rise to a civil war or *fitnah*.

When 'Ali was assassinated in 40/661, his son Hasan was immediately recognized by many of 'Ali's supporters as the rightful successor, while the majority, who constituted the Sunni group, recognized Mu'awiya, the son of Muhammad's Meccan opponent Abu Sufyan, as caliph. Mu'awiya had served as governor of Syria under the second caliphate of 'Umar, and was kin to the third caliph, 'Uthman. When Mu'awiya died and his son Yazid came to power in 60/680—the first example of a hereditary dynasty among Muslims—Husayn and, among others, al-Zubayr refused to pledge allegiance. The Shi'ah of Kufa and Basra wrote to Husayn that they had no **imam** other than him. This support proved to be insufficient and Husayn met his death at the hands of Umayyad forces at Karbala in 61/680. This event has had a profound significance in Shi'i culture, with its resonance of guilt and betrayal. Some scholars have argued that while Shi'ism as a political movement began when 'Ali was passed over for the **caliphate**, Shi'ism as a **religion** began with the **martyrdom** of Husayn.

According to one of the most distinguished modern commentators on Shi'ism, Tabataba'i, Shi'ism begins with Muhammad's invitation to 'Ali, his nephew, to become his successor as leader of the Muslim community. Most Muslims quickly selected a different caliph. Tabataba'i says that Muhammad clearly identified 'Ali as free from error and **sin** in his actions and sayings. Not only was everything that he did in perfect conformity with Islam but he was the most perfect interpreter of the religion. This leads to one of the central Shi'ite doctrines, and an integral part of Shi'ite history, the doctrine of the Imamate (*imamah*). The Shi'i Imam is the leader of the Shi'ite Muslim community and must be a direct descendant of the Prophet Muhammad and 'Ali, the first Imam. The majority of Shi'ites believe there have been twelve Imams (hence the term "Twelver") and that the twelfth Imam did not die but has entered occultation (*ghaybah*), or disappeared. He will eventually return and bring in a perfect Islamic society in which **truth** and **justice** will prevail.

These beliefs and emphases result in a different creed from Sunni Islam. While both agree on *tawhid* (divine unity), *nubuwwah* (**prophethood**), and *ma'ad* (divine judgment), the Shi'ites add the Imamate and *'adl* (justice). While various Sunni schools of **theology** have stressed justice more than others, Sunnis do not accept the doctrine of imamate, and consequently do not see the Imams as infallible or sinless, or as a source of absolute religious authority. Shi'ites believe that after the occultation of the twelfth Imam, the divine light was passed on to the *mujtahid* or legal scholar who can guide the community in how to understand their religious duties and its implications for their behavior. The **hadith** are collected differently by the two groups, although some transmitters figure in both sets of compilations; not surprisingly, the Shi'i hadith tend to be aligned with their major doctrines as Sunni hadith are with theirs.

The defense of the main principles of Shi'ism was undertaken enthusiastically by thinkers such as Nasir al-Din al-Tusi (597–672/ 1201–1274). His *Tajrid al-'aqa'id* (Freeing of the Creeds) and *Qawa'id al-'aqa'id* (Foundation of the Creeds) both deal with the nature of the Imamate and the Twelfth Imam, and were in turn the subjects of many commentaries, in particular by his student al-Hilli (648–726/ 1250 or 1251–1325). Al-Hilli is said to have played a significant role in persuading the Mongol rulers to recognize Shi'ism as the official **religion** in Persia. This made him the target of many Sunni thinkers. Ibn Taymiyyah (d. 728/1328), for example, wrote his *Minhaj* al-sunnah (The Way of the Sunnah) to refute al-Hilli's *Minhaj al-kara-mah* (The Way of Nobility), systemically attacking the whole Shi'ite enterprise, especially the role that it gives to the Imam. These debates were not only academic. Another book of al-Hilli, his *Nahj al-haqq wa-kashf al-sidq* (The Peak of Truth and the Opening to Righteous-ness) was bitterly criticized by Fadl Allah ibn Ruzbihan al-Isfahani, representing the Ash'arite Sunni school, and defended by Nur Allah Shushtari, a prolific writer of Shi'i theological texts. Nur Allah was summoned before the emperor of India, Jahangir, and put to death in 1019/1610–1611.

Apart from these polemical exchanges—which happened between thinkers and schools within Sunni Islam as well—much of the disagree-ment was not so much on doctrine but on form and choice of content. Shi'i thinkers tended to write on topics of specifically Shi'i concern, such as the nature of the Imamate, and concern themselves with texts like the *Nahj al-balaghah* (The Peak of Eloquence), traditionally attrib-uted to 'Ali. While in Sunnism *ijma'* or consensus in the community of believers served as the political foundation, in Shi'ism this legitimizing role was filled by the charismatic *imam*. Towards the end of the third/ninth century, Mu'tazilism, a theological doctrine that had previ-ously dominated the Umayyad and 'Abbasid courts, became identified with the various schools of Shi'ism. Shi'i thinkers also tended to be more sympathetic towards **Sufism** and **philosophy** in general in their theology, perhaps to distinguish themselves from the Sunni commu-nity. Sometimes, doctrinal differences led to *taqiyah*, or dissimulation, becoming a significant aspect of Shi'i thought, especially when the Shi'ah were a minority in a hostile Sunni environment.

See also: *ummah*

Further reading: Amir-Moezzi 1994; Halm 1997; Lalani 2000; Momen 1985; Tabataba'i 1987; Watt 1973

SHIRK

Shirk, sometimes translated as "idolatry," is to claim that anything or anyone has a partnership with God, or to **worship** another along-side God. *Shirk* is the opposite of *tawhid*, God's unity, the single most Islamic doctrine and the foundation on which its theology is built. The Qur'an stresses the obligation of the believer to avoid commit-ting *shirk*—that is, associating others with God: "Worship God, and do not associate any others with Him" (4:36). Another verse says,

"Do not associate others with God. To associate others is a significant wrong" (31:13). Avoiding *shirk* is a constant theme of the Qur'an: "God does not forgive any others being associated with him, but less than that He forgives . . ." (4:48).

See also: **heresy**, *kufr*

SHUKR

Gratitude involves being humble, praising God for his goodness and obeying him (39:60). We are told to be grateful to our parents (31:14) and when we do things for others we do it without expecting thanks (76:8–9). However, people are often ungrateful to God (40:61, 100:6). We have a duty to be grateful to God and this is represented both in our actions and, particularly, in **prayer**.

Gratitude is one opposite of *kufr* or unbelief, the other being *iman* or **faith**. **Sufi** thinkers such as al-Sulami (d. 412/1021) stress the importance of gratitude toward God for every breath one takes and morsel that one eats. A properly grateful attitude recognizes the divine bounty in the world and prevents one from the delusion of believing that one is self-sufficient (e.g., 96:6–7).

SIN

It is often said that Islam is a much more optimistic religion than Judaism and Christianity, since it believes that humanity is basically good. There is no "original sin," which comes to figure heavily in Christian doctrine, and thus no need for divine redemption. At 30:30 the Qur'an states that humanity was made with a pure nature (*fitrah*) and at 20:115 the reason Adam leaves the Garden of Eden is forgetfulness, nothing else. His banishment is not described as permanent, and we are not told of any necessity for him to repent, although **repentance** is declared necessary for other people who sin.

The **angels** do suggest that if humans are given the chance they will create corruption and shed blood (2:30). The **devil** anticipates that he will pervert and subjugate most people (15:39, 17:62). Adam is sometimes described as deliberately ignoring God's command, even though he is reminded of it by Satan (7:20). By eating the fruit he rebelled against God and went astray (20:121). Adam is not that enthusiastic about the level of existence that God assigns to him in the Qur'an, or so we may assume when we observe his attempts to circumvent the divine plan and become like angels or immortals (7:20, 20:120–21). Finally, in the Qur'an Adam and Eve both know they have done wrong (7:23) and feel shame (7:22, 20:121). The Qur'an notes that Satan tempts "the children of Adam" (7:26–27), and describes human beings as feeble (4:28), despairing (11:9), unjust (14:34), quarrelsome (16:4), tyrannical or overconfident (96:6), and lost (105:2).

God attempts to address and correct human wrongdoing through **prophethood** and **revelation**. Each community is sent a messenger (16:36), but almost all who hear reject the message (e.g., 15:10–11, 50:12–14). "Most people are not believers" (12:103) is the rather pessimistic conclusion, despite humanity's natural disposition toward belief. The prophet Joseph, even after preserving himself despite the enticements of his master's wife, is sometimes taken to have added, "The soul (**nafs**) is certainly an inciter to evil" (12:53). Though Joseph was ultimately able to resist temptation in this instance, the simple fact is that human beings inevitably err. Thus, "If God were to punish humans for their wrongdoing, He would not leave a single creature" (16:61).

God certainly knows about human sin (*dhanb*); on the day when the earth is thrown into chaos preceding the final judgment, "no person or **jinn** will be asked about their sins" (55:39). This does not mean that such sins do not matter but rather both that God is already aware of them and that no excuses anyone could construct at that time would make any difference. Instead, divine forgiveness can be attained through repentance during one's lifetime and, in 3:31, by loving God and following the Prophet: "Say: If you **love** God, follow me; God will love you and forgive you your sins."

See also: **hell**, **paradise**

Further reading: Calderini 1998; Cook 2000b

SINCERITY see *ikhlas*

SIRAH

Sirah refers to the biography of the prophet Muhammad. Although numerous incidents during Muhammad's lifetime are described in **hadith**, these anecdotes usually focus on events that occurred during his prophetic career. The *sirah* literature presents a full narrative of his life, including his birth (570 CE) and childhood, where he spent time with a Bedouin wet nurse. His father 'Abdullah had died while

Muhammad was still in his mother Amina's womb. Amina herself died when Muhammad was a young boy. Muhammad was raised by his paternal uncle Abu Talib (and in the company of his younger cousin 'Ali ibn Abi Talib). Muhammad grew up to be a respected man, known as *al-Amin*, "the trustworthy one." *Sirah* narratives trace his early career, his employment by the wealthy widowed merchant Khadijah, her eventual proposal to him, and their marriage. He is said to have been twenty-five and Khadijah forty. She bore him two or three sons, all of whom died in infancy, and four daughters, including Fatimah. (None of his other wives bore him children; a son by his Coptic slavegirl Mariyyah, who was a gift from an Egyptian Christian leader, also died very young.) It is through Fatimah's union with 'Ali that all Muhammad's descendants trace their lineage.

Sirah narratives chronicle Muhammad's first experience of **revelation**, his persecution at the hands of prominent Meccans, his eventual emigration to Medina, and the conflicts and raids in which the Muslims engaged. Here, the genre overlaps with the *maghazi* accounts of early military conflict. Muhammad's life at Medina, his political struggles and maneuvers, and his eventual death in his wife Aishah's arms at the age of sixty-three in 11/632 complete most such accounts.

Ibn Ishaq's *Biography of the Prophet* is the first *sirah* narrative; it is known through the recension of Ibn Hisham. Modern biographies have been written by Muslims and non-Muslims, drawing from similar early sources. Revisionist scholars, though, have argued that these sources for Muhammad's life are unreliable and that they merely parrot one another rather than offering independent corroboration of facts.

Further reading: Cook 1983; Ibn Kathir 2000; Spellberg 1994

SLAVERY

The Arabic word *'abd* refers both to a slave and to one who **worship**s God. Human beings are at base God's abject subjects. In this sense, a king and a beggar are equal. Yet this basic equality of all humans—male and female, rich and poor, black and brown, Arab and non-Arab—does not preclude social hierarchies; differences in status were taken for granted by medieval Muslim thinkers. One important distinction between human individuals, with social and legal consequences if not theological significance, is that between free and slave.

The Qur'an addresses the ownership of some people by others using various terms, including "what your (or their) right hands possess." There has been significant speculation about precisely who was encompassed by this category but it clearly included war captives. Various types of ownership were practiced in pre-Islamic Arabia, as elsewhere in the region at the time. Apart from captives, other persons were bought and sold. Among the earliest converts to Islam were slaves and freed slaves, including a black African known as Bilal who became the first muezzin, performing the call to **prayer**. While Muslims were forbidden from capturing and enslaving other Muslims, slaves could and did convert. Freeing a slave was required by the Qur'an to atone for certain misdeeds, and in such cases freeing a "believing" slave was preferred.

The Qur'an refers matter-of-factly to inequalities of status between free people and enslaved people. It permits **marriages** of slaves, including to free people, and specifies how matters such as retribution and punishment are to be handled if offenders are enslaved. It is the later jurists, however, who dealt extensively with issues relating to slavery.

Muslim slavery included permission for concubinage between masters and their own female slaves. This relationship created protections for those who bore children to their masters: the children were free and legitimate, of equal status to children born of a free wife. (Opinions differed among legal scholars as to whether a formal acknowledgment of paternity was required or whether the assumption of the master's paternity existed so long as he did not disclaim it.) The slave who bore children was referred to as *umm walad*, "mother of a child," and could not be sold; she was automatically freed upon her master's death. She could, of course, be freed before that time, and some women were.

For a few select women, concubinage could also be a route to wealth and prestige: the "favourite" concubines of the Ottoman dynasty rose to positions of power and influence within the imperial household. Having given birth to future sultans, they fulfilled important dynastic functions, made strategic political and personal alliances, and worked to manipulate the system to their own and their children's benefit.

Elite slavery was not limited to royal concubinage. The Ottoman military conscript slaves—the Janissaries—could also rise to positions of respect. The earlier Mamluk dynasty in Egypt relied upon manumitted slaves for political leadership. (The word *mamluk* means "owned.") The majority of slaves, however, existed in mundane conditions of servitude that could vary from domestic service to commercial employment to harsh physical labor.

Although slavery was never racialized in the Muslim world in the same way it was in the United States, with the exclusive association of blackness with enslavement, Bernard Lewis has shown that racial and color prejudice existed in the Middle East and affected the way slavery was organized. There were always white slaves—Circassian women were imported as concubines into Egypt into the nineteenth century and "white" as well as "black" eunuchs served in the Ottoman palace—but slavery could be organized by racial category.

Abolition took place across the Muslim world in the nineteenth and twentieth centuries. Saudi Arabia, in 1960, was the world's last nation to outlaw slavery. The processes of abolition were complex and related to, but not governed by, the situation of European colonial powers. A number of Muslim intellectuals argued for significantly restricting the practice of slavery. Rather than rejecting its religious legitimacy outright, their arguments instead hinged on the inapplicability of the institution in changed historical circumstances. Nonetheless, despite formal abolition in all nations, slavery-like conditions still prevail in a number of African countries. Some factions in civil conflicts, as in the Sudan, continue to enslave captives. These practices sometimes contravene Islamic law's explicit prohibition of enslaving other Muslims; ethnic prejudices may lead some Muslims to treat others as "not really" Muslim and hence subject to enslavement. This represents a continuation of a centuries-long tension between norm and practice.

Slavery remains a sensitive subject. Apologetics and polemics often focus on whether "Islamic" slavery was better or worse than Christian slavery. Some authors have stressed the legal protections enjoyed by Muslim slaves—which were usually although not always adhered to in practice—and the fact that large-scale plantation slavery was seldom implemented. The potential social mobility of slaves through manumission, the legitimacy of children born to concubines (although some recent research contests the general scholarly assumption that masters almost always recognized such children in accordance with the law), and the permissibility of marriages between slaves have led some to assert that Muslim slavery was more humane. On the other hand, some have attempted to blame Muslim raiders and traders for the large numbers of captured Africans sold into slavery across the Atlantic. The fact that slavery or slavery-like conditions continue to exist among some Muslim populations, mostly in Africa, provides further evidence for these critics.

What most comparisons between Muslim and Christian histories of slavery miss are not only the significant variations in slave systems within each civilization across geographic and chronological boundaries but also the deep interconnections that have existed between the two systems. Muslims enslaved Christians and Christians enslaved Muslims. Muslims enslaved pagans and animists and sold them to

Christians. Muslims were sold to Christians by non-Muslims. Neither religious tradition is free of the taint of slaveholding.

Further reading: Ali 2006; Clarence-Smith 2006; Lewis 1990; Marmon 1993; 1999; Miller 1992; Nazer and Lewis 2005; Peirce 1993; Toledano 1998; 2002; Willis 1985

STRAIGHT PATH

In the first **surah** of the Qur'an, recited daily in every **prayer**, the Muslim implores God: "guide Us on the straight path" (1:6). The concept of the *sirat al-mustaqim* has generated a great deal of commentary (*tafsir*). It represents very concisely the idea that Islam is a direct route to the **truth**, and that God provides us with guidance through the Qur'an and other earlier **revelations**.

It is sometimes said that the straight path is as narrow as the blade of a sword and stretches over **hell**. This dramatic imagery illustrates the the difficulties of living in accordance with the divine will, and the serious consequences of going awry. Other interpretations, however, stress the naturalness of belief and of the rules of Islam, emphasizing that both the **religion** and the world have been made for human beings and so are not difficult to understand. The straight path is thus in accordance with humanity's natural inclinations (*fitrah*). One must be wary of the temptations whispered by Satan in an effort to lead people "astray," but God's guidance will suffice to keep one on "the path of those with whom God is pleased" (1:7).

Further reading: Algar 1998

SUFFERING

The Qur'an discusses three major types of suffering. First, the suffering of those who are close to God is meant to deepen the faith of the believers by testing their **patience** and steadfastness in the face of life's challenges. According to the Qur'an all the tragedy, affliction, grief, loss of possessions, and fear that we experience in this life are meant to test our patience in adversity (2:155, 21:35). For those who succeed in the test and continue doing good deeds in their life God promises them freedom from fear and from sadness as their reward (2:112).

The second type of suffering seeks to jolt some people from their complacency by calling their faith into question. The Qur'an considers such a believer to be one whose faith wavers between belief and disbelief or *kufr*, especially in the event of a setback (22:11). Take the reverse experienced by Muslim combatants at the battle of Uhud, for instance. The defeat resulted in even those who had not disobeyed the Prophet suffering injury and even death. For the innocent the Uhud defeat was a test of their **faith** and not a form of punishment. Those believers who died in this and other military campaigns in the early history of Islam were regarded as martyrs (3:193).

The final type of suffering aims at dispensing **justice** by punishing evildoers or making an example of them as a warning to others. The Qur'an provides many examples in the stories of Noah, of Lot, of Hud, and of Moses, of the consequences of **sin** through the medium of natural disasters. The Qur'an elaborates as a general rule the fact that to every community that a prophet had been sent its people were visited with misfortune and hardship so that they might humble themselves. Yet after the misfortune was lifted and prosperity followed the wicked ones returned to their evil ways and in doing so doomed their communities to destruction (7:94–96).

Sometimes, though, even when it seems that the wicked do prosper and the believers do not this is only in the short term. The balance is restored in the **afterlife**. The attitude of acceptance or patient endurance of life's trials is recommended as nothing is to be gained by despairing (or, worse, giving up and committing suicide, which is prohibited). One should place one's **trust** in the overriding control and **mercy** of God. This is done by cultivating an attitude of complete submission to God as indicated in the following verse: "Say: truly my **prayer**, my sacrifice, my living, my dying belong to God, the Lord of the Universe" (6:162).

Whatever injustice or evil one may see in the world this should not lead one to think that this is an indication that God is not in control or that the **devil** has an upper hand in **creation**. The Qur'an provides a mythological content to the experience of temptation symbolized by Iblis's fall (followed by respite given to him to continue to tempt and to provoke humans to evil). Yet, despite all this, God is still in control and the satanic power only operates while it is allowed to do so by God. Ultimately therefore final victory belongs to God alone who is the supreme judge and arbiter of our affairs (17:19–20). Reward is promised to righteous people, those who do not focus their desires on the transitory things of this life but strive to achieve and devote their lives to attaining the more enduring things of the next world. Among **Sufis**, some have taken this striving a step further in their contemplative **love** of God by seeking voluntary privation through following an ascetic lifestyle. In this form of suffering, the individual seeks to purify her heart and empty it of all worldly concerns by distancing herself from worldly things.

There is one more dimension of suffering, unique to **Shi'ism**: the **martyrdom**s of 'Ali, Hasan and Husayn. The whole complex of ideas about the deaths of the infallible Imams brings Shi'ism closer to certain strands of Christianity in their shared belief in redemptive suffering— that is, the saving effects of martyrdom (for Shi'ism) and crucifixion (for Christianity). In general, Jesus for the Christians and Husayn for the Shi'is emerged victorious despite suffering cruel and humiliating defeats and deaths at the hands of their enemies. The suffering of the innocent encouraged in both faiths a belief in eventual redemption and the growth of messianic beliefs in the supernatural restoration of peace, goodwill, and justice which will come about some time in the future.

See also: **day of judgment**, **martyrdom**

Further reading: Bowker 1970

SUFISM

Sufism or Islamic mysticism takes many forms, from esoteric **philosophy** which seeks to explore the inner dimension or essence of reality to practical spiritual exercises to instill habits of piety and to develop the continual consciousness of God, or *taqwah*, that is the goal of every believer. Sufism is often highly systematized in terms of different stages of spiritual growth and awareness of the secret nature of the world. Training by a *shaykh* or spiritual advisor is generally required and a careful and cautious approach advocated to avoid the Sufi making exaggerated claims and exceeding the bounds of orthodoxy. Sufis are organized into different *tariqah*s or orders (*tariqah* literally means "path"). One way of classifying Sufi orders describes some as sober and others as drunken—ecstatic with certain spiritual states not accessible to most believers. Certainly, for most Sufis, even those who do not limit themselves to sober practices, drunkenness remains a metaphor and the dictates of **shari'ah** are observed. Even those members of the **ulama** frequently considered anti-Sufi, such as Ibn Taymiyyah, have generally regarded sober forms of Sufi practice such as recitation of litanies in *dhikr*, and techniques of pious self-scrutiny, to be acceptable and even praiseworthy.

The practice of *dhikr*, literally the remembrance of God, works on the principles that although we often talk of God, we do not really give him a leading role in our lives; we forget what we owe to him and can know of him. Through the principles of a particular Sufi path the practitioner can bring to his or her mind in a meaningful and lively manner what part God plays in our lives. In carrying out spiritual exercises through techniques provided by a guide or *murshid*, we bring back to our consciousness what we always knew: that we exist in a world under the control of God.

The Sufi is interested not so much in **knowledge** of the rational variety but in experience that brings him or her closer to God. Just knowing something is not enough; one must realize it in one's life. It should not be assumed that Sufism is anti-intellectual since much of its literature is highly abstract and heavily argumentative. Yet while argument is important, it is also limited in what it can do to nurture spiritual growth. One's understanding of the Qur'an, it is suggested, can be elevated if one looks on the text with more than just intellectual eyes. Sufi approaches to *tafsir*, Qur'anic commentary, tend to offer ways of unlocking the secrets in the Book. The mystical concept of knowledge, *'irfan*, offers to its practitioners a more direct and vivid form of awareness of reality than the more analytical approaches of the Peripatetic thinker (*faylasuf*) or the ordinary jurisprudent (*faqih*), although some Sufis were also practicing jurists.

See also: *fiqh*, **philosophy**, *ziyarah*

Further reading: Chittick 1989; Nasr 1981; Nast and Leaman 1996; Schimmel 1975; Sells 1994; 1996; Shaikh and Kugle 2006; Smith 2001; al-Sulami 1983

SUNNAH

Sunnah means normal practice, customary procedure or action, or norm sanctioned by tradition. Among the first Muslims, the term was often used to describe common custom, but then it came to be used in contrast to undesirable **innovation**, *bid'ah*. In the first centuries of Islam, *sunnah* was identified with the actions of the Prophet and his Companions. One often-quoted **hadith** urges Muslims to stick to the practices of the Prophet and of the "rightly guided" caliphs. For the **Sunni** majority, prophetic *sunnah* is the second source of Islamic practice next to the Qur'an, and it serves a key role in communal visions of adherence to a common, moderate, agreed set of doctrines and practices; Sunnis have used the phrase *ahl al-sunnah wa al-jama'ah* (the people of the *sunnah* and the community), or just *ahl al-sunnah*, to define themselves.

For the **Shi'ah**, the *sunnah* is likewise important, but understood a bit differently. It is linked to the family of the Prophet, the *ahl al-bayt*, who interpret the Book and provide successors to continue the correct line of interpretation and communal authority. They rely on reports of either the Prophet or of any of the Twelve Imams, which are called hadith. The people who are *ma'sum* or without flaw, such as the Prophet or any of the Twelve Imams, and their sayings and actions are called *sunnah*, which remains the second source for guidance.

According to the classical Sunni **ulama**, the sayings and actions of the Prophet constitute the *sunnah*. Sometimes this is extended to what he approved of, his legal judgments, as reported to later generations. Some jurists, such as al-Shafi'i (d. 204/820), regard the Qur'an and *sunnah* as equally binding sources of divine guidance. In his famous *Epistle* on legal methdology, al-Shafi'i refers to sunnah as "non-recited **revelation**"; the only distinction between properly authenticated reports of the Prophet and the Qur'an is that the former is not suitable for **recitation** in ritual **prayer**.

Pakistani modernist scholar Fazlur Rahman developed the concept of the "living *sunnah*," which includes both the hadith and the common values Muslims agree upon (*ijma'*). Rahman believes that the specific content of the *sunnah* of the early Islamic period was largely the product of Muslims. According to him, the creative power in operation was personal judgment (*ijtihad*), which took shape in the form of *ijma'* under the general guidance of the prophetic-tradition literature or hadith.

During the first two centuries of Islam, in the field of law (*fiqh*), *sunnah* was used with a broad meaning to include the sayings or doings of the Prophet, the Companions, and the first generations of Muslims. Nevertheless, al-Shafi'i reduced this wide-ranging understanding of *sunnah* by limiting hadith to the sayings, deeds, and attitudes of the Prophet and equating *sunnah* to the tradition of the Prophet. In contrast, the early Hanafi jurist Muhammad al-Shaybani (d. 189/805) viewed *sunnah* as encompassing both the practices of the Prophet and those of his Companions.

The link between Qur'an and *sunnah* relating to **abrogation** is a controversial issue. Muslims often accept that the Qur'an abrogated *sunnah* but whether *sunnah* can actually abrogate the Qur'an is debated. According to the Hanafis, a hadith that is *mutawatir* (reported by numerous authorities) or *mashhur* (linked to more than two Companions) can abrogate the Qur'an. An *ahad hadith* (reported by one transmitter) cannot abrogate any of the verses, for it has a lower degree of authenticity or reliability. On the other hand, some scholars opposed the idea of *sunnah* abrogating the Qur'an even if it is an authentic or a commonly known hadith. For al-Shafi'i, the Qur'an can only be abrogated by the Qur'an itself. His evidence is: "None of Our revelations do We abrogate or cause to be forgotten, without Our substituting something better or similar" (2.106). (Shafi'i also held, however, that the Qur'an could not abrogate the *sunnah*.)

According to the Hanafis, *sunnah* is divided into two groups. One is of actions which should be followed—to disobey would involve rejecting the *sunnah al-hudah* or guiding *sunnah*. Issues to do with prayer are considered to be covered by *sunnah* and therefore necessary. The other is of actions that are good to perform—like the reported actions of the Prophet, such as his ways of sitting, getting up, dressing, and riding—but do not have to be followed.

See also: **caliphate**

Further reading: Cook 1981; Rahman 1980

SUNNI

Somewhere between 80 and 90 percent of the world's Muslims identify as Sunni, a term derived from the collective claim to be "the people of the ***sunnah*** and the community." The term Sunni stands in contrast to **Shi'ah**, marking the main groups that originated from the schism over succession to Muhammad. While the Shi'ah reject the legitimacy of the first three caliphs—Abu Bakr, 'Umar, and 'Uthman—the Sunnis hold that these men, along with the fourth caliph 'Ali, whom the Shi'ah view as the Prophet's rightful successor, were "rightly guided". Although later caliphs were not as uniformly well-regarded, for well over a millenium, the **caliphate** functioned as a unifying Sunni political ideal, even if the reality was more fractious.

The Sunni tradition encompases a great deal of theological, philosophical, and legal diversity, with four extant legal schools (sing. ***madhhab***).

See also: **imam, philosophy,** *tafsir,* **theology**

SURAH

Surah (pl. *suwar*) means literally "row" or "fence" and is a chapter or division of the Qur'an. The Qur'an has 114 surahs of different size, the shortest consisting of three and the longest of 286 *ayat* or verses. All surahs (with the exception of the ninth) begin with the **basmalah**.

All the surahs in the Qur'an have names, although the origins of these names are unclear. A surah may have more than one name traditionally; surat al-Fatihah is also sometimes called Alhamdulillah ([All] praise is for God). This latter name stems from a significant word in the text itself. Many surah names emerge in this fashion, or from one of the first few words with which the surah begins. Surat Ya Sin (36) is named for the two mysterious letters (*huruf muqata'ah*) which appear at its beginning. Disconnected letters also make appearances in several other surahs and there are various theories as to their origins and meaning.

The surahs' organization in the Book is far from arbitrary, and generally ranges—with the exception of the brief "al-Fatihah," which comes first—from longest to shortest. Their placement does not replicate the order in which the **revelations** were given, but is taken to be the best order to express the meaning of the Book as a whole. In fact, most of the chronologically early surahs from Mecca are placed at the end of the Qur'an, while the longer Medinan surahs appear near the front of the collected Book.

Further reading: Cragg 1973; 1994, 1998; Sells 1999

TAFSIR

The word *tafsir* is derived from *fassara*, which means to explain or interpret. *Tafsir* is explanation, interpretation, and commentary on the Qur'an, and *mufassir* (pl. *mufassirun*) is commentator. Another word for interpretation is *ta'wil*. A distinction is often made between *tafsir*, which explains the "outer" (*zahir*) meanings of the Qur'an, and *ta'wil*, which treats the "inner" and hidden (*batin*) meanings. This distinction is made much of by those within the **Sufi** tradition as well as **Shi'i** groups such as the Isma'ilis who argue that the obvious interpretation of the Qur'an is often not the ultimately correct explanation. Others, such as Ibn al-'Arabi (d. 1240), insist that one must accept all linguistically possible meanings as correct, though one may privilege some over others when deciding how to apply the text.

A significant distinction often made between *ta'wil* and *tafsir* is that the former is based on rationality while *tafsir* is linked closely to what has come down directly from the Prophet himself or through his Companions or his successors as hadith. This raises the issue of whether interpretation should be based on the independent judgment of the individual or on something more traditional such as the traditions themselves. Both have precedent within early Muslim thought, and in reality the use of transmitted (*naqli*) material often involved quoting the opinions of earlier scholars, not the first Muslims; even here, in the arrangement and selection of material from earlier commentators, the use of reason (*'aql*) is clearly present.

Tafsir can be divided into various sub-types, including grammatical, narrative, legal, and mystical. These boundaries are not firm and may overlap. Works primarily concerned with the legal guidelines set forth in the Qur'an may devote special attention to grammatical issues necessary to determining the rulings with precision.

Classical *tafsir* usually proceeds verse by verse through the Qur'anic text, although other verses on the same point will be alluded to as appropriate. This verse-by-verse approach has been used by some contemporary commentators as well, including the Egyptian **fundamentalist** Sayyid Qutb (1906–1966, in his *Fi zilal al-Qur'an*, In the Shade of the Qur'an) and Indian-Pakistani thinker Abu A'la al-Mawdudi (1903–1979, in his Urdu *Tafhim-ul-Qur'an*, Understanding the Qur'an). One distinguishing feature of many modern interpreters, though, is their thematic approach. Works such as Toshiko Izutsu's *God and Man in the Qur'an*, Fazlur Rahman's *Major Themes of the Qur'an* and Amina Wadud's *Qur'an and Woman* tackle Qur'anic interpretation by marshaling all the relevant material on a given theme and discussing it together rather than atomistically.

Although any **religion** based on a text requires interpretation, many of the most significant Islamic thinkers such as Ibn Hanbal (164–241/780–855) and Ibn Taymiyyah (661–728/1263–1328) have placed restrictions on *tafsir*, worried about its tendency to seek meanings in the text that may be distant from its original purpose. According to them, the best *tafsir* is "explanation of the Qur'an by the Qur'an"—that is, using one portion of the Qur'an to elucidate another. The next best is the explanation of the Qur'an by the Prophet Muhammad. When there is no appropriate material to be found here, one may turn to reports from those close to the Prophet and his Companions. Within the **salafi** tradition, individual judgment is frowned on as a criterion for how to interpret the Book, and interpretations have to be linked with a reputable hadith or to some other part of the Qur'an itself—a resurgence of the early strand of thought favoring "transmitted" over "rational" exegesis.

Since some verses in the Qur'an are **muhkam** (clear), while others are **mutashabih**, Muslims must exert effort to understand the latter (though not at the expense of failing to adhere to the former). There are also expressions in the Book that are difficult to understand—

perhaps an expression is used that is perplexing because it is linked to the Arabic dialect of the Quraysh, the tribe of the Prophet, or because it is a foreign word. Seeming contradictions between verses require interpretive maneuvers which may include **abrogation**. One important component, then, of many exegetical works is the so-called "occasions-of-revelation" (*asbab al-nuzul*) material, which describes the circumstances under which particular surahs or verses were revealed. The chronology here is significant for deciding which verses abrogate others and which are themselves abrogated. The occasions-of-revelation information is also vital for setting verses in context, which can prove crucial to interpreting them. Of course, many verses have competing, and sometimes mutually exclusive, accounts of their revelation.

The Shi'ah often argue that the Qur'an in its original form indicated the significance of 'Ali as the chief interpreter of the Book, but that this was altered by his opponents. This stance may be accompanied by the claim that the text that we have now is not entirely authentic. More often, the standard text is accepted by all Muslims, but the Shi'i may interpret certain passages to refer to 'Ali and the significance of the family of the Prophet, and their successors, as the continuing expounders of the Book. Particular *imam*s are regarded as vital for interpretation, (who they are will depend on the particular Shi'i group), as opposed to the **Sunni** view that a consensus (*ijma'*) of scholars or leaders is sufficient to establish the appropriate understanding of the Book. 'Ali's role as an Imam comes about through the *ta'wil* of the Qur'an by disclosing layers of meaning within the text. He is regarded by his followers as the supreme *wali* (friend of God or saint). He called those close to him his *shi'a*—his followers—in the sense of initiating them into deep levels of self-awareness as a result of his spiritual guidance into the **truths** of the Qur'an.

See also: *ayah*, *sunnah*

Further reading: Amir-Moezzi 1994; Leemhuis 1988; al-Tabari 1985; Versteegh 1983

TAHARAH see **purity**

TAQIYAH

Taqiyah, or dissimulation, has been an important technique among Islamic groups who were a minority in countries ruled by other sects of Muslims, in particular by the **Shi'ah** in majority **Sunni** countries.

In order to survive in difficult cirumstances, sometimes involving direct persecution, they would not necessarily be frank about their beliefs and practices, instead pretending to follow the majority rituals and beliefs. *Taqiyah* also influenced the way in which certain books were written. Authors practicing dissimulation expressed themselves in ways that would not betray heterodox values and ideas in the work, while at the same time alerting sympathetic readers to the real nature of what was being discussed.

The doctrine was particularly developed in Isma'ili culture, which emphasized the significance of having access to the right level of interpretation or *tafsir* if one were to understand scripture properly. Only a small group of people should have access to restricted meanings. Isma'ili scholars often argued that it was important to be careful in disseminating the real meaning of religious texts since most audiences were incapable of understanding it. This is a point made forcefully also by some of the philosophers, who argued that it would be an error to disclose the real meaning of philosophical views since laypeople would not understand how to reconcile them with **religion**. Although the philosophers themselves had no difficulty in grasping these ideas, if they became widely known the result would be a decline of **faith**. In all these case it is sensible and indeed necessary to practice dissimulation.

Although the term *taqiyah* has primarily Shi'i connotations, it has also been used to describe the behavior of "moriscos"—Christian converts from Islam in the Iberian peninsula after the Reconquista and the expulsion of the Muslims in the fifteenth century—who publicly claimed a Christian identity to avoid persecution but continued to practice Islam in private. Likewise, enslaved Africans in the New World might convert nominally to Christianity but retain Muslim beliefs and practices to the extent practical under conditions of captivity.

See also: **philosophy**

Further reading: Daftary 1990; 1996; Gomez 2005; Ibn Rushd 1976

TAQLID see *fiqh*

TAQWAH

Taqwah is one of the many words in the vocabulary of Islam whose exact equivalent cannot be found in English. It has been translated as "fear of God," "piety," "righteousness," "dutifulness," "God-awareness," and "God-consciousness."

The word *taqwah* is derived from the Arabic root *waqa*, which encompasses meanings of protecting, preserving, and guarding. *Taqwah* signifies protecting oneself from moral peril, preserving one's virtue, and guarding oneself against the displeasure of God. *Taqwah* is thus a kind of awareness or consciousness by means of which one protects oneself from sliding into evil. In what is possibly the first occurrence of the word to have been revealed in the Qur'an, in surat al-Shams (91:8), *taqwah* is contrasted with wrongdoing. Wrongdoing is described as a kind of gushing forth, as though *taqwah* acts as a restraint to channel one's impulses so that they do not get out of control. But *taqwah* is far from an external constraint controlling natural tendencies. On the contrary, the Qur'an suggests that both the latter and *taqwah* come from God. God has provided us with **knowledge** of **morality**. Through *taqwah* we may acquire conscience, the moral and spiritual presence of mind necessary to keep us from going astray.

Someone with *taqwah* is alert to the perils of *shirk*, associating others with God; careful about the difference between **sin** and evil; and attentive to anything that might be spiritually damaging to him or her. After all, the Qur'an often declares that the outward observance of ritual is not sufficient for *taqwah*. After the *ayah* mentioning the change of the direction of **prayer**, the *qiblah*, from Jerusalem to Mecca, we are told:

> It is not piety [*birr*] that you turn your faces towards the east and the west, piety is rather one who believes in God, the Last Day, the **angels**, the Book, the warners, and gives his wealth out of **love** for Him to the near kin and the orphans, the poor, the wayfarer, the needy, and for those in bondage; and establishes prayer, pays obligatory alms [*zakat*]; and those who fulfill their promise when they make a promise, the patient ones in distress and affliction and in the time of war, these are the people who are truthful and these are the people who have *taqwah*.
>
> (2:177)

Here we learn that *taqwah* cannot be reduced to the performance of religious rites, but that it requires **faith** (*iman*) and practice performed out of love for God. With respect to animal sacrifice, it is written that neither the flesh nor the blood reaches God, but *taqwah* reaches him (22:37). This awareness which is *taqwah* is to be found in the heart, and by means of it the signs, symbols, and rites ordained by God may be properly respected. Without *taqwah* there is transgression. When one is motivated by hatred of one's enemies instead of love for God, self-control and awareness slip away. So *taqwah* cannot be developed without an existing disposition to be patient. *Taqwah* certainly can be seen to have political implications. It is not a meditative state that takes one away from the world, but a way of finding one's route through the world, which in its social and political dimensions requires **justice** and fairness. A constant awareness of God and God's expectations of us can help Muslims seek and follow the middle path between extremes.

The idea that one achieves nearness to God through *taqwah* (awareness of God) is to be found in many verses of the Qur'an, including: "Verily, the noblest among you in the sight of God is the one who is most deeply conscious of Him" (49:13).

See also: **charity**, **morality**, **patience**, *sabr*

TARIQAH see **Sufism**

TAWBAH see **repentance**

TAWHID

Tawhid, the oneness of God, is the single most important concept associated with Islam, and its opposite, **shirk**, associating partners with God, is the gravest **sin**. *Tawhid* is often mentioned in the Qur'an: "Your God is one God" (41:6).

The Qur'an, by emphasizing the concept of *tawhid*, challenged the main religious traditions of the time, in particular the Meccan idol worshipers with their gods located in the Holy Shrine, the **Ka'bah**, for a long period after the original monotheistic practice established by Adam and Ibrahim. The Qur'an criticizes the Christians and Jews as well as the claim of God having a son as evidence of a disbelief in *tawhid*. "And the Jews say: Ezra is the son of God and the Christians say: the Messiah is the son of God. That is their saying with their mouths. They imitate the saying of those who disbelieved of old" (9:30). However, "He is God, One, and God, the Eternal, who has not begotten, and has not been begotten, and like Him is not any one"(112:1–4). He cannot interrupt his perfect unity to participate in **creation** in the sorts of ways we do, by having children, for instance. When he wishes to create all he has to do is say "Be! And it is" (2:117).

TA'WIL see *tafsir*

TAWWAKUL see **trust**

THEOLOGY

Theology is often translated in Arabic as *kalam*, or speech, since in the early years theology was used to confront the arguments of non-Muslims in the vastly expanding Islamic empire, and to deal with the arguments between the Ash'arites, the Mu'tazilites, and the Qadarites about the nature of the basic concepts of Islam itself. Two basic tendencies predominated in early Muslim intellectual endeavors, the first largely based on reason, as with the followers of Abu Hanifa and Shafi'i, and the other based on a literal reading of **hadith**, as with the supporters of Ibn Hanbal. Both approaches are rational, in that they both rely on the resolution of theoretical issues through the application of logic, but they apply reason to different sets of concerns. The Hanbalis applied reason to the issue of hadith verification, and the precise relationship between the traditions as produced by the Prophet, his Companions, and their successors, and the implications that could be derived from that information.

Theological matters entered into Muslim debates over who should be the leader of the community and whether sinners who think they are part of the community should still be considered Muslims. As the theoretical literature became more sophisticated it started to deal with predestination and free will, the question of whether the Qur'an as the word of God was created or uncreated, and how to reconcile the divine attributes with divine unity (*tawhid*). Some of these issues were also considered in the discipline of **philosophy**.

Among theologians, the Mu'tazilites defended the principle of human free will. The Ash'arites emphasized God's omnipotence, but both schools thought that rationality was an important part of religious debate. Abu'l-Hasan al-Ash'ari (260–324/873–936) was originally a Mu'tazilite but came to reject the main principles of that approach. His school quickly became the dominant school of *kalam*. Against the Mu'tazili school, it maintained that the Qur'an is uncreated, eternal, and unchanging.

Although the Ash'arites were enthusiastic users of reason, they insisted that reason simply could not be used when dealing with some topics. They argued for the impossibility of rationally resolving some aspects of the Qur'an, in particular those parts that refer to God as having bodily parts. These should be read *bi-la kayfa*, "without asking how." They particularly criticized the Mu'tazilite theory of **justice** and its attempt to provide an objective understanding of that concept. Human beings in Ash'arite doctrine were regarded as free, but as acquiring (*kasb*) their actions from God, thus preserving divine participation in our actions. In their view, this doctrine was a middle ground between the Jabrites' emphasis on divine compulsion and the Qadarites' and Mu'tazilites' defense of free will.

Some debates that were popular in the past are no longer regarded as very relevant, and the issue of human free will, the createdness of the Qur'an, and the nature of the divine attributes are no longer live issues. Other topics remain relevant, such as the miraculous (*i'jaz*) nature of the Qur'an, the connection between traditional ways of following religion and the need for reform as societies change, and the theoretical parameters of an Islamic society and state.

See also: *qadr*, **reform**, *sunnah*

Further reading: al-Ash'ari 1953; Watt 1994, 1973; Wolfson 1976

TRUST

The English word "trust" encompasses two distinct concepts in Arabic: *amanah*, something entrusted to someone (e.g., a sacred trust), and *tawwakul*, the state of trusting and relying on someone, in this case God. As humans exercise the sacred responsibility for stewardship (**caliphate**) on earth granted to them by God, it is vital that they turn to God for assistance in fulfilling this trust.

Muslims should cultivate a state of reliance upon God. A person who "thinks they are sufficient" (96:7) is sorely mistaken and will reap the consequences of that delusion at the final judgment. Instead, one should turn to God, the "most trustworthy handhold" (2:256), in the face of life's difficulties. Surat al-Fatihah, which Muslims recite daily in **prayer**, contains the affirmation that it is God alone whom they **worship** and God alone to whom they turn for aid. This trust in God should not only appear in moments of vulnerability. Those who call on God when in peril, such as crossing the sea, but forget their creator when safe on land, are guilty and will face the consequences for their lack of **faith** on the **day of judgment**.

TRUTH

One of the beautiful names of God, *haqq* means what is true or real. The word is used more than 200 times in the Qur'an with varying applications. At its profoundest level, God is the Truth or the Reality (*Allah huwa al-haqq*) (10:32, 22:.6, 24:25). This is taken to mean that God is the sum of reality; his being must be himself and nothing else. As we are told: "everything perishes except his face" (28:88). The permanence of God in contrast to all of **creation** is one of the main arguments for the theory of *wahdat al-wujud*, the unity of being, according to which there is nothing truly in existence but God. Everything else owes its limited and contingent existence to God. This is a view that was much developed by **Sufis** in their commentaries or *tafsir* on the Qur'an.

The Qur'an is also, in another sense, truth; it is the word of God so that anyone can find in its truth the **straight path** and guidance (2:114). The truth represents what is serious: "We did not create the heavens and the Earth and all that lies between them while playing but with truth [*haqq*]" (44:37–38). The truth is real and permanent; everything else is mutable and only a matter of appearance.

Truthfulness (*sidq*) on the part of individual Muslims is also a vital part of moral behaviour, and was particularly stressed by some Sufi thinkers.

See also: *al-asma' al-husna'*, **morality,** *tawhid*

Further reading: al-Ghazali 1995a

ULAMA

Ulama (sing. *'alim*[*a*]) is the name given to the class of scholars in the Islamic sciences who have traditionally comprised the intellectual elite in the Muslim world. According to a well-known **hadith**, "The scholars [ulama] are the heirs of the prophets." Islam does not have an ordained clergy but the ulama fulfill a parallel role. Within **Shi'ism,** there is a more formalized and centralized hierarchy of scholars; within Sunni circles the organization tends to be looser.

The foundational level of **education** for a scholar was the memorization of the Qur'an, the teaching of which might happen with tutors but was eventually organized into a system of Qur'anic primary schools known as *kuttab*. Those who pursued further education did so in madrasahs. Disciplines such as hadith, grammar, and logic were central. Islamic jurisprudence or *fiqh* was a common specialization, and **rhetoric** was an important subject for those who would become not only religious scholars but literati.

In the core countries of the premodern Muslim world, higher education was centered around particular scholars, whose teaching circles might be held in the main **mosques** or adjacent centers. Although universities have become a common feature of most Middle Eastern societies, and the disciplines such as law and Qur'anic studies that formed part of the ulama's domain have become degree programs in these institutions, there have also been attempts to revive older forms of teaching and learning akin to the apprenticeship system. The Egyptian mufti 'Ali Juma'a has worked to reinstitute such learning circles at al-Azhar, the renowned Cairo university.

In the modern world the role of the ulama is in turmoil for a variety of reasons. Modern legal systems have replaced or marginalized the legal scholars and judges who were vital in earlier centuries; laws have been codified and lawyers have become a professional group. Many of the key Muslim thinkers of the nineteenth and especially twentieth centuries have not been those with the traditional formation. Mohamed Arkoun (b. 1928) in France, Abdolkarim Soroush (b. 1945) in Iran, Sayyid Qutb (d. 1966) in Egypt, and Abu A'la al-Mawdudi (d. 1979) in Pakistan represent a new class of intellectuals who are separated from one another in terms of ideology but united in arising outside of traditional networks of education that have characterized the ulama. Yet ulama remain central to key institutions and debates in the Middle East and South and Southeast Asia.

See also: **feminism**, **theology**

Further reading: Arkoun 2006; Taji-Farouki 2004; Zaman 2002

UMM AL-KITAB see **Mother of the Book**

UMMAH

The universal community of Muslims constitutes the *ummah* or community of Muhammad. Muslims are *ummah wustah*, a people following a middle way. The *ummah* has been also understood, however, to constitute the totality of those under the rule of the Muslim state (*dar al-Islam*). Muhammad is reported to have said of the Jews in Medina, where the first Muslim community was established, that they were of "Our *ummah*." Thus Muslims would be part of the *ummah* regardless of whether they lived within Muslim-ruled territory, while of non-Muslims only the *dhimmi* populations would be part of the *ummah*.

After the death of Muhammad, the Arabo-Muslim empire expanded dramatically. From the point where political unity of Muslim rule began to dissolve, the question of how the unity of the *ummah* related to the fragmented states emerged. In the modern world, this raises the question of how one's national citizenship relates to one's membership of the *ummah*. At times such as the **fasting** month of Ramadan or the annual **pilgrimage** whatever practical obstacles exist to Muslim unity are overshadowed by **rhetoric** of universal Muslim unity: one *ummah*, under God.

WAHHABISM

Muhammad ibn 'Abd al-Wahhab was an eighteenth-century religious reformer born in Najd in present-day Saudi Arabia (d. c. 1791). He was deeply critical of anything he viewed as a deviation from pure Islam, classifying as *shirk* many practices then popular in Mecca and Medina. The movement he founded has gathered both passionate adherents and impassioned critics. It is related to **salafism** and the two movements have been viewed by some scholars such as Khaled Abou El Fadl as comprising a "puritanical" strain within modern Islam. "Wahhabi" has become an epithet used by those who disdain certain forms of Muslim thought and practice, but properly pertains to a specific and relatively limited movement centered on the Gulf states.

Ibn 'Abd al-Wahhab studied in Medina with teachers at least two of whom strongly admired Ibn Taymiyyah (d. 728/1328). Some of Ibn 'Abd al-Wahhab's central teachings—especially his criticism of the custom of visiting graves—have precedent in Ibn Taymiyyah's zealous views. Ibn 'Abd al-Wahhab was particularly antagonistic to **Sufism** and **Shi'ism**, and argued that **worship** is nothing but exclusive obedience to God and his commands.

After his studies and his father's death, Ibn 'Abd al-Wahhab made a fortuitous marriage alliance, gained political protection, and began a career preaching against *shirk*. He instituted a campaign of demolishing tombs and trees associated with the Prophet and his Companions. Ibn 'Abd al-Wahhab's ideas became popular with the Sa'ud family, and when they took over what is now Saudi Arabia they made Wahhabism the basic **theology** of the country. This has developed into a system of legislation that is often regarded as harsh and extreme in its punishments.

Wahhabi theology is equally uncompromising. They self-identify as *al-Muwahhidun* or *Ahl al-Tawhid*—the "people of divine unity or one-ness." Their doctrine stresses three elements of *tawhid*: unity of lordship (*tawhid al-rububiyah*), unity of names and characteristics or attributes (*tawhid al-asma' wa'l-sifat*), and, most important, unity of worship (*tawhid al-'ibadah*).

From an external perspective, however, Wahhabi thought revolves around two concepts: opposition to **innovation** (*bid'ah*) and *shirk*. Wahhabism regards **People of the Book** as unbelievers (sing. *kafir*) since they maintain religious principles that Ibn 'Abd al-Wahhab argued are inconsistent with pure monotheism. Most importantly, Wahhabi Muslims are also intolerant toward those Muslims who disagree with them about matters of practice or doctrine. To perhaps an even greater extent than any other movement in Islamic history, Wahhabis freely use the practice of *takfir*—that is, the assertion that someone who claims to be a Muslim is in fact a disbeliever.

See also: **hadd, kufr, ziyarah**

Further reading: Abou El Fadl 2005; Abu-Rabi' 1996; Algar 2002; DeLong-Bas 2004

WAHY see **revelation**

WALAYAH, WALI, WILAYAH

Wali means many things: friend, helper, companion, partner, relation, beloved, heir, benefactor, saint, protector, or guardian. In the Qur'an, the words *wali* and its plural *awliya'* occur eighty-six times. Q. 9:71 declares male and female believers each other's *awliya'* or friends and protectors. God's exclusive status as the most influential friend and helper (*wali nasir*) is one of the major themes of Qur'anic teaching. He is the protector of those who believe (2:257), not only as a companion, but also as the supreme intercessor, who forgives compassionately (7:155). In the Qur'anic version of the birth of John the Baptist, Zacharias, having no natural son, asks God to give him a "*wali* from you, who will be my heir and will inherit from the family of Jacob" (19:5–6). Similarly, the persecuted Muslims in Mecca, after Muhammad's migration to Medina, ask God to send a *wali* and helper (4:75). In Q. 41:34, God asks believers to respond to a bad deed with something better so that the animosity is transformed, and the individual who had treated you poorly becomes your intimate friend (*wali hamim*).

In the Qur'an, *walayah* is expressed in the fable of the rich but immoral owner of two gardens and his poor but pious companion. The rich man ends up a loser despite his prosperity and power, for "ultimately, the *walayah* belongs to God, the **Truth**"(18:44).

Another verse reflects the new community in Medina in which three groups are identified in terms of *walayah*: those who emigrated and struggled on the path of God, those who gave them refuge in Medina and helped them, and those who did not emigrate. The first two, known in history as the *muhajirun* (emigrants) and the *ansar* (helpers)—are allies or friends of each other (*awliya'*), while the Prophet is advised to disregard the *walayah* of those who believed, but did not emigrate, until they really do emigrate (8:72). For the **Shiʻi**, *ayah* 5:55, revealed in Medina is significant, since it broadens the notion of *walayah*: "Your *wali* is only God, his Messenger, and those believers who perform the prayer and give alms, whilst bowing in prayers." Here the person of the Prophet plays a central role, culminating in the pledge of allegiance made to him at al-Hudaybiyah (48:9–10). This pledge (*bay'ah*) is taken to extend to the caliphs, in Shiʻi tradition to the **imams**, and for **Sufis** to their *shaykhs* or spiritual authorities.

Wilayah in the political sense relates to sovereign power and authority as reflected in the leader (*imam al-muslimin*) of the Muslim community after Muhammad and commander of the faithful (*amir al-mu'minin*). Although there is an important distinction between **Sunni** and Shiʻi views on the nature and the scope of this authority, in advocating their beliefs both communities refer to the same Qur'anic verse (2:285): "obey God and the Messenger and those in command (*ulu al-amr*)" thus called *wilayat al-amr*. In contrast to the Sunni view of *wilayah* with reference to state-building, in Shiʻi belief the transfer of *wilayah* from Muhammad to ʻAli is understood as the universal process of **revelation** to be completed by the **imams** as inheritors of the hidden substance and traditional wisdom of the previous prophets. It is only this transference that perfects the **religion** of Islam (5:3). The Shiʻi call to **prayer** reflects this as it refers to ʻAli as *wali Allah*, "God's friend."

The *awliya'* are without power or influence except that granted by God. Everything that happens, happens according to the will of God (13:16, 10:49). We are told: "he whom God guides, is on the right path; and he whom he leaves in error, you will not find for him a *wali* or guide [*murshid*]" (18:17). *Wali* means one who may be obeyed, and *murshid* is one who shows the correct path for the guidance of humankind.

Can Jews and Christians be friends of Muslims? The Qur'an says, "Oh you who believe, do not take Jews and Christians as *awliya'*. They are *awliya'* to one another, and the one among you who turns to them is of them. Truly, God does not guide wrongdoing people" (5:51). When the word *awliya'* is translated into English as "friends," as it commonly is, the verse appears very clearly to oppose friendly relations between Muslims, on the one hand, and Jews and Christians, on the other. Indeed, a number of scholars including **Wahhabis** have read it in precisely this way. A historically contextualized interpretation favored by other scholars suggests that the word *awliya'* here is better interpreted not to mean "friends" but rather "guardians" or "protectors." Before this verse was revealed, Muhammad and the Muslims had just moved as a community from Mecca to Medina. They had done so, we are told, due to their persecution by their fellow tribes and their relatives in Mecca. The Meccans feared the growing presence of the Muslims because the Muslims claimed that there was only one true God, who had no physical image, and who required the pursuit of virtue, generosity, and fair and kind treatment of the weaker members of society. This simple message was liable to overturn the social order of Mecca, based as it was upon the **worship** of multiple gods and the privilege of the strong and the wealthy. It also threatened to disrupt the business life of the vicinity, the annual **pilgrimage** when people from all over the Arabian peninsula would come to worship the idols at the **Ka'bah**—a cubical structure which Muslims hold was originally built by Abraham and his son, Ishmael, as a temple to the one God. Religion in Arabia, Muslims hold, went into a sharp decline and this monotheist venue became instead the site of polytheism and idolatry. In warning the Muslims not to get too close to those of other faiths such as the Jews and Christians, the point is not that one cannot be friends with them, but rather that one should not rely on them as protectors to help a nascent community survive and flourish.

See also: **People of the Book**

Further reading: Crone and Hinds 2003

WORSHIP

The language of worship or *'ibadah* is also that of service; at base, the believer is a slave (*'abd*) of God. Worship comprises both formal ritual **prayer** and other required acts such as the payment of alms and **fasting** during the month of Ramadan as well as supererogatory acts, those beyond what is required. In addition to standard prayers one can undertake supplication or keep prayer vigils at night, one can give **charity** beyond the obligatory *zakat*, one can fast additional days of the year. **Recitation** of the Qur'an can be an important component of individual or collective devotional practice. *Dhikr*, remembrance and praise of God, may likewise be done individually or in **Sufi** circles.

In theory, though, every act that a Muslim undertakes should be done in a spirit of pious consciousness of God's oversight of all one's deeds. Invoking God's name and attributes of **mercy** by repeating the *basmalah* before beginning any action underscores and reinforces this attitude.

See also: **slavery**, *taqwah*

ZAKAT see charity

ZINA' see sex

ZIYARAH

Prior to the modern period, tomb visitation or *ziyarah* was a common element in Muslim practice, although it has long been controversial in some circles. *Ziyarah* involves visiting the graves of saints or *walis* (friends of God). There are *ziyarah* guides—some lead visits to particular tombs on special days—and guidebooks pinpointing the specific locations of great reservoirs of blessing or **barakah**. Proofs of sanctity may include mysterious lights or pleasant smells experienced around graves. The *zuwwar* or visitors might come to pray and seek active assistance and intercession of the saints on their behalf. They might take keepsakes from the vicinity of graves, such as earth to cure certain illnesses. Or they might simply want to benefit from close proximity to the divine blessing that is supposed to surround the tomb. It is mainly a belief in the possibility of catching a glimpse of the **afterlife**, or attaining some emanation of its promise of **paradise** through *ziyarah* that made these visits to the cemetery so attractive. Its form of blessing is the *barzakh* (intermediary state) between the sacred and the profane. The tomb represents the link between this world (the *dar al-dunyah*), where the body is outward and the spirit is unseen, and the *dar al-barzakh*, where the spirit is outward and the bodies are hidden in their graves.

The legality of such activities, extending as they do to people actually spending nights at cemeteries and holding extensive prayer services there, is not accepted by all. Ibn Taymiyyah condemned such practices, which were very popular in Egypt in his time. The **Wahhabi** movement founded by Ibn 'Abd al-Wahhab also took a strong stance on visitation of graves, in that instance those of the Prophet and his Companions, charging that it constituted a dangerous **inno-**

vation. At the heart of this debate over the cemetery and the cult of saints was a disagreement on the very concept of sanctity in Islam.

Further reading: Eklund 1941; Smith and Haddad 1981; Taylor 1999

BIBLIOGRAPHY

Note: Arabic sources are alphabetized without attention to the prefix "al" or the letter 'ayn.

Abdel Haleem, M. (1999) *Understanding the Qur'an: Themes and Style*, London: I.B. Tauris.

Abderraziq, A. (1994) *L'Islam et les fondements du pouvoir*, Paris: La Découverte.

Abdul-Ghafur, S. (ed.) (2005) *Living Islam Out Loud: American Muslim Women Speak*, Boston: Beacon Press.

Abdul-Rauf, H. (2000) "The Linguistic Architecture of the Qur'an," *Journal of Qur'anic Studies*, 2: 2, 37–51.

Abdul-Rauf, H. (2001) *The Qur'an Outlined: Theme and Text*, London: Taha Publishers.

Abou El Fadl, K. (2001a) *Conference of the Books: The Search for Beauty in Islam*, Lanham, MD: University Press of America.

Abou El Fadl, K. (2001b) *Speaking in God's Name: Islamic Law, Authority, and Women*, Oxford: Oneworld Publications.

Abou El Fadl, K. (2001c) *Rebellion and Violence in Islamic Law*, Cambridge: Cambridge University Press.

Abou El Fadl, K. (2004) *Islam and the Challenge of Democracy*, Boston: Beacon Press.

Abou El Fadl, K. (2005) *The Great Theft: Wrestling Islam from the Extremists*, San Francisco: Harper San Francisco.

Abu-Rabi', I. (1996) *Intellectual Origins of Islamic Resurgence in the Modern Arab World*, Albany: State University of New York Press.

Abu-Rabi', I. (2004) *Contemporary Arab Thought*, London: Pluto Press.

Abu Zayd, N. (1998) *Mafhum al-nass: Dirasa fi 'ulum al-Qur'an*, Bayrut: al-Markaz al-thaqafi al-'arabi.

Abugideiri, H. (2004) "On Gender and the Family," in *Islamic Thought in the Twentieth Century*, ed. Taji-Farouki and Nafi, 223–59.

Ahmed, L. (1992) *Women and Gender in Islam: Historical Roots of a Modern Debate*, New Haven, CT: Yale University Press.

Ahmed, S. (1998) "Ibn Taymiyyah and the Satanic Verses," *Studia Islamica*, 87, 67–124.

Algar, H. (1998) *Surat al-Fatiha*, New York: Islamic Publications International.

Algar, H. (2002) *Wahabbism: A Critical Essay*, Oneonta, NY: Islamic Publications International.

Ali, K. (2003) "Progressive Muslims and Islamic Jurisprudence: The Necessity for Critical Engagement with Marriage and Divorce Law," in *Progressive Muslims*, ed. Safi, 163–89.

Ali, K. (2004) "'A Beautiful Example': The Prophet Muhammad as a Model for Muslim Husbands," *Islamic Studies*, 43:2: 273–91.

Ali, K. (2006) *Sexual Ethics and Islam: Feminist Reflections on Qur'an, Hadith, and Jurisprudence*, Oxford: Oneworld Publications.

Alvi, S. and S. McDonough (eds.) (2003) *The Muslim Veil in North America: Issues and Debates*, Toronto: Women's Press.

Amir-Moezzi, M.A. (1994) *The Divine Guide in Early Shi'ism*, trans. David Streight, Albany: State University of New York Press.

Arkoun, M. (2006) *Islam: To Reform or to Subvert?*, London: Saqi Books.

Armstrong, K. (2002) *Islam: A Short History*, New York: The Modern Library.

al-Ash'ari (1953) *The Theology of al-Ash'ari: The Arabic Texts of al-Ash'ari's Kitab al-Luma' and Risalat Istihsan al-khawd fi 'ilm al-kalam*, ed. J. McCarthy, Beirut: Imprimerie catholique.

Aslan, A. (1998) *Religious Pluralism in Christian and Islamic Philosophy: The Thought of John Hick and Seyyed Hossein Nasr*, London: RoutledgeCurzon.

Aslan, R. (2006) *No God but God: The Origins, Evolution, and Future of Islam*. Random House.

Awn, P.J. (1983) *Satan's Tragedy and Redemption: Iblis in Sufi Psychology*, Leiden: Brill.

Austin, A. (1984) *African Muslims in Antebellum America: A Sourcebook* (London and New York: Garland Publishing.

Austin, A. (1997) *African Muslims in Antebellum America: Transatlantic Stories and Spiritual Struggles* (New York and London: Routledge.

Ayoub, M. (1987) "Martyrdom in Christianity and Islam," in *Religious Resurgence: Contemporary Cases in Islam, Christianity, and Judaism*, R. Antoun. and M. Hegland (eds.), Syracuse New York: Syracuse University Press, 67–76.

Ayoub, M. (1992) *The Qur'an and Its Interpreters*, Albany: State University of New York Press.

al-'Azm, S. (1998) *al-'Ilmaniyya wa al-mujtama' al-madani* (Secularism and Civil Society), Cairo: Markaz al-Dirasat al-Qanuniyya li-Huquq al-Insan, Cairo.

Badawi, J. (1971) *The Status of Woman in Islam*, Plainfield, IN: Muslim Students Association of U.S. and Canada.

Badran, M. (1996) *Feminists, Islam, and Nation: Gender and the Making of Modern Egypt*, Princeton, NJ: Princeton University Press.

al-Baqillani, Abu Bakr Muhammad (1994) *I'jaz al-Qur'an*, Beirut: Dar Ihya' al-'Ulum.

Baranzagi, N. (2004) *Women's Identity and the Qur'an: A New Reading*, Gainesville: University Press of Florida.

Barlas, A. (2002) *"Believing Women" in Islam: Unreading Patriarchal Interpretations of the Qur'an*, Austin: University of Texas Press.

Beeston, A. et al. (eds.) (1983) *The Cambridge History of Arabic Literature: Arabic Literature to the End of the Umayyad Period*, Cambridge: Cambridge University Press.

Bell, R. (1937) *The Qur'an, Translated with a Critical Re-arrangement of the Surahs*, Edinburgh: T. and T. Clark.

Bianchi, R. (2004) *Guests of God: Pilgrimage and Politics in the Islamic World*, Oxford: Oxford University Press.

Black, A. (2001) *The History of Islamic Political Thought*, Edinburgh: Edinburgh University Press.

Bonner, M. (2006) *Jihad in Islamic History: Doctrines and Practice*, Princeton, NJ: Princeton University Press.

Bowker, J. (1970) *Problems of Suffering in Religions of the World*, Cambridge: Cambridge University Press.

Bowker, J. (1993) *The Meanings of Death*, Cambridge: Cambridge University Press.

Bowen, D. (1981) "Muslim Juridical Opinions Concerning the Status of Women as Demonstrated by the Case of *'Azl*," *Journal of Near Eastern Studies*, 40: 4, 323–28.

Brockopp, J. (ed.) (2003) *Islamic Ethics of Life: Abortion, War, and Euthanasia*, Columbia: University of South Carolina Press.

Brown, D. (1996) *Rethinking Tradition in Modern Islamic Thought*, Cambridge: Cambridge University Press.

Brown, D. (1998) "The Triumph of Scripturalism: The Doctrine of Naskh and its Modern Critics," in Earle H. Waugh and Frederick M. Denny (eds.), *The Shaping of an American Islamic Discourse: A Memorial to Fazlur Rahman*, Atlanta: Scholars Press, 49–66.

Bulliet, R. (1995) *Islam: The View from the Edge*, Columbia: Columbia University Press.

Bunt, G. (2003) *Islam in the Digital Age: E-jihad, Online Fatwas and Cyber Islamic Environments*, London: Pluto Press.

Burton, J. (1977) *The Collection of the Qur'an*, Cambridge: Cambridge University Press.

Burton, J. (1985) "The interpretation of Q87, 6–7 and the theories of naskh," *Der Islam*, 62, 5–19.

Burton, J. (1990) *The Sources of Islamic Law: Islamic Theories of Abrogation*, Edinburgh: Edinburgh University Press.

Calderini, S. (1998) "Woman, 'Sin' and 'Lust': The Fall of Adam and Eve According to Classical and Modern Muslim Exegesis," in Michael A. Hayes et al. (eds.), *Religion and Sexuality*, Roehampton Institute London Papers 4, Sheffield, UK: Sheffield Academic Press, 49–63.

Campanini, M. (2003) *Islam e politica*, Bologna: Il Mulino.

Campanini, M. (2007) *The Qur'an: The Basics*, trans. O. Leaman, London: Routledge.

Chittick, W. (1989) *The Sufi Path of Knowledge*, Albany: State University of New York Press.

Clarence-Smith, W. (2006) *Islam and the Abolition of Slavery*, Oxford: Oxford University Press.

Cook, D. (2005) *Understanding Jihad*, Berkeley: University of California Press.

Cook, D. (2007) *Martyrdom in Islam*, Cambridge: Cambridge University Press.

Cook, M. (1981) *Early Muslim Dogma*, New York: Cambridge University Press.

Cook, M. (1983) *Muhammad*, New York: Oxford University Press.

Cook, M. (2000a) *The Koran: A Very Short Introduction*, New York: Oxford University Press.

Cook, M. (2000b) *Commanding Right and Forbidding Wrong in Islamic Thought*, Cambridge: Cambridge University Press.

cooke, m. (2000) *Women Claim Islam: Creating Islamic Feminism through Literature*, New York: Routledge.

Corbin, H. (1986) *Histoire de la philosophie islamique*, Paris: Gallimard.

Coulson, N. (1964) *A History of Islamic Law*, Edinburgh: Edinburgh University Press.

Cragg, K. (1973) *The Mind of the Quran: Chapters in Reflection*, London: George Allen and Unwin.

Cragg, K. (1994) *The Event of the Qur'an*, Oxford: Oneworld Publications.

Cragg, K. (1998) *Readings in the Qur'an*, London: Collins Religious Publishing.

Crone, P. and M. Hinds (2003) *God's Caliph: Religious Authority in the First Centuries of Islam*, Cambridge: Cambridge University Press.

Crone, P. and M. Hinds (2004) *Medieval Islamic Political Thought*, Edinburgh: Edinburgh University Press.

Curtis, E. (2002) *Islam in Black America: Identity, Liberation, and Difference in African-American Muslim Thought*, Albany: State University of New York Press.

Curtis, E. (2006) *Black Muslim Religion in the Nation of Islam 1960–1975*, Chapel Hill: University of North Carolina Press.

Daftary, F. (1990) *The Isma'ilis: Their History and Doctrines*, Cambridge: Cambridge University Press.

Daftary, F. (ed.) (1996) *Medieval Isma'ili History and Thought*, Cambridge: Cambridge University Press.

Dannin, R. (2002) *Black Pilgrimage to Islam*, Oxford: Oxford University Press.

DeLong-Bas, N. (2004) *Wahhabi Islam: From Revival and Reform to Global Jihad*, New York: Oxford University Press.

Denny, F.D. (1985) "Ethics and the Qur'an Community and World View," in *Ethics in Islam*, ed. Hovannisian, 103–21.

Denny, F.D. (1994) *An Introduction to Islam*, New York: Macmillan.

Diouf, S. (1998) *Servants of Allah: African Muslims Enslaved in the Americas*, New York: New York University Press.

Dunne, B. (1998) "Power and Sexuality in the Middle East," *Middle East Report*, 206 (Spring), 8–11, 37.

Eklund, R. (1941) *Life between Death and Resurrection According to Islam*, Uppsala: Almqvist and Wiksell.

Enayat, H. (1982) *Modern Islamic Political Thought*, London: Macmillan.

Esack, F. (1998) *Qur'an, Liberation and Pluralism*, Oxford: Oneworld Publications.

Esack, F. (2001) "Islam and Gender Justice: Beyond Simplistic Apologia," in J. Raines and D. Maguire (eds.), *What Men Owe to Women: Men's Voices from World Religions*, New York: State University of New York Press.

Esack, F. (2005a) *The Qur'an: A User's Guide*, Oxford: Oneworld Publications.

Esack, F. (2005b) *Islam, HIV and AIDS: Reflections Based on Compassion, Responsibility and Justice*, Cape Town: Positive Muslims.

Esposito, J. (ed.) (1987) *Islam in Asia: Religion, Politics, Society*, Oxford: Oxford University Press.

Esposito, J. (ed.) (1995) *Oxford Encyclopedia of the Modern Islamic world*, Oxford: Oxford University Press.

Esposito, J. (ed.) (2003) *The Oxford Dictionary of Islam*, New York: Oxford University Press.

Esposito, J. and J. Voll (1996) *Islam and Democracy*, New York: Oxford University Press.

Esposito, J. with N. DeLong-Bas (2001) *Women in Muslim Family Law*, 2nd edition, Syracuse, NY: Syracuse University Press.

Fadel, M. (1998) "Reinterpreting the Guardian's Role in the Islamic Contract of Marriage: The Case of the Maliki School," *Journal of Islamic Law*, 3: 1, 1–26.

al-Fadli, 'A. (2002) *Introduction to Hadith*, trans. Nazmina Virjee, London: Islamic College for Advanced Studies.

Fakhry, M. (1991) *Ethical Theories in Islam*, Leiden: Brill.

Faruki, K. "Legal Implications for Today of *al-Ahkam al-Khamsa* (The Five Values)," in *Ethics in Islam*, ed. Hovannisian, 65–72.

al-Faruqi, L. (1994) *Women, Muslim Society, and Islam*, Plainfield, IN: American Trust Publications.

al-Faruqi, M. (2000) "Women's Self-Identity in the Qur'an and Islamic Law," in *Windows of Faith*, ed. G. Webb.

J. Fetzer and J. Soper (2004) *Muslims and the State in Britain, France and Germany*, Cambridge: Cambridge University Press

Filaly-Ansari, A. (1996) *L'Islam est-il hostile à la laïcité?*, Casablanca: Le Fennec.

Friedmann, Y. (2003) *Tolerance and Coercion in Islam: Interfaith Relations in the Muslim Tradition*, Cambridge: Cambridge University Press.

Fyzee, A. (1955) *Outlines of Muhammadan Law*, London: Oxford University Press.

Gätje, H. (1976) *The Qur'an and Its Exegesis: Selected Texts with Classical and Modern Muslim Interpretations*, ed. and trans. A. Welch, London: Routledge and Kegan Paul.

al-Ghazali, Abu Hamid (1980) *Qistas al-mustaqim*, trans. R. McCarthy as "The correct balance," in *Freedom and fulfillment*, Boston: Twayne: 287–332.

al-Ghazali, Abu Hamid (1984) *Marriage and Sexuality in Islam: A Translation of al-Ghazali's Book on the Etiquette of Marriage from the Ihya'*, ed. and trans. Madelain Farah, Salt Lake City: University of Utah Press.

al-Ghazali, Abu Hamid (1985) *Ihya''ulum al-din*, ed. A. al-Sirwan, Beirut: Dar al-qalam.

al-Ghazali, Abu Hamid (1995a) *The Ninety-Nine Beautiful Names of God*, trans. and ed. David Burrell and Nazih Daher, Cambridge, UK: The Islamic Texts Society.

al-Ghazali, Abu Hamid (1995b) *The Remembrance of Death and the Afterlife* (book 40 of *The Revival of Religious Sciences*) trans. T.J. Winter, Cambridge, UK: The Islamic Texts Society.

al-Ghazali, Abu Hamid (1998) *The Proper Conduct of Marriage in Islam (Adab an-Nikah): Book Twelve of Ihya' 'Ulum ad-Din*, trans. Muhtar Holland, Fort Lauderdale, FL: Al-Baz Publishing.

Ghazali, Ahmad (1986) *Inspirations (Sawanih)*, trans. N. Pourjavady, London: KPI.

Goldziher, I. (1967) *Muslim Studies*, Vol. 1, London: George Allen and Unwin.

Gomez, M. (2005) *Black Crescent: The Experience and Legacy of African Muslims in the Americas*, Cambridge: Cambridge University Press.

Graham, W. (1977) *Divine Word and Prophetic Word in Early Islam*, The Hague: Mouton.

Gray, Peter B. (2004) "HIV and Islam: Is HIV Prevalence Lower among Muslims?," *Social Science & Medicine*, 58, 1751–56.

Gregorian, V. (2003) *Islam: A Mosaic not a Monolith*, Washington, DC: Brookings Institute.

Groff, P. (2007) *A–Z Islamic Philosophy*, Edinburgh: Edinburgh University Press.

Gwynne, R. (2004) *Logic, Rhetoric and Legal Reasoning in the Qur'an: God's Arguments*, London: RoutledgeCurzon.

Haddad, Y. (ed.) (2002) *Muslims in the West: From Sojourners to Citizens*, New York: Oxford University Press.

Haeri, S. (1989) *Law of Desire: Temporary Marriage in Shi'i Iran*, Syracuse, NY: Syracuse University Press.

Haeri, S. (1995) "The Politics of Dishonor: Rape and Power in Pakistan," in Mahnaz Afkhami (ed.), *Faith and Freedom: Women's Human Rights in the Muslim World*, Syracuse, NY: Syracuse University Press, 161–74.

Hallaq, W. (1997) *A History of Islamic Legal Theories*, Cambridge: Cambridge University Press.

Hallaq, W. (2001) *Authority, Continuity and Change in Islamic Law*, Cambridge: Cambridge University Press.

Hallaq, W. (2004) "Can the Shari'a Be Restored?," in Yvonne Yazbeck Haddad and Barbara Freyer Stowasser (eds.), *Islamic Law and the Challenges of Modernity*, Walnut Creek, CA: AltaMira Press, 21–53.

Halm, H. (1997) *Shi'a Islam: From Religion to Revolution*, trans. Allison Brown, Princeton, NJ: Markus Wiener.

Hashmi, S. (ed.) (2002) *Islamic Political Ethics: Civil Society, Pluralism, and Conflict*, Princeton, NJ: Princeton University Press.

Hassan, R. (1991) "Muslim Women and Post-patriarchal Islam," in Paula M. Cooey et al. (eds.), *After Patriarchy: Feminist Transformations of the World Religions*, Maryknoll, NY: Orbis Books.

Hawting, G. and A. Shareef (eds.) (1993) *Approaches to the Qur'an*, London: Routledge.

al-Hibri, A. (1993) "Family Planning and Islamic Jurisprudence," in Azizah Y. al-Hibri, Daniel C. Maguire, and James Martin-Schramm (eds.), *Religious and Ethical Perspectives on Population Issues*, Washington, DC: The Religious Consultation on Population, Reproductive Health and Ethics, 2–11.

al-Hibri, A. (1997) "Islam, Law, and Custom: Redefining Muslim Women's Rights," *American University Journal of International Law and Policy*, 12: 1, 1–44.

al-Hibri, A. (1999) "Islamic Law and Muslim Women in America," in Marjorie B. Garber and Rebecca L. Walkowitz (eds.), *One Nation under God? Religion and American Culture*, New York: Routledge, 128–42.

al-Hibri, A. (2000) "An Introduction to Muslim Women's Rights," In *Windows of Faith*, ed. Webb, 51–71.

Hidayatullah, A. (2003) "Islamic Conceptions of Sexuality," in David W. Machacek and Melissa M. Wilcox (eds.), *Sexuality and the World's Religions*, Santa Barbara, CA: ABC-Clio, 255–92.

Hodgson, M. (1974) *Ventures of Islam*, Chicago: University of Chicago Press.

Hoodbhoy, P. (1991) *Islam and Science: Religious Orthodoxy and the Battle for Rationality*, Karachi: Zed Books.

Hourani, A. (1982) *Arabic Thought in the Liberal Age 1798–1939*, Cambridge: Cambridge University Press.

Hourani, G. (1985) *Reason and Tradition in Islamic Ethics*, Cambridge: Cambridge University Press.

Hovannisian, R. (ed.) (1985) *Ethics in Islam*, Malibu, CA: Undena Publications.

Howarth, G. and O. Leaman (eds.) (2000) *Encyclopedia of Death and Dying*, London: Routledge.

Hoyland, R. (2001) *Arabia and the Arabs: From the Bronze Age to the Coming of Islam*, London: Routledge.

Hunwick, J. (2003–4) "'I wish to be seen in our land called Afrika': 'Umar b. Sayyid's Appeal to Be Released from Slavery (1819)" *Journal of Arabic and Islamic Studies*, 5, 62–77.

Ibn Kathir, I. (n.d.) *Tafsir al-Qur'an al-' azim* (Interpretation of the Great Qur'an), 4 vols., Cairo: Dar al-taqwa.

Ibn Kathir, I. (2000) *The Life of the Prophet Muhammad* (al-Sirah al-Nabaw-iyyah), 4 vols., trans. Trevor Le Gassick as *History of the Prophet*, Reading (UK): Centre for Muslim Contribution to Civilization, Garnet Publishing.

Ibn Khaldun (1958) *The Muqaddimah: An Introduction to History*, New York: Pantheon.

Ibn Rushd (1976) *Fasl al-maqal*, trans. G. Hourani, *Averroes on the Harmony of Religion and Philosophy*, London: Luzac.

Ibn Rushd (1994–96) *The Distinguished Jurist's Primer: A Translation of* Bidayat al-Mujtahid, 2 vols., trans. Imran Ahsan Khan Nyazee, Reading, UK: Centre for Muslim Contribution to Civilization, Garnet Publishing.

Ilkkaracan, P. (2002) "Islam and Women's Sexuality: A Research Report from Turkey," in Patricia Beattie Jung et al. (eds.), *Good Sex: Feminist Perspectives from the World's Religions*, New Brunswick, NJ: Rutgers University Press, 61–76.

Imam, A. (2002) "The Muslim Religious Right ('Fundamentalists') and Sexuality," in Patricia Beattie Jung et al. (eds.), *Good Sex: Feminist Perspectives from the World's Religions*, New Brunswick, NJ: Rutgers University Press, 15–30.

Iqbal, M. (1965) *The Reconstruction of Religious Thought in Islam*, Lahore: Ashraf.

Irwin, R. (2006) *Dangerous Knowledge: Orientalism and Its Discontents*, Woodstock, NY: Overlook Press.

Izutsu, T. (1959) *The Structure of the Ethical Terms in the Koran*, Montreal: McGill University Press.

Izutsu, T. (1964) *God and Man in the Koran: Semantics of the Koranic Weltan-schauung*, The Keio Institute of Cultural and Linguistic Studies, Tokyo.

Izutsu, T. (1966) *Ethico-Religious Concepts in the Qur'an*, Montreal: McGill University Press.

Jackson, S. (2002) *On the Boundaries of Theological Tolerance in Islam: Abu Hamid al Ghazali's Faysal al Tafriqa* (Studies in Islamic Philosophy, Vol. 1), New York: Oxford University Press.

Jackson, S. (2005) *Islam and the Blackamerican: Looking toward the Third Resur-rection*, New York: Oxford University Press.

Jamal, A. (2001) "The Story of Lot and the Qur'an's Perception of the Morality of Same-Sex Sexuality," *Journal of Homosexuality*, 41: 1, 1–88.

Johansen, B. (1996) "The Valorization of the Body in Muslim Sunni Law," in D. Stewart, B. Johansen, and A. Singer (eds.), *Law and Society in Islam*, Princeton, NJ: Markus Wiener Publishers, 71–112.

Jomier, J. (1997) *The Great Themes of the Qur'an*, London: SCM Press.

al-Juwayni (1950) *Kitab al-irshad ila qawati al-adilla fi usul al-i'tiqad*, ed. M. Musa and A. 'Abd al-Hamid, Cairo, Maktabat al-Khanji.

Kahf, M. (1999) *Western Representations of the Muslim Woman: From Terma-gant to Odalisque*, Austin: University of Texas Press.

Kamali, M. (1991) *Principles of Islamic Jurisprudence*, Cambridge, UK: The Islamic Texts Society.

Kamali, M. (2006) *An Introduction to Shari'ah*, Kuala Lumpur: Ilmiah Publishers.

Keddie, N. (ed.) (1972) *Scholars, Saints, and Sufis*, Berkeley: University of California Press.

Keddie, N. (1983) *An Islamic Response to Imperialism: Political and Religious Writings of Sayyid Jamal al-Din "al-Afghani,"* Berkeley: University of California Press.

Keddie, N. and B. Baron (eds.) (1991) *Women in Middle Eastern History: Shifting Boundaries in Sex and Gender*, New Haven, CT: Yale University Press 1991.

Kedourie, E. (1966) *Afghani and Abduh: An Essay on Religious Unbelief and Political Activism in Modern Islam*, London: Frank Cass.

Keller, Nuh Ha Mim (trans. and ed.) (1994 [1991]) Ahmad ibn Naqib al-Misri, *Reliance of the Traveller: A Classic Manual of Islamic Sacred Law*, Beltsville, MD: Amana Publications.

Kermani, N. (1999) *Gott ist schön. Das ästhetische Erleben des Koran*, Munich: Beck.

Khadduri, M. (1984) *The Islamic Conception of Justice*, Baltimore, MD: Johns Hopkins University Press.

Khalidi, O. (2000) "Approaches to Mosque Design in North America," in Y. Haddad and J. Esposito (eds.), *Muslims on the Americanization Path*, New York: Oxford University Press, 317–34.

Khan, S. (2000) *Muslim Women: Crafting a North American Identity*, Gainesville: University Press of Florida. Republished as *Aversion and Desire: Negotiating Muslim Female Identity in the Diaspora*, Toronto: Women's Press (2002).

Khan, S. (2006) Zina, *Transnational Feminism, and the Moral Regulation of Pakistani Women*, Vancouver: University of British Columbia Press.

al-Khu'i, A. (1998) *The Prolegomena to the Qur'an*, trans. A. Sachedina, Oxford: Oxford University Press.

Köse, A. (1996) *Conversion to Islam: A Study of Native British Converts*, London: Kegan Paul International.

Kugle, S. (2003) "Sexuality, Diversity, and Ethics in the Agenda of Progressive Muslims," in *Progressive Muslims*, ed. Safi, 190–234.

Kurzman, C. (ed.) (1998) *Liberal Islam*, New York: Oxford University Press.

Kurzman, C. (ed.) (2002) *Modernist Islam: A Source Book*, New York: Oxford University Press.

Lalani, A. (2000) *Early Shi'i Thought: The Teachings of Imam Muhammad al-Baqir*, London: I.B. Tauris.

Leaman, O. (1999) *Brief Introduction to Islamic Philosophy*, Oxford: Polity Press.

Leaman, O. (2001) *An Introduction to Classical Islamic Philosophy*, Cambridge: Cambridge University Press.

Leaman, O. (2004) *Islamic Aesthetics*, Edinburgh: Edinburgh University Press.

Leaman, O. (ed.) (2006) *The Qur'an: An Encyclopedia*, London: Routledge.

Leemhuis, F. (1988) "Origins and Early Development of the *Tafsir* Tradition," in *Approaches to the History of the Interpretation of the Qur'an*, ed. Rippin, 13–30.

Lev, Y. (2005) *Charity, Endowments, and Charitable Institutions in Medieval Islam*, Gainseville: University Press of Florida.

Levtzion, N. (ed.) (1979) *Conversion to Islam*, London: Holmes and Meier.

Lewinstein, K. (2002) "The Reevaluation of Martyrdom in Early Islam," in *Sacrificing the Self: Perspectives on Martyrdom and Religion*, ed. M. Cormack, M. 78–91, Oxford: Oxford University Press.

Lewis, B. (1988) *The Political Language of Islam*, Chicago: University of Chicago Press.

Lewis, B. (1990) *Race and Slavery in the Middle East: An Historical Enquiry*, Oxford: Oxford University Press.

Lewis, B. (1996) *Cultures in Conflict: Christians, Muslims, and Jews in the Age of Discovery*, Oxford: Oxford University Press.

Lucas, S. (2004) *Constructive Critics, Hadith Literature, and the Articulation of Sunni Islam*, Leiden: Brill.

Macaulay, D. (2003) *Mosque*, Boston: Houghton Mifflin.

McDonough, S. (1984) *Muslim Ethics and Modernity: A Comparative Study of the Ethical Thought of Sayyid Ahmad Khan and Mawlana Mawdudi*, Waterloo, Ontario: Canadian Corporation for Studies in Religion, Wilfred Laurier Press.

Madelung, W. (1997) *The Succession to Muhammad: A Study of the Early Caliphate*, Cambridge: Cambridge University Press.

Madigan, D. (2001) *The Qur'an's Self-Image: Writing and Authority in Islam's Scripture*, Princeton, NJ: Princeton University Press.

Maghen, Z. (2004) *Virtues of the Flesh: Passion and Purity in Early Islamic Jurisprudence*, Leiden: Brill.

Mahfouz, N. (1990) *Palace Walk*, New York: Anchor Books.

Mahmood, S. (2004) *Politics of Piety: Islamic Revival and the Feminist Subject*, Princeton, NJ: Princeton University Press.

Mahmutćehejić, R. (2006) *On Love in the Muslim Tradition*, New York: Fordham University Press.

Malik, I. (2004) *Islam and Modernity: Muslims in Europe and the United States*, London: Pluto Press.

Malti-Douglas, F. (1992) *Woman's Body, Woman's Word: Gender and Discourse in Arabo-Islamic Writing*, Princeton, NJ: Princeton University Press.

Mardin, S. (2000) *The Genesis of Young Ottoman Thought: A Study in the Modernization of Turkish Political Ideas*, Syracuse, NY: Syracuse University Press.

Marlow, L. (1997) *Hierarchy and Egalitarianism in Islamic Thought*, Cambridge: Cambridge University Press.

Marmon, S. (1993) *Eunuchs and Sacred Boundaries in Islamic Society*, Oxford: Oxford University Press.

Marmon, S. (1999) "Domestic Slavery in the Mamluk Empire: A Preliminary Sketch," in *idem* (ed.), *Slavery in the Islamic Middle East*, Princeton, NJ: Markus Wiener, 1–23.

Marshall, D. (1999) *God, Muhammad and the Unbelievers: A Qur'anic Study*, London: Curzon.

Mashhour, A. (2005) "Islamic Law and Gender Equality—Could There Be a Common Ground? A Study of Divorce and Polygamy in Sharia Law and Contemporary Legislation in Tunisia and Egypt," *Human Rights Quarterly*, 27, 562–96.

Masud, M., et al. (1996) "Muftis, Fatwas, and Islamic Legal Interpretation," in *Islamic Legal Interpretation*, ed. Masud, Messick, and Powers, 3–32.

Masud, M., B. Messick, and D. Powers (eds.) (1996) *Islamic Legal Interpretation: Muftis and Their Fatwas*, Cambridge, MA: Harvard University Press.

Maurer, B. (2006) *Pious Property: Islamic Mortgages in the United States*, New York: Russell Sage Foundation Publications.

Mawdudi, S. (1982) *The Meaning of the Qur'an*, trans. S. Akbar, Lahore: Islamic Publication Ltd.

Melchert, C. (2006) *Ahmad ibn Hanbal*. Oxford: Oneworld.

Mernissi, F. (1992) *Islam and Democracy: Fear of the Modern World*, trans. Mary Jo Lakeland, Reading, MA: Addison-Wesley Publishing Company.

Mernissi, F. (1993) *The Veil and the Male Elite: A Feminist Interpretation of Women's Rights in Islam*, Reading, MA: Addison-Wesley Publishing Company.

Mernissi, F. (1995) *Dreams of Trespass: Tales of a Harem Girlhood*, Reading, MA: Addison-Wesley Publishing Company.

Mernissi, F. (1996) *Women's Rebellion and Islamic Memory*, London and New York: Zed Books.

Miller, J. (1992) "Muslim Slavery and Slaving: A Bibliography," *Slavery and Abolition*, 13: 1 (April), 249–71.

Mir, M. (1987) *Dictionary of Qur'anic Terms and Concepts*, New York: Garland.

Mir-Hosseini, Ziba (1999) *Islam and Gender: The Religious Debate in Contemporary Iran*, Princeton, NJ: Princeton University Press.

Mir-Hosseini, Ziba (2000) *Marriage on Trial: A Study of Islamic Family Law*, revised edition, London: I.B. Tauris.

Mir-Hosseini, Ziba (2003) "The Construction of Gender in Islamic Legal Thought: Strategies for Reform," *Hawwa: Journal of Women in the Middle East and the Islamic World*, 1: 1, 1–28.

Mir-Hosseini, Ziba (2006) "Muslim Women's Quest for Equality: Between Islamic Law and Feminism," *Critical Inquiry* 32, 629–45.

Moghissi, H. (1999) *Feminism and Islamic Fundamentalism: The Limits of Postmodern Analysis*, London: Zed Books.

Mohamed, Y. (1996) *Fitrah: The Islamic Concept of Human Nature*, London: Taha Publishers.

Mohamed, Y. (2004) *The Path to Virtue*, Kuala Lumpur: ISTAC.

Momen, M. (1985) *An Introduction to Shi'i Islam*, New Haven: Yale University Press.

Moors, A. (1995) *Women, Property, and Islam: Palestinian Experiences, 1920–1990*, New York: Cambridge University Press.

Moors, A. (1999) "Debating Islamic Family Law: Legal Texts and Social Practices," in Margaret L. Meriwether and Judith E. Tucker (eds.), *Social History of Women and Gender in the Modern Middle East*, Boulder, CO: Westview, 141–75.

Moosa, E. (2003) "The Debts and Burdens of Critical Islam," in *Progressive Muslims*, ed. Safi, 111–27.

Moosa, E. (2005) *Al-Ghazali and the Poetics of Imagination*, Chapel Hill: University of North Carolina Press.

Motzki, H. (1998) "Child Marriage in Seventeenth-Century Palestine," in *Islamic Law and Legal Interpretation*, ed. Masud, Messick, and Powers, 129–40.

Motzki, H. (ed.) (2004) *Hadith*, The Formation of the Classical Islamic World, Vol. 28, Burlington, VT: Ashgate.

Moussalli, A. (2001) *The Islamic Quest for Pluralism, Democracy and Human Rights*, Gainesville: University Press of Florida.

Muqtedar Khan, A. (ed.) (2006) *Islamic Democratic Discourse*, Lanham, MD: Lexington.

Murata, S. (1987) "Temporary Marriage (Mut'a) in Islamic Law," *Alserat*, 13: 1 (Spring).

Murata, S. (1991) "The Angels," in S.H. Nasr (ed.), *Islamic Spirituality: Foundations*, New York: Crossroad Publishing, 324–44.

Murata, S. (1992) *The Tao of Islam: A Sourcebook on Gender Relationships in Islamic Thought*, Albany: State University of New York Press.

Murata, S. and W.C. Chittick (1994) *The Wisdom of Islam*, New York: Paragon House.

Murray, S. and W. Roscoe (eds.) (1997) *Islamic Homosexualities: Culture, History, and Literature*, New York: New York University Press.

Musallam, B.F. (1983) *Sex and Society in Islam: Birth Control before the Nineteenth Century*, Cambridge: Cambridge University Press.

Mutahhari, M. (1985) *Fundamentals of Islamic Thought*, trans. R. Campbell, Berkeley: Mizan.

An-Na'im, A. (ed.) (2002a) *Islamic Family Law in a Changing World*, London: Zed Books.

An-Na'im, A. (2002b) "Shari'a and Islamic Family Law: Tradition and Transformation," in *Islamic Family Law*, ed. An-Na'im.

Nadvi, S. (2001) *Women Companions of the Holy Prophet and Their Sacred Lives*, New Delhi: Islamic Book Service.

Nahas, O. (2004) "Yoesuf: An Islamic Idea with Dutch Quality," in Samantha Wehbi (ed.), *Community Organizing against Homophobia and Heterosexism: The World through Rainbow-Colored Glasses*, Binghamton, NY: Harrington Park Press, 53–64.

Nasr, S. and O. Leaman (eds.) (1996) *History of Islamic Philosophy*, London: Routledge.

Nasr, S.H. (1981) *Islamic Life and Thought*, London: George Allen and Unwin.

Nazer, M. and D. Lewis (2005) *Slave: My True Story*, Cambridge, MA: Public Affairs.

Nelson, K. (1985) *The Art of Reciting the Qur'an*, Austin: University of Texas Press.

Netton, I. (1992) *Popular Dictionary of Islam*, Richmond, UK: Curzon Press.

Nielsen, J. (1999) *Towards a European Islam*, London: Macmillan.

Nielsen, J. (2004) *Muslims in Western Europe*, Edinburgh: Edinburgh University Press.

Nielsen, J., with S. Allievi (eds.) (2003) *Muslim Networks and Transnational Communities in and across Europe*, Leiden: Brill.

Nielsen, J., with B. Maréchal, S. Allievi, and F. Dassetto (eds.) (2003) *Muslims in the Enlarged Europe*, Leiden: Brill.

Nizami (1997) *The Story of Layla and Majnun*, trans. R. Gelpke et. al., New Lebanon, NY: Omega Publications.

Nomani, A. (2005a) *Standing Alone in Mecca: An American Woman's Struggle for the Soul of Islam*, San Francisco: Harper San Francisco.

Nomani, A. (2005b) "Being the Leader I Want to See in the World," in *Living Islam Out Loud*, ed. Abdul-Ghafur, 139–52.

Nursi, Bediuzzaman Said (1990) *Resurrection and the Hereafter*, trans. Hamid Algar, Istanbul: Sözler Neşriyat.

Peirce, L. (1993) *The Imperial Harem: Women and Sovereignty in the Ottoman Empire*, New York: Oxford University Press.

Peirce, L. (2003) *Morality Tales: Law and Gender in the Ottoman Court of Aintab*, Berkeley: University of California Press.

Peters, F. (1994) *The Hajj: The Muslim Pilgrimage to Mecca and the Holy Places*, Princeton, NJ: Princeton University Press.

Peters, F. (ed.) (1999) *The Arabs and Arabia on the Eve of Islam*, Brookfield: Ashgate.

Peters, R. (1996) *Jihad in Classical and Modern Islam*, Princeton, NJ: Markus Winter.

Peters, R. and G. De Vries (1976–77) "Apostasy in Islam," *Die Welt des Islams*, 17.4, 1–25.

al-Qaradawi, Y. (1989) *Al-sabr fi al-Qur'an*, Cairo: Maktabat wahba.

al-Qaradawi, Y. (1994) *The Lawful and the Prohibited in Islam*, trans. K. El-Helbawy, M.M. Siddiqui, and S. Shukry, Indianapolis: American Trust Publications, also widely available online.

Quraishi, A. (2000) "Her Honor: An Islamic Critique of the Rape Laws of Pakistan from a Woman-Sensitive Perspective," in *Windows of Faith*, ed. Webb, 102–35.

al-Qurtubi, Abu 'Abd Allah Muhammad (1997) *al-Jami' li ahkam al-Qur'an*, vols. 1–20, Beirut: Dar al-Kitab al-'Arabi.

Qutb, S. (1981) *In the Shade of the Qur'an*, London: MWH.

Rahman, F. (1965) *Islamic Methodology in History*, Islamabad, Pakistan: Islamic Research Institute.

Rahman, F. (1966) *Islam*, Chicago: University of Chicago Press.

Rahman, F. (1980) *Major Themes of the Qur'an*, Minneapolis: Bibliotheca Islamica.

Rahman, F. (1982) *Islam and Modernity*, Chicago: University of Chicago Press.

Rahman, F. (1985) "Law and Ethics in Islam," in *Ethics in Islam*, ed. Hovannisian, 3–15.

Rapoport, Y. (2005) *Marriage, Money, and Divorce in Medieval Islamic Society*, Cambridge: Cambridge University Press.

al-Razi, Fakhr al-Din (1990) *Al-Mabahith al-Mashriqiyyah*, ed. M. al-Baghdadi, Beirut: Dar al-Kitab al-'Arabi.

Reeves, M. (2001) *Muhammad in Europe: A Thousand Years of Western Myth-Making*, London: Garnet Publishing.

Reinhart, K. (1983) "Islamic Law as Islamic Ethics," *Religious Ethics*, 11, 186–203.

Reinhart, K. (1995) *Before Revelation: The Boundaries of Muslim Moral Thought*, Albany: State University of New York Press.

Reis, J. *Muslim Slave Rebellion in Brazil*, Baltimore: Johns Hopkins University Press, 1993.

Rippin, A. (ed.) (1988) *Approaches to the History of the Interpretation of the Qur'an*, Oxford: Oxford University Press.

Rippin, A. (2005) *Muslims: Their Religious Beliefs and Practices*, 2nd edition, London: Routledge.

Rippin, A. (ed.) (2006) *The Blackwell Companion to the Qur'an*, Oxford: Blackwell Publishing.

Rippin, A. (ed.) (2007a) *Defining Islam: A Reader*, London: Equinox.

Rippin, A. (ed.) (2007b) *The Islamic World*, London: Routledge.

Rippin, A., N. Calder, and J. Mojaddedi (eds.) (2003) *Classical Islam: A Sourcebook of Religious Literature*, London: Routledge.

Rispler-Chaim, V. (1992) "*Nušuz* between Medieval and Contemporary Islamic Law: The Human Rights Aspect," *Arabica*, 39, 315–27.

Rizvi, S. (1982) "Adultery and Fornication in Islamic Jurisprudence: Dimensions and Perspectives," *Islamic and Comparative Law Quarterly*, 2: 4 (March).

Roald, A. (2001) *Women in Islam: The Western Experience*, New York: Routledge.

Robinson, N. (1996) *Discovering the Qur'an: A Contemporary Approach to a Veiled Text*, London: SCM Press.

Roded, R. (1994) *Women in Islamic Bibliographical Collections: From Ibn Sa'd to Who's Who*, Boulder, CO, and London: Lynnne Reinner Publishers.

Rosenthal, E. (1962) *Political Thought in Medieval Islam: An Introductory Outline*, Cambridge: Cambridge University Press.

Rosenthal, F. (1946) "On Suicide in Islam," *Journal of the American Oriental Society*, 66, 239–59.

Rosenthal, F. (1960) *The Muslim Concept of Freedom Prior to the Nineteenth Century*, Leiden: Brill.

Rosenthal, F. (1970) *Knowledge Triumphant: The Concept of Knowledge in Medieval Islam*, Leiden: Brill.

al-Rouhayeb, K. (2005) *Before Homosexuality in the Arab-Islamic World, 1500–1800*, Chicago: University of Chicago Press.

Rouse, C. (2004) *Engaged Surrender: African American Women and Islam*, Berkeley: University of California Press.

Ruthven, M. (2000) *Islam: A Very Short Introduction*, Oxford: Oxford University Press.

Sachedina, A. (2001) *The Islamic Roots of Democratic Pluralism*, New York: Oxford University Press.

Saeed, A. and H. Saeed (2004) *Freedom of Religion, Apostasy and Islam*, Aldershot, UK: Ashgate.

Safi, O. (ed.) (2003) *Progressive Muslims: On Justice, Gender, and Pluralism*, Oxford: Oneworld Publications.

Safi, O. (2007) "I and Thou in a Fluid World: Beyond 'Islam versus the West'," in V. Cornell, series ed., *Voices of Islam: Voices of Change*, ed. O. Safi, vol. 5 of *Voices of Islam*, Westport, CT: Praeger, 199–222.

Said, E. (1978) *Orientalism*, London: Penguin.

Sanneh, L. (2005) "*Shari'ah* Sanctions and State Enforcement: A Nigerian Islamic Debate and Intellectual Critique," in Ron Geaves et al. (eds.), *Islam and the West Post 9/11*, Aldershot, UK: Ashgate.

al-Sayyid-Marsot, A. (ed.) (1979) *Society and the Sexes in Medieval Islam*, Malibu, CA: Undena Publications, 64–68.

Schacht, J. (1986) *An Introduction to Islamic Law*, Oxford: Clarendon Press.

Schimmel, A. (1975) *Mystical Dimensions of Islam*, Chapel Hill: University of North Carolina Press.

Sells, M. (1994) *Mystical Languages of Unsaying*, Chicago: University of Chicago Press.

Sells, M. (1996) *Early Islamic Mysticism*, New York: Paulist Press.

Sells, M. (1999) *Approaching the Qur'an: The Early Revelations*, Ashland, OR: White Cloud Press.

al-Shafi'i, Muhammad b. Idris (1993) *Al-Umm*, 9 vols., Beirut: Dar al-Kutub al-'Ilmiyyah.

Shah, N. (ed.) (2006) *Women, the Koran and International Human Rights Law*, Leiden: Nijhoff.

Shaikh, Sa'diyya (1997) "Exegetical Violence: Nushuz in Qur'anic Gender Ideology," *Journal of Islamic Studies*, 17, 49–73.

Shaikh, Sa'diyya (2003a) "Family Planning, Contraception, and Abortion in Islam: Undertaking *Khilafah*," in Daniel C. Maguire (ed.), *Sacred Rights: The Case for Contraception and Abortion in World Religions*, Oxford: Oxford University Press, 105–28.

Shaikh, Sa'diyya (2003b) "Transforming Feminism: Islam, Women, and Gender Justice," in *Progressive Muslims*, ed. Safi, 147–62.

Shaikh, Sa'diyya and Scott Kugle (eds.) (2006) *Journal for Islamic Studies*, thematic issue: Engaged Sufism, Vol. 26.

Sha'rawi, Huda (1986) *Harem Years: The Memoirs of an Egyptian Feminist (1879–1924)*, trans. and ed., with intro., Margot Badran, London: Virago Press.

Shirazi, Faegheh (2001) *The Veil Unveiled: The Hijab in Modern Culture*, Gainesville: University Press of Florida.

Sidahmed, Abdel Salam (2001) "Problems in Contemporary Applications of Islamic Criminal Sanctions: The Penalty for Adultery in Relation to Women," *British Journal of Middle East Studies*, 28: 2, 187–204.

Skovgaard-Petersen, Jakob (1997) *Defining Islam for the Egyptian State: Muftis and Fatwas of the Dar al-Ifta*, Leiden: Brill.

Smart, N. (1999) *World Philosophies*, London: Routledge.

Smith, J. and Y. Haddad (1981) *The Islamic Understanding of Death and Resurrection*, Albany: State University of New York Press.

Smith, M. (2001) *Muslim Women Mystics: The Life and Work of Rabi'a and Other Women Mystics in Islam*, Oxford: Oneworld Publications.

Sonbol, Amira El Azhary (1996a) "Adults and Minors in Ottoman Shariah Courts and Modern Law," in *Women, the Family, and Divorce Laws*, ed. Sonbol, 236–56.

Sonbol, Amira El Azhary (ed.) (1996b) *Women, the Family, and Divorce Laws in Islamic History*, Syracuse, NY: Syracuse University Press.

Sonbol, Amira El Azhary (2003) *Women of Jordan: Islam, Labor, and the Law*, Syracuse, NY: Syracuse University Press.

Spectorsky, Susan A. (ed. and trans.) (1992) *Chapters on Marriage and Divorce: Responses of Ibn Hanbal and Ibn Rahwayh*, Austin: University of Texas Press.

Spellberg, D.A. (1994) *Politics, Gender, and the Islamic Past: The Legacy of 'A'isha bint Abi Bakr*, New York: Columbia University Press.

Stowasser, B. (1993) "Women's Issues in Modern Islamic Thought," in *Arab Women*, ed. Tucker, 3–28.

Stowasser, B. (1994) *Women in the Qur'an: Traditions and Interpretations*, New York: Oxford University Press.

Stowasser, B. (1996) "Women and Citizenship in the Qur'an," in *Women, the Family, and Divorce Laws*, ed. Sonbol, 23–38.

al-Sulami, Muhammad ibn al-Husayn (1983) *The Book of Sufi Chivalry (Futuwwah): Lessons to a Son of the Moment*, trans. Tosun Bayrak al-Jerrahi al-Halveti, New York: Inner Traditions International.

al-Tabari, Abu Ja'far Muhammad b. Jarir (1985) *al-Jami' al-bayan an ta'wil ay al-Qur'an* (The Completion of Commentaries on the Verses of the Qur'an), Beirut: Dar al-fikr.

Tabatabai, S. (1987) *The Qur'an in Islam*, London: Zahra Publications.

Taji-Farouki, Suha (ed.) (2004) *Modern Muslim Intellectuals and the Qur'an*, The Institute of Ismaili Studies, London: Oxford University Press.

Taji-Farouki, Suha and Basheer M. Nafi (eds.) (2004) *Islamic Thought in the Twentieth Century*, London: I.B. Tauris.

Talbani, A. (1996) "Pedagogy, Power and Discourse: Transformation of Islamic Education," *Comparative Education Review*, 40: 1, 66–82.

Taylor, C. (1999) *In the Vicinity of the Righteous: Ziyara and the Veneration of Muslim Saints in Late Medieval Egypt*, Leiden: Brill.

Toledano, Ehud (1998) *Slavery and Abolition in the Ottoman Middle East*, Seattle: University of Washington Press.

Toledano, Ehud (2002) "Representing the Slave's Body in Ottoman Society," in *Slavery and Abolition*, 23: 2 (August), 57–74.

Trimingham, J. (1959) *Islam in West Africa*, Oxford: Clarendon Press.

Trimingham, J. (1964) *Islam in East Africa*, Oxford: Clarendon Press.

Trimingham, J. (1965a) *Islam in the Sudan*, Oxford: Clarendon Press.

Trimingham, J. (1965b) *Islam in Ethiopia*, Oxford: Clarendon Press.

Trimingham, J. (1968) *The Influence of Islam on Africa*, Oxford: Clarendon Press.

Tucker, Judith E. (ed.) (1993) *Arab Women: Old Boundaries, New Frontiers*, Bloomington: Indiana University Press.

Tucker, Judith E. (1994) *Gender and Islamic History*, Essays on Global and Comparative History, Washington, DC: American Historical Association.

Tucker, Judith E. (1998) *In the House of the Law: Gender and Islamic Law in Ottoman Syria and Palestine*, Berkeley: University of California Press.

al-Turabi, H. (1983) "The Islamic State," in J. Esposito (ed.), *Voices of Resurgent Islam*, New York: Oxford University Press.

Turner, J. (1997) *The Holy War Idea in Western and Islamic Traditions*, University Park: Pennsylvania State University.

Versteegh, C.H.M. (1983) *Arabic Grammar and Qur'anic Exegesis in Early Islam*, Leiden: Brill.

Vogel, F. and Hayes, S. (1999) *Islamic Law and Finance: Religion, Risk, and Return*, Leiden: Brill.

Wadud, A. (1999) *Qur'an and Woman: Rereading the Sacred Text from a Woman's Perspective*, New York: Oxford University Press.

Wadud, A. (2000) "Alternative Qur'anic Interpretation and the Status of Muslim Women," in *Windows of Faith*, ed. Webb, 3–21.

Wadud, A. (2006) *Inside the Gender Jihad: Women's Reform in Islam*, Oxford: Oneworld Publications.

Wansborough, J. (2004) *Qur'anic Studies: Sources and Methods of Scriptural Interpretation*, Amherst, MA: Prometheus.

Watt, M. (1973) *Formative Period of Islamic Thought*, Edinburgh: Edinburgh University Press.

Watt, M. (1994) *Islamic Creeds: A Selection*, Edinburgh: Edinburgh University Press.

Webb, Gisela (ed.) (2000) *Windows of Faith: Muslim Women Scholar-Activists in North America*, Syracuse, NY: Syracuse University Press.

Welch, A. (1980) "Allah and Other Supernatural Beings: The Emergence of the Qur'anic Doctrine of Tawhid," *Journal of the American Academy of Religion*, 47, 733–58.

Wensinck, A. (1965) *The Muslim Creed, Its Genesis and Historical Development*, London: Frank Cass.

Wheeler, B. (2002) *Prophets in the Qur'an: An Introduction to the Qur'an and Muslim Exegesis*, New York: Continuum.

Wild, S. (ed.) (1996) *The Qur'an as Text: Islamic Philosophy, Theology, and Science*, Leiden: Brill.

Wild, S. (2001) *Mensch, Prophet und Gott*, Münster: Gerda Henkel Vorlesung.

Willis, John Ralph (1985) "The Ideology of Enslavement in Islam," in *idem* (ed.), *Slaves and Slavery in Muslim Africa*, vol. 1: *Islam and the Ideology of Enslavement*, London: Frank Cass, 1–15.

Wolfe, Michael and the producers of Beliefnet (eds.) (2002) *Taking Back Islam: American Muslims Reclaim Their Faith*, Emmaus, PA: Rodale Press.

Wolfson, A. (1976) *The Philosophy of the Kalam*, London: Harvard University Press.

Wynn, Lisa (1996) "Marriage Contracts and Women's Rights in Saudi Arabia," in *Shifting Boundaries in Marriage and Divorce in Muslim Communities*, vol. 1 (Women Living under Muslim Laws Special Dossier), Montpellier, France: Women Living under Muslim Laws, 106–20.

Yamani, Mai, with Andrew Allen (eds.) (1996) *Feminism and Islam: Legal and Literary Perspectives*, New York: New York University Press.

Zakariyya', F. (1993) *Laïcité ou Islamisme*, Cairo: al-Fikr.

al-Zamakhshari, Abu al-Qasim (1995) *al-Kashshaf*, Beirut: Dar al-Kutub al-'Ilmiyyah.

Zaman, Muhammad Qasim (2002) *The Ulama in Contemporary Islam: Custodians of Change*, Princeton, NJ: Princeton University Press.

Zebiri, K. (2003) "Towards a Rhetorical Criticism of the Qur'an," *Journal of Qur'anic Studies*, 5, 95–120.

Zomeño, Amalia (1997) "Kafa'a in the Maliki School: A Fatwa from Fifteenth-Century Fes," in R. Gleave and Eugenia Kermeli (eds.), *Islamic Law: Theory and Practice*, London and New York: I.B. Tauris, 87–106.

Translations of the Qur'an

Abdel Haleem, M. (2004) *The Qur'an*, Oxford: Oxford University Press.

Ali, Abdullah Yusuf (1989) *The Holy Qur'an: Text, Translation and Commentary*, Washington, DC: Amanah Publications.

Ali, Ahmed (1988) *Al-Qur'an: A Contemporary Translation*, Princeton, NJ: Princeton University Press.

Arberry, A. (1955) *The Koran Interpreted*, London: George Allen and Unwin.

Asad, Muhammad (1980) *The Message of the Qur'an*, Gibraltar: Dar al-Andalus.

The Qur'an Translated, With a Critical Rearrangement of the Surahs (1937), trans. Richard Bell, Edinburgh: T. and T. Clark.

Cleary, T. (1994) *The Essential Koran*, New York: Harper Collins.

Cleary, T. (2004) *The Qur'an*, Louisville, KY: Fons Vitae.

Dawood, N.J. (1956) *The Koran*, Harmondsworth, UK: Penguin.

The Qur'an: The First American Version (1985), translation and commentary by T.B. Irving (al-Hajj Ta'lim 'Ali), Brattleboro, VT: Amana Books.

The Meaning of the Glorious Koran, an Explanatory Translation (1952) by Marmaduke Pickthall, London: George Allen and Unwin.

The Koran, trans. J.M. Rodwell (1909), London: J.M. Dent and Sons (reprint edition, 1974).

Hadith collections are available in numerous Arabic editions. The "authentic" (*sahih*) compilations of Bukhari and Muslim have been translated into English multiple times; portions of other works have also appeared in English. Bukhari and Muslim's collections can be found in searchable databases online.

Abu Dawud Sulayman b. al-Ash'ath al-Sijistani (1952) *Sunan Abi Dawud*, 2 vols., Cairo: n.p.

Bukhari, [Muhammad b. Isma'il] (1987) *The Translation of the Meanings of Sahih al-Bukhari*, Arabic–English, 8 vols., trans. Muhammad Muhsin Khan, revised edition, New Delhi: Kitab Bhavan.

Ibn Abi Shayba, Abu Bakr 'Abd Allah b. Muhammad (1995) *Al-Kitab al-Musannaf fi'l-Ahadith wa'l-Athar*, 9 vols., Beirut: Dar al-Kutub al-'Ilmiyyah.

Ibn Majah, Abu 'Abd Allah Muhammad ibn Yazid al-Qazwini (1952) *Sunan ibn Majah*, ed. Muhammad Fu'ad 'Abd al-Baqi. [Cairo]: Dar Ihya' al-Kutub al-'Arabiyya.

Muslim [b. al-Hajjaj al-Qushayri] (1995 [1977]) *Sahih Muslim, Being Traditions of the Sayings and Doings of the Prophet Muhammad as Narrated by His Companions and Compiled under the title Al-Jami'-us-Sahih*, 4 vols., trans. 'Abdul Hamid Siddiqi. New Delhi: Kitab Bhavan.

Muslim [b. al-Hajjaj al-Qushayri] (n.d. [1963?]) *Sahih Muslim*, 8 vols. in 2, Egypt: Maktabah wa Matbu'ah Muhammad 'Ali Sabih wa awlad.

al-Nasa'i, Ahmad b. Shu'ayb (n.d.) *Sunan al-Nasa'i, bi sharh al-Hafiz Jalal al-Din al-Suyuti wa Hashiyah al-Imam al-Sindi*, 8 vols. in 4, ed. Hasan Muhammad al-Mas'udi, Beirut: Dar Ihya' al-Turath al-'Arabi.

al-Tirmidhi, Abu 'Isa Muhammad b. 'Isa (1937) *Al-Jami' al-Sahih, wa huwa Sunan al-Tirmidhi*, ed. Ahmad Muhammad Shakir, Cairo: Matbu'ah Mustafa al-Babi.

Useful websites include:
www.uga.edu/islam.
www.rippin.ca.
www.academicinfo.net/Islam.html.
www.islamworld.net.
www.jannah.org/sisters/index.html.
www.al-islam.com.
www.virtuallyislamic.com.
www.iranica.com.
www.muslimphilosophy.com.

INDEX OF TERMS

Ubiquitous expressions such as Allah have not been indexed, and since they are also so frequent the page numbers for Qur'an and surah given here are restricted to the specific entry for that topic in the book.

INDEX OF PERSONAL NAMES

In alphabetizing Arabic names, no notice is taken of 'ayn, hamza, or the prefix al-.

Fifty Eastern Thinkers
Diané Collinson, Kathryn Plant and Robert Wilkinson

Close exposition and analysis of fifty major thinkers in eastern
philosophy and religion form the core of this introduction to a
fascinating area of study. The authors have drawn on the major
eastern traditions, examining founder figures such as:

- Zoroaster
- Confucius
- Muhammad.

Through to modern thinkers such as

- Mao Zedong
- Nishitani
- Gandhi.

General introductions to the major traditions and a glossary of
philosophical terms, as well as bibliographies and recommended
further reading for each thinker, make this a comprehensive
and accessible work of reference.

ISBN10: 0–415–20284–1
ISBN13: 978–0–415–20284–8

Available at all good bookshops
For ordering and further information please visit
www.routledge.com

Fifty Key Figures in Islam
Roy Jackson

If you would like to learn more about the Muslim culture, people and teachings, then this is the perfect resource for you. Roy Jackson explores the lives and thoughts of fifty influential figures in Islam and surveys a heritage which spans 1,500 years. *Fifty Key Figures in Islam* could not have come at a more interesting time in history.

Fully cross-referenced, for each figure the book provides:

- Biographical details
- A presentation and analysis of their main ideas
- An account of their impact and influence within and, if appropriate, beyond the Islamic tradition
- List of major works and additional reading.

ISBN10: 0–415–35468–4
ISBN13: 978–0–415–35468–4

Available at all good bookshops
For ordering and further information please visit
www.routledge.com